Film Stardom in Southeast Asia

International Film Stars
Series Editor: Homer B. Pettey and R. Barton Palmer

This series is devoted to the artistic and commercial influence of performers who shaped major genres and movements in international film history. Books in the series will:

- Reveal performative features that defined signature cinematic styles
- Demonstrate how the global market relied upon performers' generic contributions
- Analyse specific film productions as case studies that transformed cinema acting
- Construct models for redefining international star studies that emphasise materialist approaches
- Provide accounts of stars' influences in the international cinema marketplace

Titles available:

Close-Up: Great Cinematic Performances Volume 1: America
edited by Murray Pomerance and Kyle Stevens

Close-Up: Great Cinematic Performances Volume 2: International
edited by Murray Pomerance and Kyle Stevens

Chinese Stardom in Participatory Cyberculture
by Dorothy Wai Sim Lau

Geraldine Chaplin: The Gift of Film Performance
by Steven Rybin

Tyrone Power: Gender, Genre and Image in Classical Hollywood Cinema
by Gillian Kelly

Film Stardom in Southeast Asia
edited by Jonathan Driskell

www.euppublishing.com/series/ifs

Film Stardom in Southeast Asia

Edited by
Jonathan Driskell

EDINBURGH
University Press

Edinburgh University Press is one of the leading university presses in the UK. We publish academic books and journals in our selected subject areas across the humanities and social sciences, combining cutting-edge scholarship with high editorial and production values to produce academic works of lasting importance. For more information visit our website: edinburghuniversitypress.com

© editorial matter and organisation Jonathan Driskell, 2022, 2024
© the chapters their several authors, 2022, 2024

Grateful acknowledgement is made to the sources listed in the List of Illustrations for permission to reproduce material previously published elsewhere. Every effort has been made to trace the copyright holders, but if any have been inadvertently overlooked, the publisher will be pleased to make the necessary arrangements at the first opportunity.

Edinburgh University Press Ltd
The Tun – Holyrood Road
12(2f) Jackson's Entry
Edinburgh EH8 8PJ

First published in hardback by Edinburgh University Press 2022

Typeset in 12/14 Arno and Myriad by
IDSUK (Dataconnection) Ltd, and
printed and bound by CPI Group (UK) Ltd
Croydon, CR0 4YY

A CIP record for this book is available from the British Library

ISBN 978 1 4744 4219 0 (hardback)
ISBN 987 1 4744 4220 6 (paperback)
ISBN 978 1 4744 4221 3 (webready PDF)
ISBN 978 1 4744 4222 0 (epub)

The right of Jonathan Driskell to be identified as the author of this work has been asserted in accordance with the Copyright, Designs and Patents Act 1988, and the Copyright and Related Rights Regulations 2003 (SI No. 2498).

Contents

List of illustrations — vii
Acknowledgements — ix

Introduction — 1
   Jonathan Driskell

Chapter 1 Spectral stars, haunted screens: Cambodian golden age cinema — 19
   Annette Hamilton

Chapter 2 P. Ramlee, the *star*: Malay stardom and society in the 1950s–60s — 36
   Jonathan Driskell

Chapter 3 Shake it like Elvis: Win Oo, the culturally appropriate heart-throb of the Burmese socialist years — 51
   Jane M. Ferguson

Chapter 4 Trà Giang's stardom in wartime Vietnam: simple glamour, socialist modernity and acting agency — 67
   Qui-Ha Hoang Nguyen

Chapter 5 Seeking a passport: the transnational career of Kiều Chinh — 84
   Pujita Guha

Chapter 6 Three kinds of stardom in Indonesia — 104
   David Hanan

Chapter 7 The Indonesian sex bomb: female sexuality in cinema 1970s–90s — 124
   Thomas Barker

Chapter 8 Nora Aunor and Sharon Cuneta as migrant workers: stars and labour export in Filipino commercial films   149
Katrina Ross Tan

Chapter 9 One more second chance: love team longevity and utility in the era of the television studio   166
Chrishandra Sebastiampillai

Chapter 10 The changing status of the Thai *luk khrueng* (Eurasian) performer: a case study of Ananda Everingham   182
Mary J. Ainslie

Chapter 11 Fight like a girl: Jeeja Yanin as a female martial arts star   203
Katarzyna Ancuta

Notes on contributors   220
Index   223

Figures

Figure 1.1	King Norodom Sihanouk. Image courtesy of CasaDei Productions © 1996	22
Figure 1.2	Dy Saveth in *Puos Keng Kang*. Image courtesy of Kim Tia	28
Figure 2.1	P. Ramlee sings 'Selamat Panjang Umur' in *Antara dua Darjat*	44
Figure 2.2	P. Ramlee in *Ibu Mertuaku*	47
Figure 3.1	Win Oo in a publicity still for *Tein Hlwa Moe Moe Lwin*	59
Figure 4.1	Trà Giang. Photo courtesy of Trà Giang	68
Figure 4.2	Trà Giang and President Hồ Chí Minh. Photo courtesy of Trà Giang	69
Figure 5.1	My-Lan meets Thuần at the hospital ward. Screenshot from *Người Tình Không Chân Dung*	89
Figure 5.2	Mai and Loan talking against the war-torn landscape. Screenshot from *Chiếc Bóng Bên Đường*	91
Figure 5.3	A room in the exhibition commemorating the history of Independence Palace, Saigon. Photo by Pujita Guha	100
Figure 6.1	Betawi singer and comedian Benyamin S, in *Ambisi*. Image courtesy of Sinematek Indonesia	106
Figure 6.2	Rhoma Irama in *Satria Bergitar*. Image courtesy of Sinematek Indonesia	114
Figure 6.3	Rhoma Irama in *Nada dan Dakwah*. Image courtesy of Sinematek Indonesia	115
Figure 6.4	Image from Teguh Karya's second feature film, *Cinta Pertama*. Image courtesy of the Teater Populer collective	117

Figure 6.5	Members of the Teater Populer group in 1985. Photo by David Hanan	119
Figure 7.1	Original poster for *Si Genit Poppy* featuring Yati Octavia and Debbie Cynthia Dewi	129
Figure 7.2	Original poster for *Akibat Pergaulan Bebas*. Image courtesy of Rapi Films	130
Figure 7.3	Original poster for *Napas Perempuan* with Eva Arnaz in supporting role	131
Figure 7.4	Original poster for *Roro Mendut* starring Meriam Bellina	133
Figure 7.5	Original poster for the WARKOP DKI film *Depan Bisa Belakang Bisa* featuring the three comedians and Eva Arnaz. Image courtesy of Soraya Intercine Films	134
Figure 7.6	Original poster for *Pergaulan Metropolis 2* starring Inneke Koesherawaty. Image courtesy of Soraya Intercine Films	142
Figure 7.7	Front cover of issue 1 of *Alia* magazine (July 2003) featuring Inneke Koesherawaty in headscarf	143
Figure 8.1	The young Nora Aunor in the 1970s. Photo courtesy of Oliver Inocentes	153
Figure 8.2	Sharon Cuneta, a new star in the 1980s. Photo courtesy of Jerrick David and Angelo de Guzman	158
Figure 9.1	Cruz and Alonzo star in *A Second Chance*. Star Cinema and ABS-CBN Film Productions Inc.	169
Figure 9.2	The iconic quote from the Cruz and Alonzo film *One More Chance*. Star Cinema and ABS-CBN Film Productions Inc.	173
Figure 11.1	Spin-kicking into fame: Jeeja in her impressive screen debut in *Chocolate*	204
Figure 11.2	Jeeja in bike-fu action from a fight sequence featuring bike acrobatics in *This Girl is Badass*	211
Figure 11.3	Jeeja (right) and Theerada Kittisiriprasert (left) as a cute 'Chinese' fighting duo in *The Protector 2*	213
Figure 11.4	Jeeja and Kazu Patrick Tang showcasing their impressive martial arts skills in *Raging Phoenix*	215

Acknowledgements

I would like to thank the following: the staff at Edinburgh University Press, particularly Gillian Leslie, Fiona Conn, Sam Johnson, Caitlin Murphy and Richard Strachan, for all their help during the completion of this book; the series editors, Homer B. Pettey and R. Barton Palmer, for their comments and feedback on the manuscript; the School of Arts and Social Sciences, Monash University Malaysia, which funded the initial workshop on 'Film Stardom in Southeast Asia' held in November 2016, which led to this publication; other individuals who have helped in a variety of ways, including Thomas Barker, Louis Bayman, Agata Frymus, Stephanie Hemelryk Donald, Gaik Cheng Khoo, Chrishandra Sebastiampillai, Leong Wai Lun, Jiyni Lim, and Robert and Sue Driskell.

Introduction
Jonathan Driskell

Southeast Asian cinema has become increasingly well known to audiences beyond the region, owing to several recent high-profile successes. Apichatpong Weerasethakul has won major prizes at Cannes, including the Palme d'Or for *Uncle Boonmee Who Can Recall His Past Lives* (2010); Brillante Mendoza won the Best Director award at Cannes for *Kinatay* (Butchered, 2009); in 2013 Anthony Chen won the Caméra d'Or at Cannes for *Ilo Ilo* (2013), the same year that Rithy Panh won the Un Certain Regard section at the same festival for *The Missing Picture* (2013). Many other Southeast Asian directors have achieved international critical success over the years too, including Lino Brocka, Ishmael Bernal, Lav Diaz, Wisit Sasanatieng, Pen-Ek Ratanaruang, Eric Khoo, Amir Muhammad, Yasmin Ahmad, Garin Nugroho, Nia Dinata and Trần Anh Hùng. Taken together, these filmmakers offer an impressive view of the region's filmmaking. This is a critically acclaimed and artistically – as well as often politically – accomplished cinema, which has understandably attracted considerable academic interest.

Yet while such successes have demonstrated that the region's cinema can compete on the global stage, they only provide a partial view of its cinematic achievements. Southeast Asian cinemas have also been successful in attaining a significant share of the domestic film market – a notable accomplishment, considering the strength of global film industries, such as Hollywood, Hong Kong cinema and Indian cinemas, which have all attained a strong presence in the region. The success of domestic industries has been evident throughout Southeast Asia, especially in the countries with the larger film industries, such as the Philippines, Thailand and Indonesia, but even historically in some of the region's smaller cinematic nations, which have experienced golden ages during which large quantities of films were produced. The Burmese film industry grew in the post-independence era, reaching an apex of ninety-two films in 1962 alone (Ferguson 2020: 83); before the Khmer Rouge took over

Cambodia in 1975 there was an output of over 400 films; in Singapore, the Malay film industry of the late-1940s to the 1970s produced over 360 films. Although the reasons for this success are complex and varied, these examples indicate that an important component of the region's cinema is its popular, mainstream filmmaking, aimed at a domestic audience.

Another key index of the success of these cinemas is the presence of film stars. The first Southeast Asian film stars appeared during the colonial era, notably in the Philippines, where they were used in early silent productions, including in the first locally produced Philippine feature film, *Dalagang Bukid* (Country Maiden, José Nepomuceno, 1919), which featured *sarsuwela* (musical theatre) star Honorata de la Rama (Deocampo 2011: 519). Similarly, in Indonesia, Roekiah and Rd Mochtar were significant early examples, who achieved fame following the release of *Terang Boelan* (Full Moon, Albert Balink, 1937) (Woodrich 2017). However, it was in the post-Second World War period following decolonisation, the period this book largely focuses on, that domestic national cinemas began to grow in strength, and this was accompanied by the development of film stardom.

This book's main argument is that the star phenomenon is of central importance to understanding film in Southeast Asia. Stars constitute one of its main atractions and in doing so can shed light on the workings of the region's movie industries, give insight into the meanings and appeal of its films, and can reveal much about its representational and political dimensions. To outline this book's contribution to existing scholarship in more detail, I will discuss its place within two main areas of inquiry, star studies and work on Southeast Asian cinema, before finishing with an overview of the book's contents.

Stardom beyond Hollywood

While academic discussion of ideas related to stardom slowly emerged during the twentieth century, with early work written by Max Weber, Roland Barthes and Edgar Moran (see Redmond and Holmes 2007), it accelerated following the publication of Richard Dyer's *Stars* (1979) and *Heavenly Bodies: Film Stars and Society* (1986, 2004). In these books Dyer offers a theorisation of the star phenomenon, examining the contribution stars make to the films they appear in and the ways they take on ideological significance in the societies from which they emerge. In addition to discussing stars' film appearances, Dyer's (2004: 2) work also stresses the importance of other areas of culture in which star personas are constructed:

> The star phenomenon consists of everything that is publicly available about stars. A film star's image is not just his or her films, but the promotion of those films and of the star through pin-ups, public appearances, studio hand-outs and so on, as well as interviews, biographies and coverage in the press of the star's doings and 'private' life.

Dyer's influential body of work has led to the creation of a whole field known as star studies, which encompasses a wide range of topics and approaches. Several edited collections and introductory volumes have been published (Redmond and Holmes 2007; Shingler 2012; Yu and Austin 2017) and work has examined a plethora of issues, including audiences (Stacey 1994), the relationship between stars and the film industry (McDonald 2013), star labour (Clark 1995; McLean 2004) and star performance (Naremore 1988; Klevan 2005; Pomerance and Stevens 2018a and 2018b). In recent years star studies has grown further, with universities now offering modules on the subject, book series devoted to it (for example, BFI's Film Stars series and Edinburgh University Press's International Film Stars series – to which this volume belongs) and the creation of the *Celebrity Studies* journal (in 2010), which frequently includes new research on film stardom.

The earliest academic work on the subject focused largely on Hollywood, with Dyer's two books dealing almost entirely with Hollywood stars. The global impact of Hollywood stardom is undeniable. It has created some of the world's most famous stars and during its studio era crafted an influential star system where studios had their own stables of stars contracted to them. However, scholarship has also emerged exploring the role stardom has played in cinemas beyond Hollywood. One of the first full-length studies of national stardom was *Stars and Stardom in French Cinema* by Ginette Vincendeau (2000), which outlines the nationally specific features of the French star system, involving connections between the stage and screen, the role of French national identity, its connections with cinephilia, and its alternative models of star creation and management, in the absence of the vertically integrated studios that existed in Hollywood. Other works followed, with studies looking at stardom in the United Kingdom (Macnab 2000; Babington

2001), Italy (Landy 2008; Gundle 2013) and Germany (Ascheid 2003; Carter 2004).

In recent years research has examined stars from all over the world, an important trajectory for the field, not only because it brings to the fore cinemas that are often obscured by Hollywood, but also because it provides the opportunity to re-examine ideas relating to film stardom itself. Investigating stars in such contexts raises the question of whether existing theories are sufficient or if fresh analytical tools are required, an issue that is tackled in a variety of ways within these studies. One of the books that has been most upfront about this is *Stars in World Cinema*, which includes chapters on stars from a wide range of countries – from across South America, Europe, Africa and Asia (including a chapter on stardom in the Philippines (Lim 2015)). In the introduction Andrea Bandhauer and Michelle Royer (2015: 3) write:

> This book is based on a desire to advance polycentrism in Star Studies, starting from insiders' viewpoints. Hence our contributors are all scholars whose research is based on an in-depth knowledge of the culture and language of the stars and star systems they study, and of the global articulations between stars and cultural practices.

Also of relevance to this collection is scholarship on Asian stardom, including a special issue of *Celebrity Studies* on the subject published in 2021 and work specifically on Indian stars and stardom (Majumdar 2009; Viswamohan and Wilkinson 2020; Dudrah et al. 2015; Lawrence 2020), which provides useful insights into analysing film stars in a non-Hollywood context. In *Stardom in Contemporary Hindi Cinema*, for example, Viswamohan and Wilkinson (2020: 3) explain that some aspects of stardom in the Hindi cinema are similar to what is found in Hollywood: 'stars act as test cases of the models of celebrity developed elsewhere. Oftentimes, they seem to solidify these models, with the Indian film star in question made more meaningful through reference to the existing paradigms of celebrity.' On the other hand, they explain how it also possesses its own unique features through discussion of *darsan* (a term borrowed from Hinduism referring to a form of devotion based on looking), *parda* (a form of veiling that describes how Indian stars negotiate the public–private dichotomy central to stardom) and 'insidership' (describing the power of 'dynasties' or film families, such as the Kapoors and the Bachchans). There have also been studies of East

Asian stars and stardom (González-López and Smith 2018; Leung and Willis 2014; Feng 2017; Lau 2018; Farquhar and Zhang 2010) and one of these, *Chinese Film Stars*, acknowledges and draws upon ideas developed in Dyer's work, with its introductory chapter even commenting that the book's title is a tribute to Dyer's *Stars* (Farquhar and Zhang 2010: 3). Beyond these, there is also work on Southeast Asian stars, which I discuss further in the following section.

This book, then, seeks to contribute to existing research on stardom beyond Hollywood by investigating the stars of Southeast Asia. The work discussed above demonstrates that while Hollywood stardom continues to be a key reference point for cinemas all over the world, we cannot assume that Hollywood models are universal and, as I explain below, the chapters in this volume investigate some of the unique features of the stardom that exists in the region. In doing so, this book also contributes to research on Southeast Asian cinema more generally, particularly by shifting attention towards the region's *popular* cinema.

Popular Southeast Asian cinema

Scholarship on Southeast Asia's filmmaking initially focused on individual national cinemas. This work has grown in volume and there is now a significant body of writing on the cinemas of Indonesia, the Philippines, Thailand, Singapore and Malaysia, as well as, increasingly, Vietnam and Cambodia, and in recent years work has been emerging on Myanmar, Laos, Brunei and East Timor (see Khoo 2020 for a comprehensive overview of this literature). In addition, as the field has developed, there has been a move towards a regional perspective, which has positioned individual national cinemas within Southeast Asian cinema more generally. This shift is evident from the establishment in 2004 of the Association of Southeast Asian Cinemas, which holds regular conferences on the subject, as well as from a wealth of publications on Southeast Asian cinema, including general overviews (Hanan 2001; Giminez and Margirier 2012), studies of particular time periods (Lim and Yamamoto 2012; Khoo et al. 2020), its independent cinema (Baumgärtel 2012; Ingawanij and McKay 2012; Meissner 2021) and collections on its horror films (Bräunlein and Lauser 2016; Ancuta and Campos 2015).

While Southeast Asia has been examined from a regional perspective across several academic disciplines, including history, anthropology, media and communications, and politics, viewing the region as a coherent whole can be problematic. At worst Southeast Asia can be seen as an artificial construct, which groups together eleven extremely different countries within an arbitrarily defined territory, particularly as these territories exhibit huge diversity along ethnic, religious, linguistic, political and economic lines. At the same time, these countries do share some notable connections. The region has to some extent been brought together through the establishment and work of the Association of Southeast Asian Nations (ASEAN), an economic union formed in 1967. Moreover, ten (out of eleven) Southeast Asian nations were colonised by Western powers and gained independence at various stages in the post-Second World War period. The one country that was not colonised, Thailand, was still heavily impacted by these developments – for further discussion see Harrison and Jackson (2010) as well as Mary Ainslie's contribution to this book (Chapter 10). While France, Holland, Portugal, Spain, the United Kingdom and the USA all held parts of Southeast Asia at different points in time, they each had a different social, cultural and political impact on the places they colonised, which has further heightened the variety that makes up the region. Nevertheless, this is also a shared history, which has shaped the region's development, both during colonisation and in the years since, when the newly independent nations embarked upon nation-building projects during the Cold War period and beyond. For this reason, decolonisation and postcolonialism have been key themes in work looking at Southeast Asian film from a regional perspective (Sim 2020; Khoo et al. 2020; Galt 2021).

Whether examining the cinema from a regional or a national point of view, a significant emphasis within existing literature on Southeast Asian cinema is the role played by its critically acclaimed films and filmmakers – its leading directors and film movements, especially the independent cinemas that have emerged since the early 2000s (Baumgärtel 2012; Ingawanij and McKay 2012; Meissner 2021). As Khoo (2020: 10) points out, the accomplishments of individual filmmakers have played a major role in contributing to the recent development of the discipline:

> The international success and prominence of contemporary Southeast Asian filmmakers and auteurs such as Apichatpong Weerasethakul, Lav Diaz, Rithy Panh, Anthony Chen and Garin Nugroho, many of whom have won prestigious awards in film festivals in Europe, Asia and elsewhere, also spawned local and international interest, sparking scholarly curiosity.

The centrality of authorship is evident from the wealth of scholarship on some of the directors mentioned above, as well as from the tendency to structure the histories of Southeast Asian cinema using its top filmmakers as the key reference points (Khoo 2020). At the same time, as with elsewhere, where academic studies of national cinemas have turned towards the 'popular' (Dyer and Vincendeau 1992; Shaw and Dennison 2004; Bayman and Rigoletto 2013), there are examples of studies that focus on aspects of Southeast Asia's popular cinemas. A survey of recent literature shows that this is becoming an increasingly prominent part of the field and while it is not possible to list all these works here, it is worth mentioning some recent examples. Ainslie and Ancuta's *Thai Cinema: The Complete Guide* (2018) gives space to the New Thai Cinema and the Independent Cinema, and a section on 'Key Directors' includes entries on auteurs such as Nonzee Nimibutr, Pen-Ek Ratanaruang and Apichatpong Weerasethakul, but also devotes lengthy sections to genres such as Heritage/Nostalgia, Horror, Muay Thai/Action, and Comedy/Romantic Comedy. Similarly, in *Indonesian Cinema after the New Order* (2019) Thomas Barker examines post-1998 Indonesian cinema as 'Pop Culture': a market-driven entertainment form, distinct from the state cinema of the authoritarian era that preceded it. One of the region's popular genres that has received considerable attention is horror, including a book on the Pontianak film (a type of Southeast Asian monster) by Rosalind Galt (2021), and collections looking at horror cinema from across the region (Bräunlein and Lauser 2016; Ancuta and Campos 2015). Moreover, one of the most recent books, *Southeast Asia on Screen*, includes a section devoted specifically to 'Popular Pleasures', further emphasising this tendency.

With film stars being a defining feature of much popular cinema, research on the region's stardom can make a significant contribution to work on popular Southeast Asian cinema. Several pieces have already been published on the Philippines – the Southeast Asian country with one of the richest histories of stardom – especially on Nora Aunor, including work by Lim (2015), Sebastiampillai (2019 and 2020) and Tadiar (2002) (see also Katrina Ross Tan's contribution to this volume in Chapter 8), as well as on Weng Weng, a 2 foot 9 inch star of Philippine exploitation cinema, who appeared in James Bond parodies (Smith 2012). One of the most distinctive features of Philippine stardom is its emphasis on 'love teams', star pairings that appear in several films together, a phenomenon that has been examined by Sebastiampillai (2019) and forms the basis of her contribution to this book (Chapter 9). Work has also emerged on stardom in Indonesian cinema, on Benyamin S (Hanan and Koesasi 2011) and Rhoma Irama (Frederick 1982; Weintraub 2010) (both are discussed by David Hanan in Chapter 6 of this book), on Thai stars, such as Mitr Chaibancha (Harrison 2010) and the internationally renowned Tony Jaa (Steimer 2021), as well as on the Malaysian star Henry Golding (Sebastiampillai 2021). However, given that Southeast Asia has produced huge numbers of film stars over the years, there is significant potential for additional studies, hence the current volume.

Film stardom in Southeast Asia

This book seeks to contribute to existing scholarship in star studies and on Southeast Asian cinema by exploring a few key questions: How do Southeast Asian film stars contribute to the film industries they work in? In what ways are Southeast Asian films shaped by their stars, through their extra-filmic personas and/or their star performances? How do the region's stars give insight into the social and political contexts of life in Southeast Asia? On the one hand these issues are investigated through case studies of individual stars, with chapters exploring some of the region's key figures, as well as some less well known, but fascinating examples. At the same time, this volume seeks to provide a more general picture of the region's stardom: taken together, the book's chapters look at stars in eight (out of eleven) Southeast Asian countries (Burma, Cambodia, Indonesia, Malaysia, the Philippines, Singapore, Thailand, Vietnam); chapters examine stars from across a broad time period, from the mid-1950s to the present day; the book also looks at a wide-range of *types* of star, through consideration of stars associated with different genres (comedy, romance, martial arts, horror, melodrama, among others). In addition, many themes, such as postcolonialism, authoritarianism, royalty, religion and race – commonly explored in work on Southeast Asia – are examined in novel ways, with film stars offering new avenues for considering these issues, as I explain more fully below.

As outlined in the first section of this introduction, scholarship on stardom beyond Hollywood has taken many forms, with some work drawing on existing ideas derived from star studies and others seeking to move away from these. This book invites both possibilities: it sees the utility of existing star studies theories, but also allows authors – all specialists in their respective cinemas – to base their analyses on historical context and broader understandings of the region's cinema. In doing so, the book's chapters demonstrate several ways in which Southeast Asian stardom offers continuities with existing ideas of stardom, while also offering something unique.

The book's chapters have been arranged in a rough chronological order (rough because some cover several decades, while others focus on shorter periods of time), allowing readers to follow some of the historical developments of stardom, while also making comparisons across the individual nations, some of which I highlight in the paragraphs that follow. While a couple of contributions offer contextualising information that goes back to before the Second World War, the book's chapters largely span a sixty-five-year period from the mid-1950s to the present day. This period has witnessed huge variety across the region's cinema and embodied through its film stars, which is unsurprising, given the diversity that Southeast Asia has to offer. Simultaneously, as noted earlier, the region's colonial history and nation-building projects as newly independent nations also point towards certain shared experiences. The chapters that follow demonstrate some of the ways in which film stardom can be a useful tool for engaging with these developments.

The first three chapters introduce an important way in which stardom has been shaped by this postcolonial context through discussion of stars whose personas contain tensions between local, traditional values on the one hand, and cosmopolitan, modern ideas on the other. In Chapter 1, Annette Hamilton provides a broad history of Cambodian stardom from the 1940s up to the present day, exploring some of the diverse factors that have shaped its production of stars. One of its distinctive features, before the rise of the Khmer Rouge in 1975, was the connection between stardom and royalty, owing to the films of King Norodom Sihanouk, who made and – along with other members of the royal family – starred in films during this time. In addition, Cambodian stardom has represented local culture, superstitions, and traditions, especially through the popular 'snake film' genre, while also articulating modern ideas common to stardom elsewhere in the world. Hamilton explores this through discussion of Dy Saveth, one of the country's most prominent pre-Khmer Rouge era stars. As Hamilton notes, with the rise of the Khmer Rouge, much of the country's film heritage has been lost, but recent films such as *Golden Slumbers* (Davy Chou, 2011) and *The Last Reel* (Kulikar Sotho, 2014) (which also feature Dy Saveth) have offered nostalgic reflections on this period and the chance to reconnect with the lost stardom of the past.

In Chapter 2, I discuss P. Ramlee, the biggest star of the Singapore-based 'golden age' of Malay cinema of the 1950s and 1960s and still a legendary figure in modern-day Malaysia. While existing work on the multi-talented Ramlee has focused predominantly on his roles as a director and musician, this chapter investigates his intertextual star persona, made up of his appearances in films as well as in extra-filmic materials, such as newspapers and fan magazines, and his performance style, which carried significant meaning in his films and stardom more generally. The chapter outlines some of the distinctive features of Malay stardom, such as its vertically integrated studios, which played a central role in the creation and promotion of its stars, and its connections with local cultural forms, such as the *bangsawan* theatre. In doing so, I show how stardom, particularly through its emphasis on notions of individualism, contributed to tensions in Ramlee's persona between a traditional Malay image, based in *kampung* (village) communities, and a more modern, urban identity.

Related issues are explored in Chapter 3 by Jane Ferguson through her discussion of Win Oo, the biggest star of the Burmese cinema between 1962 and 1988, albeit in a significantly different national context, with Win Oo's stardom coinciding with the duration of Ne Win's repressive military dictatorship. Ferguson shows how Win Oo's stardom can offer a different perspective on this period, which, as she comments, is usually defined in terms of 'repression, conflict, and economic stagnation'. On the one hand, the military regime sought to use the cinema to promote its ideological agenda, known as the 'Burmese way to Socialism', through the nationalisation of the cinema, censorship and the promotion of Burmese socialist realist film. However, as Ferguson argues, Win Oo's stardom offered something different. While still distinctly Burmese, appearing in films with Buddhist themes and values, his star persona emphasised a cosmopolitan look and ideas, with him sharing similarities with such Hollywood stars as Elvis Presley and James Dean. While emerging from significantly different social and political contexts, Win Oo shares clear similarities with P. Ramlee. They were both multi-talented individuals who contributed to all aspects of the film production process; they were romantic leads who were also famous for their music and singing; they were icons of modernity and cosmopolitanism, who were also distinctly traditional.

Since the Second World War, Southeast Asia has experienced many armed conflicts, including wars of independence (in Indochina and Indonesia), proxy wars relating to the Cold War (in Vietnam, Cambodia and Laos) and internal conflicts, owing to contesting visions for the new postcolonial nations (the Malayan Emergency). The next two chapters investigate connections between war and stardom in Southeast Asia, through case studies on stardom in relation to the Vietnam War and its aftermath. In Chapter 4, Qui-Ha Hoang Nguyen discusses the North Vietnamese star Trà Giang. While stardom has commonly been seen as an extension of capitalism, with stars embodying notions of individualism, conspicuous consumption and glamour, Nguyen explains that Trà Giang's persona instead stressed ideas that were important to the revolutionary cause: in her films she frequently took on mother-fighter roles and off-screen was presented as an ideal worker figure, who lived a modest and simple life. As with the examples of stardom already considered, Trà Giang also embodied ideas relating to modernity, though here it was a 'socialist modernity', where women were encouraged, as part of the national cause, to take on an active professional life, and in doing so Trà Giang attained a degree of gender equality. She played an active role in the creative process, allowing her to inject her portrayals of the communist mother figure with an emotional resonance that helped her connect with audiences and which challenged the 'Statue-like' portrayals of communism commonly found in cinema. While the stardom of Win Oo – which existed within a socialist framework – was compatible with the entertainment and glamour associated with Hollywood stardom, Nguyen presents a significantly different picture of the socialist stardom that existed in North Vietnam, one that was based on a more simple, modest aesthetic and the promotion of revolutionary ideals.

In Chapter 5, Pujita Guha explores another dimension of stardom in relation to the Vietnam War through her discussion of Kiều Chinh. While Trà Giang's stardom was a product of the North Vietnamese state, Kiều Chinh's stardom speaks primarily of the South Vietnamese diasporic experience. Although born in the north of Vietnam, she first became a national star in the anti-communist Saigon-based film industry, where she was a glamorous icon of 1960s style and appeared in commercial genre films, such as *Từ Sài Gòn Đến Điện Biên Phủ* (From Saigon to Dien Bien Phu, Ying Chang, 1967), alongside Thẩm Thúy Hằng, another major star of the South Vietnamese cinema. In addition, Kiều Chinh appeared in several international and transnational productions at this time, including

A Yank in Vietnam (Marshall Thompson, 1964), *Operation C.I.A.* (Christian Nyby, 1965), *Destination Vietnam* (Lamberto V. Avellana, 1968) and *The Evil Within* (Lamberto V. Avellana, 1970), before moving to the USA upon the fall of Saigon in 1975. There, Kiều Chinh continued her acting career, as an Asian American diaspora star, appearing in several films and television shows, including episodes of *M*A*S*H* (Alan Alda, 1977) and *Dynasty* (Richard and Esther Shapiro, 1983), and the films *The Joy Luck Club* (Wayne Wang, 1993) and *Journey from the Fall* (Ham Tran, 2006). However, for Guha, ultimately Kiều Chinh was a 'passportless' star, whose stardom represented a prolonged period of displacement, first from North to South Vietnam and then from South Vietnam to California, a career which sheds light on the region's experiences of war, displacement and exile.

One of the defining features of postcolonial Southeast Asia is the rise of authoritarian politics, evident through such figures as Ne Win (Burma), Pol Pot (Cambodia), Mahathir Mohamad (Malaysia), Ferdinand Marcos (the Philippines) and Lee Kuan Yew (Singapore), along with one of the most well-known examples of this phenomenon, Suharto (Indonesia), whose New Order regime (1966–98) rose to power following an attempted military coup in 1965. The next two chapters explore how different kinds of Indonesian stardom functioned within this context. In Chapter 6, David Hanan looks at three types of stardom popularised in Indonesia during the New Order: the singer and comedy star Benyamin S, who possessed a down-to-earth image that was linked with the Betawi culture to which he belonged, thus offering a key example of the role that regional identities within nations can play in Southeast Asian stardom; Rhoma Irama, a singer who appeared in musical films and who represented an individualised form of 'superstardom', albeit with a distinctly Indonesian dimension, owing to the *dangdut* music and Islamic themes found in his films; three stars who rose to fame from Teguh Karya's Teater Populer theatre collective – Christine Hakim, Slamet Rahardjo and Tuti Indra Malaon – who starred in some of Karya's most critically acclaimed work. In doing so, Hanan points towards the multiple star systems at work in Indonesian cinema and the ways these connected with the nation's regional and national cultures, its generic contexts, including comedy and musical films, and the work of established directors, such as Teguh Karya.

In Chapter 7, Thomas Barker considers another type of stardom to emerge under the New Order: the *bom seks* (sex bomb). These female stars were known for their *'berani'* (bravery) – their willingness to appear in sexual roles, often in a state of undress. Through an examination of newspaper and magazine articles from the 1970s to 1990s, Barker explains the various factors that brought about this form of stardom, including the modernisation of Indonesian society under the Suharto regime, the influence of relaxed import restrictions, which witnessed the screening of 'risqué' films from Japan and Italy, as well as issues relating to state policy, tradition, religion and commercial forces. Barker examines the defining features of the *bom seks*, including discussion of the post-*bom seks* career trajectories of some key examples. While positioning these stars within their cinematic contexts, discussing some of the genres and films in which they appeared, Barker explains how these stars reveal transformations in Indonesia relating to sexuality and gender roles, and how these relate to developments that occurred under the New Order regime.

The final four chapters bring us into the twenty-first century, with the first two looking at contemporary Philippine star vehicles, and the next two examining instances of Thai stardom that emerged after the New Thai Cinema of the late 1990s. In Chapter 8, Katrina Ross Tan examines the stardom of Nora Aunor and Sharon Cuneta through the roles they took in Overseas Filipino Worker (OFW) films, with Nora starring in *The Flor Contemplacion Story* (Joel Lamangan, 1995) and Sharon Cuneta in *Caregiver* (Chito S. Roño, 2008). As Tan argues, these films functioned as star vehicles at critical moments in their careers, representing comebacks for both stars. While both have attained huge levels of fame in the Philippines, with Nora being known as 'the Superstar' and Sharon as 'the Megastar', there are significant differences in their stardom. Dark skinned and small in stature, Nora's rise to fame in the 1970s represented a new kind of stardom in which she looked and spoke like the masses, rather than the light-skinned ideal represented by the nation's *mestizo/a* (mixed-race) stardom. Sharon, a *mestiza* star, became famous in the 1980s and had to modify her image to appeal to Nora's audience, as Tan explains. In their OFW films both stars take on the role of the *'babaeng martir'* (the long suffering female), but for different ideological purposes: while Nora's portrayal in *The Flor Contemplacion Story* offers a call for collective action by foregrounding the difficulties OFWs face, in *Caregiver* Sharon Cuneta presents the work of the OFW in more glamorous and desirable terms, as part of an aspirational narrative that individualises, rather than collectivises, the figure of the OFW.

In Chapter 9 Chrishandra Sebastiampillai also explores key features of Philippine stardom, including the role played by the television studio ABS-CBN in the Philippine star system, the influence of the Catholic Church, the use of stardom and social media to promote recent films, as well as a phenomenon distinct to Philippine cinema, the 'love team': star couples who appear together in film after film (and who may, or may not, be a couple in real life). Sebastiampillai focuses on one of the most popular love teams of recent years, made up of John Lloyd Cruz and Bea Alonzo, two stars who, like Sharon, possess the *mestizo/a* appearance that is still characteristic of stardom in the Philippines. Discussing *A Second Chance* (Cathy Garcia Molina, 2015), the sequel to their hugely successful *One More Chance* (Cathy Garcia Molina, 2007), Sebastiampillai demonstrates the connections between love teams, star vehicles and the romance genre, and considers the role their stardom plays in relation to the film's narrative, which, as she points out, disrupts traditional Philippine notions of gender.

The book's final two chapters consider contemporary stardom in Thailand. Issues relating to race, raised in Chapters 8 and 9, are explored in Chapter 10 by Mary Ainslie through a discussion of the *luk khrueng* (Thai Eurasian) stardom of Ananda Everingham. Ananda is potentially the biggest star of recent Thai cinema, having achieved several major box office hits, including the internationally well-known horror film *Shutter* (*Shutter Kòt tit Winyaan*, Banjong Pisanthanakun, 2004). With mixed Australian and Laotian heritage, he is also a prime example of Thailand's *luk khrueng* stardom. Ainslie provides a historical overview of the *luk khrueng*, who emerged in the post-Second World War years, rose to prominence in the 1980s and is now a ubiquitous figure in Thai cinema. Using Ananda as a case study to discuss the changing status of the *luk khrueng* performer, Ainslie examines his position in the post-1997 New Thai film industry, his feminisation, in line with common gender stereotypes about the *luk khrueng*, and his more recent diversification, with him taking on roles that move beyond common connotations associated with this figure. In discussing Ananda in relation to the contradictory ideas associated with the *luk khrueng*, Ainslie explains the connections between Thai stardom and recent transformations in Thai society.

In Chapter 11, the book's final chapter, Katarzyna Ancuta examines links between stardom and genre through a discussion of Jeeja Yanin, a *muay thai* star who has appeared in such films as *Chocolate* (Prachya Pinkaew, 2008) and *Raging Phoenix* (Rashane Limtrakul, 2009), while also taking roles in several other high profile films including *Never Back Down: No Surrender* (Michael Jai White, 2016) and *Triple Threat* (Jesse V. Johnson, 2019). Ancuta situates Jeeja in relation to female martial arts stardom, while also exploring her place within Thailand's masculinist *muay thai* cinema, which has been made internationally famous by films like *Ong-Bak* (Prachya Pinkaew, 2003) and stars such as Tony Jaa. Explaining this genre's emphasis on a masculine and nationalistic ideology, which largely excludes women, Ancuta asks what happens when it features a female star such as Jeeja. While Jeeja has achieved considerable fame, she has been less able to capitalise on her stardom than many of the Thai stars whose careers have been based on their roles in popular television dramas and, as Ancuta notes, she has achieved more success abroad than at home. As such, she gives insight into the dynamics of stardom in contemporary Thailand, as well as into notions of gender and national identity in recent Thai cinema.

In sum, the chapters that make up this volume demonstrate the important role film stars have played across Southeast Asia at different points in time, from the 1950s to the present day. They also show how scholarship on the region's stardom can help to broaden the geographical scope of existing star studies and can make a valuable contribution to the growing body of work on popular cinema in Southeast Asia, facilitating a fuller understanding of the region's filmmaking and the societies from which it has emerged.

References

Ainslie, Mary J. and Katarzyna Ancuta (eds) (2018), *Thai Cinema: The Complete Guide*, London: I. B. Tauris.

Ancuta, Katarzyna and Patrick Campos (eds), (2015), 'Locating Southeast Asian Horror: Special Issue', *Plaridel* 12:2.

Ascheid, Antje (2003), *Hitler's Heroines: Stardom and Womanhood in Nazi Germany*, Philadelphia: Temple University Press.

Babington, Bruce (2001), *British Stars and Stardom: From Alma Taylor to Sean Connery*, Manchester: Manchester University Press.

Bandhauer, Andrea and Michelle Royer (eds) (2015), *Stars in World Cinema: Screen Icons and Star Systems Across Cultures*, London: I. B. Tauris.

Barker, Thomas (2019), *Indonesian Cinema after the New Order: Going Mainstream*, Hong Kong: Hong Kong University Press.

Baumgärtel, Tilman (ed.) (2012), *Southeast Asian Independent Cinema: Essays, Documents, Interviews*, Hong Kong: Hong Kong University Press.

Bayman, Louis and Sergio Rigoletto (eds) (2013), *Popular Italian Cinema*, Basingstoke, New York: Palgrave Macmillan.

Bräunlein, Peter and Andrea Lauser (eds) (2016), *Ghost Movies in Southeast Asia and Beyond: Narratives, Cultural Contexts, Audiences*, Leiden: Koninklijke Brill.

Carter, Erica (2004), *Dietrich's Ghosts: The Sublime and the Beautiful in Third Reich Film*, London: British Film Institute.

Clark, Danae (1995), *Negotiating Hollywood: The Cultural Politics of Actors' Labor*, Minneapolis: University of Minnesota Press.

Deocampo, Nick (2011), *Film: American Influences on Philippine Cinema*, Manila: Anvil Press.

Dudrah, Rajinder, Elke Mader and Bernhard Fuchs (eds) (2015), *SRK and Global Bollywood*, Oxford: Oxford University Press.

Dyer, Richard (1979), *Stars*, London: British Film Institute.

Dyer, Richard (1986), *Heavenly Bodies: Film Stars and Society*, New York: St Martin's Press.

Dyer, Richard (2004), *Heavenly Bodies: Film Stars and Society*, 2nd edn, London: Routledge.

Dyer, Richard and Ginette Vincendeau (eds) (1992), *Popular European Cinema*, London: Routledge.

Farquhar, Mary and Yingjin Zhang (eds) (2010), *Chinese Film Stars*, New York: Routledge.

Feng, Lin (2017), *Chow Yun-Fat and Territories of Hong Kong Stardom*, Edinburgh: Edinburgh University Press.

Ferguson, Jane (2020), 'Pearl tears on the silver screen: war movies and expanding Burmese militarism in the early independence years', in Gaik Cheng Khoo, Thomas Barker and Mary J. Ainslie (eds), *Southeast Asia on Screen: From Independence to Financial Crisis (1945–1998)*, Amsterdam: Amsterdam University Press, pp. 75–92.

Frederick, William H. (1982), 'Rhoma Irama and the Dangdut style: aspects of contemporary Indonesian popular culture', *Indonesia* 34, pp. 102–30.

Galt, Rosalind (2021), *Alluring Monsters: The Pontianak and Cinemas of Decolonization*, New York: Columbia University Press.

Gimenez, Jean-Pierre and Gaëtan Margirier (eds) (2012), *Southeast Asian Cinema*, Lyon: Asia-Expo.

González-López, Irene and Michael Smith (2018), *Tanaka Kinuyo: Nation, Stardom and Female Subjectivity*, Edinburgh: Edinburgh University Press.

Gundle, Steven (2013), *Mussolini's Dream Factory: Film Stardom in Fascist Italy*, New York, Oxford: Berghahn Books.

Hanan, David (ed.) (2001), *Film in South East Asia: Views from the Region*, Manila: SEAPAVAA.

Hanan, David and Basoeki Koesasi (2011), 'Betawi Moderen: songs and films of Benyamin S from Jakarta in the 1970s – further dimensions of Indonesian popular culture', *Indonesia* 91, pp. 35–76.

Harrison, Rachel V. (2010), 'The man with the golden gauntlets: Mit Chaibancha's *Insi Thorng* and the hybridization of Red and Yellow perils in Thai Cold War action cinema', in Tony Day and Maya H. T. Liem (eds), *Cultures at War: The Cold War and Cultural Expression in Southeast Asia*, Ithaca: Cornell Southeast Asia Program Publications, pp. 195–226.

Harrison, Rachel V. and Peter A. Jackson (eds) (2010), *The Ambiguous Allure of the West: Traces of the Colonial in Thailand*, Hong Kong: Hong Kong University Press.
Ingawanij, May Adadol and Benjamin McKay (eds) (2012), *Glimpses of Freedom: Independent Cinema in Southeast Asia*, Ithaca: Cornell Southeast Asia Program Publications.
Khoo, Gaik Cheng (2020), 'Introduction: Southeast Asia on screen: from independence to financial crisis (1945–1998)', in Gaik Cheng Khoo, Thomas Barker and Mary J. Ainslie (eds), *Southeast Asia on Screen: From Independence to Financial Crisis (1945–1998)*, Amsterdam: Amsterdam University Press, pp. 9–31.
Khoo, Gaik Cheng, Thomas Barker and Mary J. Ainslie (eds) (2020), *Southeast Asia on Screen: From Independence to Financial Crisis (1945–1998)*, Amsterdam: Amsterdam University Press.
Klevan, Andrew (2005), *Film Performance: From Achievement to Appreciation*, London: New York: Wallflower.
Landy, Marcia (2008), *Stardom, Italian Style: Screen Performance and Personality in Italian Cinema*, Bloomington: Indiana University Press.
Lau, Dorothy Wai Sim (2018), *Chinese Stardom in Participatory Cyberculture*, Edinburgh: Edinburgh University Press.
Lawrence, Michael (ed.) (2020), *Indian Film Stars: New Critical Perspectives*, London: British Film Institute.
Leung Wing-Fai and Andy Willis (eds) (2014), *East Asian Film Stars*, New York: Palgrave Macmillan.
Lim, Bliss Cua (2015), 'Sharon's Noranian turn: stardom, race, and language in Philippine cinema', in Andrea Bandhauer and Michelle Royer (eds), *Stars in World Cinema: Screen Icons and Star Systems Across Cultures*, London: I. B. Tauris, pp. 169–83.
Lim, David and Hiroyuki Yamamoto (eds) (2012), *Film in Contemporary Southeast Asia: Cultural Interpretation and Social Intervention*, New York: Routledge.
McDonald, Paul (2013), *Hollywood Stardom*, Chichester: Wiley-Blackwell.
McLean, Adrienne (2004), *Being Rita Hayworth: Labor, Identity, and Hollywood Stardom*, New Brunswick: Rutgers University Press.
Macnab, Geoffrey (2000), *Searching for Stars: Stardom and Screen Acting in British Cinema*, London: Cassell.
Majumdar, Neepa (2009), *Wanted Cultured Ladies Only!: Female Stardom and Cinema in India, 1930s–1950s*, Urbana, Chicago: University of Illinois Press.
Meissner, Nico (2021), *Independent Filmmaking in South East Asia: Conversations with Filmmakers on Building and Sustaining a Creative Career*, Oxford, New York: Routledge.
Naremore, James (1988), *Acting in the Cinema*, Berkeley, London: University of California Press.
Pomerance, Murray and Kyle Stevens (eds) (2018a), *Close-up: Great Cinematic Performances, Volume 1: America*, Edinburgh: Edinburgh University Press.
Pomerance, Murray and Kyle Stevens (eds) (2018b), *Close-up: Great Cinematic Performances, Volume 2: International*, Edinburgh: Edinburgh University Press.
Redmond, Sean and Su Holmes (eds) (2007), *Stardom and Celebrity: A Reader*, London: SAGE Publications.

Sebastiampillai, Chrishandra (2019), 'Love Teams in 1970s Philippine Cinema', unpublished PhD thesis, Monash University.

Sebastiampillai, Chrishandra (2020), 'Nora Aunor vs Ferdinand Marcos – popular youth films of 1970s Philippine cinema', in Gaik Cheng Khoo, Thomas Barker and Mary J. Ainslie (eds), *Southeast Asia on Screen: From Independence to Financial Crisis (1945–1998)*, Amsterdam: Amsterdam University Press, pp. 215–31.

Sebastiampillai, Chrishandra (2021), 'Crazy rich Eurasians: white enough to be acceptable, Asian enough to be an asset', *Celebrity Studies* 12:2, pp. 219–33.

Shaw, Lisa and Stephanie Dennison (eds) (2004), *Popular Cinema in Brazil, 1930–2001*, Manchester: Manchester University Press.

Shingler, Martin (2012), *Star Studies: A Critical Guide*, London: British Film Institute, Palgrave Macmillan.

Sim, Gerald (2020), *Postcolonial Hangups in Southeast Asian Cinema: Poetics of Space, Sound, and Stability*, Amsterdam: Amsterdam University Press.

Smith, Iain Robert (2012), '"You're really a miniature Bond": Weng Weng and the transnational dimensions of cult film stardom', in Kate Egan and Sarah Thomas (eds), *Cult Film Stardom: Offbeat Attractions and Processes of Cultification*, London: Palgrave Macmillan.

Stacey, Jackie (1994), *Star Gazing: Hollywood Cinema and Female Spectatorship*, London: Routledge.

Steimer, Lauren (2021), *Experts in Action: Transnational Hong Kong-Style Stunt Work and Performance*, Durham, NC: Duke University Press.

Tadiar, Neferti X. M. (2002), '*Himala* (miracle): the heretical potential of Nora Aunor's star power', *Signs: Journal of Women in Culture and Society* 27:3, pp. 703–41.

Vincendeau, Ginette (2000), *Stars and Stardom in French Cinema*, London; New York: Continuum.

Viswamohan, Aysha Iqbal and Claire M. Wilkinson (eds) (2020), *Stardom in Contemporary Hindi Cinema: Celebrity and Fame in Globalized Times*, Singapore: Springer.

Weintraub, Andrew (2010), *Dangdut Stories: A Social and Musical History of Indonesia's Most Popular Music*, New York: Oxford University Press.

Woodrich, Christopher Allen (2017), 'Negotiating the path of fame: tradition and modernity in the public persona of Roekiah (1917–1945)', *International Journal of Humanity Studies* 1:1, pp. 17–28.

Yu, Sabrina Qiong and Guy Austin (eds) (2017), *Revisiting Star Studies: Cultures, Themes and Methods*, Edinburgh: Edinburgh University Press.

Chapter 1

Spectral stars, haunted screens: Cambodian golden age cinema

Annette Hamilton

Popular visions of Cambodia: Angelina Jolie, Hollywood star, swinging through vast fake caverns in *Lara Croft: Tomb Raider* (Simon West, 2001), a fictional adventure based on a video game. Another view: black and white images, mug shots, thousands of anonymous Khmer faces pinned to gloomy prison walls. This is the 'meaning' of Cambodia to most Westerners, reflected in the two most common tourist experiences: the ancient temples of Angkor Wat near Siem Reap, the torture and execution centre Tuol Sleng in Phnom Penh.[1] Ancient monuments, modern genocide: few know, or could imagine, that this country once was entertained by a wild escapist romantic cinema which grew, flourished and disappeared in the space of little more than a decade. Among the small national film industries of Southeast Asia, Cambodia's has been one of the least known.[2]

This chapter offers an overview of cinema in Cambodia especially during the period regarded as its 'golden age', and discusses the specific nature of stardom in that era. As is the case with popular cinema everywhere, it was a cinema where stars could shine. The basic structures of stardom, familiar from Hollywood cinema, emerged, but in the Cambodian case distinct and unique inflections arose from the historical moment of this cinema's existence. The great stars of Cambodian cinema embodied special qualities which came from their own charisma and skills. However, we also now recognise them as spectres, ghostly reminders of a past gone but not forgotten. These stars live on in memorial fragments today, bearing a tragic load through the knowledge of their fates, and the fates of their films. Most of the great stars (and directors, writers, musicians, dancers) did not merely fade away into the obscurity of age, decline and change of fashion. Instead, they disappeared in 1975 when the Khmer Rouge eliminated them along with their glittering and fantastical films. Today, we can recuperate only a glimpse of the stars and the films. A labour of research and memory slowly fills the archive with moments, passages, images and reminders. The painstaking reconstruction and appreciation of Cambodian cinema has been developing through archival searches around the world and interviews with the few remaining survivors.[3]

From its inception, cinema prompted thoughts of magic, illusion, ghosts and revenants. Cinematic techniques – the close-up, slow motion, time-lapse, cutting and editing – opened up a new way of seeing and announced the power of the uncanny in the imagination of modernity. Derrida's *Specters of Marx* (1994) introduced the 'spectral turn' in critical philosophy. It took almost two decades for this thinking to enter cultural analysis (see for instance Gordon 2008; del Pilar Blanco and Peeran 2013) and then a short step to reintroducing the spectral in media and cinema studies (Leeder 2015 and 2017). The Internet and its inherently unstable digital environment has newly enabled the spectral through re-inscription of the archive (Leeder 2017:182). The archive wields great powers of revaluation and interpretation. New domains of reflection and cultural identification arise with unpredictable results (see Røssaak 2010; Ernst 2012; Ernst 2017).[4]

In a small lane not far from the central Phnom Penh markets is a humble building dedicated to the recuperation of Cambodia's visual heritage. The Khmer Rouge regime (1975–9) destroyed almost all existing film material, including the many hundreds of feature films made in the kingdom, rare early documentary footage, films of theatrical performances, pamphlets, posters and countless other ephemeral documents. In 2006 the Bophana Audio-Visual Resource Centre was established to comb the world for film and audio material from Cambodia and provide it in an accessible digitised form to anyone who wishes to see it.

At various times between 2011 and 2013 I pored over flickering images on the small monitors, listening to crackling texts and music through headphones, taking notes on the narrow uncomfortable desk. Every afternoon schoolchildren would arrive, sometimes just for fun and sometimes for their school projects. A few other researchers appeared now and then. Rithy Panh, revered for his films reconstructing Khmer Rouge histories and the aftermath, has an office and screening facilities at the Centre which acts as a seedbed of documentary cinema for a new generation of Khmer students, many of them working on projects related to the Khmer Rouge years.[5] It requires continued maintenance in the difficult tropical environment. By late afternoon the viewing room reflects a trembling bluish-grey light from the monitors as ghostly images of a vanished past are summoned into the here and now.

Cinema in Cambodia

In the short but glittering history of Khmer cinema the predominant influences came from French, Hindi and to a lesser extent Chinese sources. Hollywood films never seem to have been as popular with the Khmer audience. Film was introduced into the French colonies (Protectorates) as part of France's 'civilising mission'. Its early circulation and the almost immediate debates about its dangers especially in what is now Vietnam is a fascinating story which remains to be written.[6]

In Cambodia film became a widespread and popular form of entertainment with little overt political implications. The immediate popularity of film set the stage for a visual culture which saw film as a new way of linking past and present, nation and mythology.

The short Khmer word for film is 'kon' (cf. Thai 'khon'), a term sometimes used for the traditional shadow puppet play (Wille 2009: 18).[7] As elsewhere in Southeast Asia, the puppet theatre is composed of a group of highly trained artists who have elements of spirituality and the sacred attached to them. The modern movie screen seemed to be readily accepted as another form of shadow-play.

The first modern cinema in Cambodia was set up on the riverfront in Phnom Penh in 1909. Although the audiences were largely European, the outdoor location made it readily accessible to locals. Cinemas were established in all the main cities and towns by 1920 and mobile cinemas brought film to people in more remote regions. By 1951 seven cinemas existed in Phnom Penh, five screening French and other Western movies, the others presenting Chinese films (Wille 2009: 21).

By the 1940s some Khmer had begun filming themselves (Muan and Daravuth 2001a, 2001b). In the 1950s the United States Information Service began promoting film as a useful adjunct to anti-communist education and development. US mobile cinecars showed films about life in America and local people were trained as cameramen, editors and sound technicians. By the beginning of the 1960s there were trained cinema technicians, an adequate infrastructure and eager audiences (Wille 2009: 22–4).

Norodom Sihanouk: the king's films and the origins of stardom

With the accession to the throne of the young King Norodom Sihanouk (Figure 1.1) the influence of the movies was set to expand exponentially. Sihanouk adored cinema and wanted Khmer to make their own films. To help the infant industry he ensured that quotas were introduced to limit the number of foreign films in the kingdom. Nevertheless movies from France, the USA, India, China and Thailand played in most large villages, towns and cities.

At Sihanouk's invitation French 'exoticist' film director Marcel Camus filmed *L'Oiseau de paradis* (Dragon Sky, Marcel Camus, 1962) in Cambodia in 1961 with a Khmer cast and trainee crew. Many went on to glittering careers, including Meas Sam E, Nary Hem, Nop Nem, Saksi Sbong and Bopha Devi. The number of movie production companies also expanded, with up to sixty companies making local films (interview with Yvon Hem, 3 July 2007, reported in Wille 2009: 21). Most popular were movies based on traditional mythologies, especially those with fantastic and supernatural aspects which could, by the magic of cinema, be brought onto the screen with apparent realism.

Figure 1.1 King Norodom Sihanouk in *Norodom Sihanouk: Roi Cinéaste*, written by Frédéric Mitterrand, directed by Jean-Baptiste Martin, produced by Marie Mitterrand and Jean-Baptiste Martin. Image courtesy of CasaDei Productions © 1996.

There were many technical problems, especially arising from a shortage of equipment and difficult conditions, in large part due to lack of temperature and humidity control. Most films were sent to Hong Kong or France for processing. Live narrators were often used until 1968. Then a sound studio was opened with simultaneous recording of sound and voice (Muan and Daravuth 2001a: 101).

Norodom Sihanouk's films form a very specific corpus quite unlike anything else made in Cambodia before or since. His films have been subjected to much negative assessment over the years. They are among the few to survive in complete form following the Khmer Rouge takeover in 1975. He took them with him into exile and continued to work on them, particularly when he was hosted by Kim Il-Sung in North Korea. Some consider his obsession with filmmaking to be one of the main reasons for his downfall, as he inhabited imaginary worlds of past and present while the state slid into disaster (Osborne 1994: 6). Nevertheless, his best films are now appreciated for their lively entertainment value and depiction of Cambodia as it was before the catastrophes of the Khmer Rouge era.

Studies of stardom in Western cinema take so much for granted – the industrial basis, the studio system, commercialisation, national distribution, the segmentation of the audience, fandom (see Gledhill 1991; King 2014). The rise of stardom in Cambodia began with Sihanouk's belief in the importance of film as a modern means to express his own absolute identity with the nation. Stars? Who could be greater stars than the members of the royal family and its retainers? Consequently he made himself, his family, friends and courtiers the stars of his films. In the documentary *Norodom Sihanouk: Roi Cinéaste* (Norodom Sihanouk: King and Filmmaker, Jean-Baptiste Martin, 1997) the king explains why whenever he appeared as the principal male lead, Monique, his wife, took the female lead. He states, in his breathy soft French, that Monique did not want to perform love scenes with any other man. In fact, it would have been scandalous had she done so. There are not many love scenes in the king's films, and he and Monique demonstrate only the most modest expressions of affection.

Norodom Sihanouk's daughter Bopha Devi, a renowned classical dancer, starred in his first film, *Apsara* (Norodom Sihanouk, 1966).[8] *Apsara* is the term for a female spirit of the clouds and waters in Hindu and Buddhist belief. *Apsaras* appear in dance, literature and painting in many Asian cultures. Sihanouk used the traditional figure of the *Apsara* to comment on modern life in Cambodia. In colour with a well-constructed soundtrack, parts of the dialogue are spoken in the Khmer inflected French common in the 1960s. The film also starred the king and queen, along with Nhiek Tioulong, a well-known actor often cast as a philanderer, and Saksi Sbong, who became a favourite star following this film. It links the mystic past with a present day where Jaguars and Cadillacs proceed down modern roads through a graceful clean city. It is a traditional love story but also an ironic celebration of the raffish behaviour of Sihanouk's circle. *Apsara* reveals Sihanouk's ideas about the modern nation state and a vision of national independence. Most of the king's films include reference to Angkor Wat, and this film opens with the National Independence Monument in Phnom Penh with its Angkorean-style carvings, linking Sihanouk's recuperation of the great traditions of the Khmer empire with modernist Phnom Penh.

The king's son Crown Prince Sihamoni played the lead in one of his early films, *Le Petit Prince* (The Little Prince, Norodom Sihanouk, 1967). A beautiful delicate boy of around twelve at the time, he comported himself on-screen with great charm and dignity, as he continues to do as King of Cambodia today. In *Norodom Sihanouk: Roi et Cineaste* he reflects on his time as an actor in his father's films with affectionate nostalgia. *Le Petit Prince* might make us squirm a thousand times over, watching the common people offering prostrations and grovelling before the royal prince, but this would have reflected reality, as many newsreel films of the time show.

Sihanouk wanted his stars to be part of the reality of the society although he did prefer experienced actors for some roles. One of his favourites was Dy Saveth, who was a well-known actress in the small but developing commercial film world. His films also featured a number of local expatriate dignitaries. In his urban films they are seen in nightclubs or eating in restaurants with important Cambodians. Prominent army generals also feature. Sihanouk was widely condemned by his Phnom Penh political rivals for using army personnel in his films. Milton Osborne (1979: 48) mentions an incident in which Sihanouk diverted army helicopters from their mission to transport wounded soldiers from the front in order to use them in his first major film, *Apsara*, made in 1966.[9]

Sihanouk's films were intended to have a national political effect. They appealed to many levels of Khmer society, creating deeper identification with audiences who were already highly attuned to seeing movies as a kind of contact with sacred elements of Cambodian history. He tried to make sure his films were shown throughout Cambodia at cinemas in provincial towns and cities and through the mobile country cinemas. He also wanted his films to be seen around the world and they were featured in socialist-bloc film festivals, such as in Moscow. The many occasions when parts of the story are set in Angkor highlights the emotional connection Sihanouk hoped to make between ancient Khmer traditions, modernity and the monarchy.

His films, with their royal stars, negotiated the link between the sacred world of traditional monarchical power and the expression of nationhood and identity in modern times. The lead actors are framed in such a way as to open up the link between this never-to-be-forgotten sacred history and the beauties of the nation.

Modern life and transcendent powers

Sihanouk's films referred to ancient themes of monarchical power on the one hand, and postcolonial modernity on the other. The popular, non-royal cinema similarly oscillated between depictions of contemporary life in urban Cambodia, and encounters with the pre-colonial, pre-modern world of spirits, ghosts and shapeshifters. The popular stars appeared in film after film, usually in similar roles: the handsome male lead, the vampy seductress, the superior woman. So far, so Hollywood (or Europe): but these stars had something more, a supplement beyond glamour. Their power was believed to arise from their direct contact with supernatural forces, the same presiding powers which were believed to be embodied in royalty and the nation itself.

Between around 1960 and 1970 more than 300 films were produced by Cambodian filmmakers.[10] Their roots can be found in Western melodrama although they demonstrate much more strongly a stylistic and narrative influence from the emerging popular Hindi and Thai cinema. Most of these films have long disappeared and others exist only in fragments, but the sparse remainder reflect an unfettered pleasure in the ability of film to offer revivified forms of cultural expression.

For the popular audience, the graceful *Apsaras* and dance-hall aristocrats were one thing, but behind them pulsed the vibrant heart of the unknowable, the forces of the uncanny, witchcraft and cruelty, vengeance or generosity of the unpredictable powers which lie behind the everyday world. Popular stars carried the honour and burden of representing these forces.

Filmmakers came from several backgrounds. A few emerged from Sihanouk's personal interest in filmmaking. Sihanouk had arranged for several of his favourites to study cinematography in France (Wille 2009: 24).[11] A second group came from the United States Information Service film training programme, and a third was composed of talented and enthusiastic amateurs who had little or no formal training, although several had worked for French production companies. The relation between directors and stars was as important in Cambodia as it was in Hollywood. Directors favoured certain stars and placed them in certain kinds of roles which came to define the essential characteristics for which they became adored. As Dyer has pointed out, these contribute to the 'star persona' common in star systems everywhere.

One of the outstanding directors of the period was Ly Bun Yim. He fled the Khmer Rouge and was able to return to Cambodia in 1994, where he has continued to train and support a new generation. In the 1960s and early 1970s his films explored all the fantastic possibilities of cinema technology for the mystical world of popular folklore. He explored the boundaries between past and present, animal and human, ghostly and everyday life. In 1965 he made *Sobasith* (the name of the principal male character) starring Kong Sam Oeun and Virak Dara, both of whom became huge stars in their subsequent movies.

Kong Sam Oeun played famous legendary heroes, deeply embedded in Khmer popular culture and beloved by urban and rural people alike. It is no surprise then that he became one of the primary and most beloved male stars in Cambodian cinema of the time. He was talented, good looking and had a 'sexy' quality, like moodily handsome young men in American cinema of the 1950s. He starred in a controversial film directed by Ly You, *L'Etang sacré* (The Sacred Pond, Ly You, 1970), where he appeared almost naked in a sexually charged scene. But in most of his films he represents a superior masculine position, a hero who acts with morality to restore righteousness. Part of the meaning of these films derives from the audience understanding that the stars represent characters linking imagined past and the experienced present and function as allegories of the nation.[12]

In 1970 came one of the most decisively important films of the era, *The Snake King*, starring Dy Saveth. If Kong Sam Oeun is the heartthrob male lead of the golden era, Dy Saveth is its presiding goddess. And where Kong Sam Oeun was sacrificed and disappeared during the Khmer Rouge era, Dy Saveth survived, and has gone on to remain one of the most vital star figures of Cambodian cinema history.

Dy Saveth: Snake films and beyond

The theme of snake–human transformation forms part of the deep structure of Southeast Asian mythology, almost certainly part of a pre-dynastic and indigenous belief system focused on water, clouds, snakes and gender. Legends of the Naga Snake and its role in establishing kingdoms and nations reappear in numerous folktales, performances, dances, enactments and rituals in the region.[13]

The snake theme was well known in Khmer folktales and stories, and appeared in cinema many times over. The first and most famous of the Snake films is titled in Khmer *Puos Keng Kang* (Tea Lim Koun, 1970). In English (or French equivalent) it has been referred to as 'The Giant Snake', 'The Snake King' or 'The Snake King's Wife'.[14] The original film, two hours and eighteen minutes long, was made in 1969/70 and starred female lead Dy Saveth with Chea Yuthorn as the male lead. Director Tea Lim Koun was a Cambodian of Chinese origin, known as a 'father' of Khmer cinema. The film was enormously successful in Cambodia, Thailand and beyond. The soundtrack included famous songs sung by Sinn Sisamouth and Ros Serey Sothea.[15] The film has a very complicated plot and a happy ending. The Snake King, a giant python capable of transforming into a human man with shiny reflective skin, falls in love with a beautiful village woman who is mistreated by her boorish husband. She conceives a child with the Snake King. The daughter grows into a lovely girl whose hair consists of baby snakes (Figure 1.2). The girl falls in love with a young man from an aristocratic family but although she is able to conceal her half-snake/half-human identity most of the time, certain events cause her powers to be revealed.[16]

Due to its success, a follow-up version was made as a Cambodian-Thai co-production in 1972. Titled *Puos Keng Kang Peak Phii* (The Snake Man Part 2, Tea Lim Koun, 1972), it was known by several English titles, including 'Giant Snake 2', 'Snake Girl 2: Revenge'. Dy Saveth and Chea Yuthorn again starred, along with famous Thai actress Aranua Namwong. The story continues where the last film ended. The happiness of the lead couple turns to sadness and terror due to black magic.

After Khmer Rouge rule ended in 1979 there was no feature film made for over a decade.[17] In 2001 the first full length feature returned to the theme of the Snake King. Director Fai Sang Am's new version of the original tale, again a Cambodian-Thai co-production, starred beautiful seventeen-year-old Cambodian actress Pich Chanbomey and famous Thai heartthrob Winai Krabutr. Fai Sam Ang also directed a 2005 follow

Figure 1.2 Dy Saveth in *Puos Keng Kang*. Image courtesy of Kim Tia.

up, *The Snake King's Grandchild*. Dy Saveth no longer appeared in the Snake films, but her original screen presence was significantly defined by them.

Dy Saveth was born in 1944. She came from a performance family: her grandmother and sisters had been classical dancers in the royal palace, but she was far more attracted to film. She viewed every film possible in Phnom Penh in the 1950s but never imagined she could become a star herself. Yet so it happened, almost overnight, following her being crowned as the first Miss Cambodia at the age of fifteen in 1959.[18]

Her star power was enormous. She appeared in over a hundred feature films, including *L'Oiseau de paradis* in 1962 and in Norodom Sihanouk's *Shadow Over Angkor* in 1967, playing the first wife of General 'Dap' Mchulpich.[19] She also had a lead role in Sihanouk's *Crepuscule* (Twilight) in 1969. Following her role in *The Snake King* she starred in thirty-three films, including several more Snake films and two Chinese-Khmer co-productions.

Dy Saveth was a perfect hybrid of the traditional female performer and the modern charismatic star, full of the youthful cosmopolitan spirit so evident in some of the films of the era, including especially Sihanouk's *La Joie de Vivre* (The Joy of Living, 1969) (although Saveth did not appear in it). But her links to classical dance and to the royal court, including a level of patronage from Sihanouk himself, resulted in her being poised at the junction between the traditional Cambodian imaginary and the urgency of contemporary sixties life. Her graceful presence always offered a counterpart to the sometimes boorish and overblown acting common in many popular movies. She never featured as a promiscuous or dangerous woman, and seemed able to project herself as beneficent, with a quality of maternal kindness blended with a polite superiority.

After the 1970 coup against Sihanouk, Dy Saveth went on working although the growing chaos throughout the country meant that budgets became very limited and travel restrictions made movement difficult. There were dangers in going to the movies: cinemas became a target for Khmer Rouge grenade attacks and the government considered closing them, along with nightclubs. Ly Bun Yim convinced them otherwise. He argued that closing the cinemas would be a sign that the Khmer Rouge had already won (Wille 2009: 31). Nevertheless, cinema owners began to close their premises down of their own accord as the situation in Phnom Penh deteriorated rapidly.

Recuperating the golden years: movies about Khmer stars and movies

Davy Chou is an important figure in the recent development of film in Cambodia. His family moved from Cambodia to France when he was young, and his film-making has been inspired in part by his late grandfather, Van Chann, who was prominent in Cambodian film production in the 1960s. This led him to begin researching the history and remaining material of the era which formed the basis for his beautiful and informative documentary, *Golden Slumbers* (*Le Sommeil d'Or*, Davy Chou, 2011).[20]

In 2010 he moved to Cambodia to locate survivors of its golden age film industry and was fortunate to be able to film and interview Ly Bun Yim, Dy Saveth, Liv Sreng and Yvon Hem (who died in 2012). Dy Saveth provides rich insight into the conditions of the early film industry and an account of her continued role in the Cambodian film world today. *Golden Slumbers* has been screened in many festivals around the world and remains a unique record of loss and destruction of a vital indigenous film industry. The film envelops the viewer in the quality of hauntedness: the abandoned movie theatres, fragments of film, images of lost stars from posters and photographs, extracts from the few remaining films, Davy Chou's sense of engagement with his own missing past.

Dy Saveth returns audiences once again to those themes in a second recent film dealing with the old movies, this time a feature film, *The Last Reel* (Kulikar Sotho, 2014). The debut film from director Kulikar Sotho, who previously worked on international productions including *Lara Croft: Tomb Raider*, *The Last Reel* begins in modern Cambodia when a young woman avoids an arranged marriage and runs away to an abandoned movie theatre in Phnom Penh.[21] She meets an old projectionist, who shows her a film from the golden era which, he says, is missing the last reel. She discovers that her mother was the lead actress and tries to complete the film by shooting the last part. Dy Saveth plays Sotho's mother, whose face also appears in the lost film. Released in 2014, the film has won many prizes for its director, the first Khmer female director since Dy Saveth's directorial work on two films in the 1970s.

Conclusion

Movie stars in Cambodia were something more than mere celebrities. Like movie stars everywhere, they were exceptional, fabulous, different. But because they were thought to participate in a deeper kind of power, conveyed through centuries of history, monarchy, forces of the supernatural and magic, they embodied a transcendence beyond the everyday, an ability to project via the screen the mysterious forces of Khmer consciousness and history to the inner imaginative world of their audiences.

Stardom has a strange relationship with temporality. Normally, stars, like all human beings, age. They emerge when young, at their most compelling, beautiful and handsome. As they appear in movie after movie, they get older, just as the audience members do. But in Cambodia the Khmer Rouge era terminated the normal expected flow of time and being. The beloved and beautiful stars for the most part disappeared entirely. There was no opportunity to watch them develop their talents or grow older. They once were, and then they were not. Between 1975 and 2010 their existence survived only in memory, the lyrics of a few popular songs and in scattered recollections. The stars became spectres. When movies continue to exist we can experience the stars as forever young in their original bodies and forms; time has not really passed and their ghostly presence remains forever with us. But in Cambodia stars and their movies were mostly destroyed and all that remained was a ghostly supplement in the imagination. The living presence of great star Dy Saveth, her return to Cambodia and continued work in film and cultural education, offers support to the recuperation of culture and memory for a new generation.

References

Austin, Jessica (2014), 'Gender and the Nation in Popular Cambodian Heritage Cinema', unpublished MA thesis, University of Hawai'i at Manoa.
Barnes, Leslie (2016), 'The image of a quest: the visual archives of Rithy Panh', *Australian Humanities Review* 59, pp. 190–208.
Barnes, Leslie (2018), 'Un cinéma sans image: palimpsestic memory and the lost history of Cambodian film', in Kathryn Kleppinger and Laura Reeck (eds), *Post-Migratory Cultures in Postcolonial France*, Liverpool: Liverpool University Press, pp. 79–95.
Baumgärtel, Tilman (ed.) (2012), *Southeast Asian Independent Cinema: Essays, Documents, Interviews*, Hong Kong: Hong Kong University Press.
Benzaquen, Stéphanie (2012), 'Remediating genocidal images into artworks: the case of the Tuol Sleng mugshots', in Joram ten Brink and Joshua Oppenheimer (eds), *Killer Images: Documentary Film, Memory and the Performance of Violence*, New York: Wallflower Press, pp. 206–23.
Blum-Reid, Sylvie (2003), *East-West Encounters: Franco-Asian Cinema and Literature*, London: Wallflower Press.
Chandler, David (1991), *The Tragedy of Cambodian History: Politics, War and Revolutions since 1945*, New Haven, CT: Yale University Press.
Chou, Chea (2005), 'Film Industry in Cambodia: Moviegoers' Perspectives', unpublished BA thesis, Royal University of Phnom Penh.
del Pilar Blanco, Maria and Esther Peren (eds) (2013), *The Spectralities Reader: Ghosts and Haunting in Contemporary Cultural Theory*, London: Bloomsbury.
Derrida, Jacques (1994) [*Spectres de Marx*, 1993], *Specters of Marx: The State of the Debt, the Work of Mourning, and the New International*, London: Routledge.
Ernst, Wolfgang (2012), *Digital Memory and the Archive*, Minneapolis and London: University of Minnesota Press.
Ernst, Wolfgang (2017), *The Delayed Present: Media-induced Tempor(e)alities and Techno-traumatic Irritations of 'the Contemporary'*, Berlin: Sternberg Press.
Gaudes, Rüdiger (1993), 'Kaundinya, Preah Thaong, and the Nagi Soma: some aspects of a Cambodian legend', *Asian Folklore Studies* 52:2, pp. 333–58.
Gledhill, Christine (ed.) (1991), *Stardom: Industry of Desire*, New York: Routledge.
Goloubev, Victor (1924), 'Les Légendes de la Nagi et de l'Apsaras', *Bulletin de l'École française d'Extrême-Orient* 24, pp. 501–10.

Gordon, Avery F. (2008), *Ghostly Matters: Haunting and the Sociological Imagination*, Minneapolis: University of Minnesota Press.
Hamilton, Annette (2012a), 'A national cinema in Cambodia?', in Gaëtan Margirier and Jean-Pierre Giminez (eds), *Le Cinéma d'Asie du Sud-Est /Southeast Asian Cinema*, Lyons: Asia-Expo, pp. 68–73.
Hamilton, Annette (2012b), 'A short history of Cambodian cinema', in Gaëtan Margirier and Jean-Pierre Giminez (eds), *Le Cinéma d'Asie du Sud-Est/ Southeast Asian Cinema*, Lyons: Asia-Expo, pp. 92–108.
Hamilton, Annette (2013a), 'Witness and recuperation: Cambodia's new documentary cinema', *Concentric: Literary and Cultural Studies* 39:1, pp. 7–30.
Hamilton, Annette (2013b), 'Cambodian genocide: ethics and aesthetics in the cinema of Rithy Panh', in Axel Bangert, Robert S. C. Gordon and Libby Saxton (eds), *Holocaust Intersections: Genocide and Visual Culture at the New Millennium*, UK: Legenda (MHRA/Maney Publishing), pp. 170–90.
Hamilton, Annette (2018), 'Fragments in the archive: the Khmer Rouge years', *Plaridel* 15:1, pp. 1–14.
'Interview with Dy Saveth' (2007), *Touchstone Magazine, The Insider's Guide to Heritages, Arts and Cultures*, July–September, pp. 41–5.
Jarvis, Helen and Peter Arfanis (2002), 'Publishing in Cambodia – A Survey and Report', *Publishing in Cambodia Project*, Phnom Penh: Center for Khmer Studies, Reyum Institute, Toyota Foundation, December.
Khut, Sornnimul (ed.) (2010), *Kon: The Cinema of Cambodia*, Phnom Penh: VS Vann Sophea Printing House.
King, Barry (2014), *Taking Fame to Market: On the Pre-history and Post-history of Hollywood Stardom*, New York: Palgrave Macmillan.
Knee, Adam (ed.) (2018), 'Cinema and the archives in Southeast Asia', *Plaridel* 15:1.
Leeder, Murray (ed.) (2015), *Cinematic Ghosts: Haunting and Spectrality from Silent Cinema to the Digital Era*, London: Bloomsbury Academic.
Leeder, Murray (2017), *The Modern Supernatural and the Beginnings of Cinema*, London: Palgrave Macmillan.
Muan, Ingrid and Ly Daravuth (2001a), 'A survey of films in Cambodia', in David Hanan (ed.), *Film in South East Asia: Views from the Region*. Manila: SEAPAVAA, pp. 93–106.
Muan, Ingrid and Ly Daravuth (2001b), *Cultures of Independence: An Introduction to Cambodian Arts and Culture in the 1950s and 1960s*, Phnom Penh: Reyum.
Osborne, Milton (1979), *Before Kampuchea: Preludes to a Tragedy*, Sydney: George Allen and Unwin.
Osborne, Milton (1994), *Sihanouk: Prince of Light, Prince of Darkness*, Thailand: Silkworm Books.
Pavie, Auguste (1969), *Les Douze Jeunes Filles ou l'Histoire de Neang Kangrey, Extrait de Mission Pavie, Indochine, tome 1*, Phnom Penh: Éditions de l'Institut bouddhique.
Peou, Chivoin (2008), 'Contemporary Cambodian Cinema: Gender and Generations', unpublished PhD thesis, Carbondale: Southern Illinois University.
Porée-Maspéro, Evelyne (1950), 'Nouvelle étude sur la Nagi Soma', *Journal Asiatique* 238, pp. 237–67.
Przyluski, Paul (1925), 'La princesse l'odeur du poisson et la Nagi dans les traditions de l'Asie Orientale', *Études Asiatiques* 2, pp. 265–84.

Romey, Eliza (2001), 'King, artist, filmmaker: the films of Norodom Sihanouk', in David Hanan (ed.), *Film in South East Asia: Views from the Region*, Manila: SEAPAVAA, pp. 107–18.

Røssaak, Ievind (ed.) (2010), *The Archive in Motion: New Conceptions of the Archive in Contemporary Thought and New Media Practices*, Oslo: Novus Press.

Wille, Kirstin (2009), *Film Production in Cambodia: Conditions and Structure of the Cambodian Film Production Market – Demand and Supply in Consideration of Film Genre*, Ehrfurt: Schriftenreihe der Thüringisch-Kambodschanischen Gesellschaft.

Notes

1. The iconic uses of the Tuol Sleng images and their incorporation into artworks is discussed by Benzaquen (2012).
2. On Cambodia see Muan and Daravuth (2001a and 2001b); Romey (2001); Jarvis and Arfanis (2002); Blum-Reid (2003); Chou (2005); Peou (2008); Wille (2009); Khut (2010); Baumgärtel (2012); Hamilton (2012a, 2012b, 2013a, 2013b, 2018); Austin (2014).
3. Since around 2010 many fragments of golden era films, and some whole films, have appeared on YouTube, in different quality and condition, often uploaded anonymously. Many have no titles, or the titles do not match those of the original films. Some have subtitles in French, Khmer and/or English. Some have been filmed from a live showing, for example during a film festival. Bootleg copies of some films now circulate on CD/DVD in Cambodian markets and beyond. Two recently uploaded compilations (2017) use selected scenes from a variety of lesser known golden era movies. Under the title *Heritage Film Reel Cambodia Old Film Clips 1960s – Golden Era* and *Women in Cambodian Cinema 1960–1974* the clips were compiled and edited by Jessica Austin (see Austin 2014) using material from the Preah Soriya Historical Society with a credit to Bophana Audio-Visual Centre, although it is unclear what role Bophana Centre had in the project. Available at <https://www.youtube.com/watch?v=6lj-ucTRsVE> and <https://www.youtube.com/watch?v=ZM_GpZ89yvg> (last accessed 30 October 2018).

    Readers wishing to explore a wider range of film material will find many of the titles mentioned in the filmography available on my website (Cinemasandcultures.com) on YouTube in part or in whole, including the full original movie of Norodom Sihanouk's *Apsara*, uploaded in five parts by Jatikhmer Entertaniment, Phnom Penh. Available at <https://www.youtube.com/watch?v=ey07ZfePMaU&t=46s> (last accessed 30 October 2018). This was his first feature film and his use of staff and equipment from the Royal Cambodian Air Force is evident throughout. Note particularly in Part 4 at 8.30 scenes from inside Cambodian air force planes. See also: select clips from Ly Bun Yim's *Neang Kong Ray* with Virak Dara: available at <https://www.youtube.com/watch?v=TyvOCge2x7c> (last accessed 30 October 2018); and Kong Sam Oeun and Dy Saveth in *Neang Preay Sawh Pous* (Girl with Snake Hair): available at <https://www.youtube.com/watch?v=fDgD0D_DZ5g> (last accessed 30 October 2018). Although the male lead is said to be Kong Sam Euon in the written text, it is likely that this is an edited version of the original 'Snake' film with Dy Saveth and Chea Yuthorn (1969/70).

4. Issues around archives in Southeast Asia were discussed in a recent special issue of *Plaridel* (Knee 2018).
5. Many thanks to Rithy Panh and the wonderful staff at Bophana for their kindness, support and insights.
6. This author has carried out a partial survey of the many boxes of materials relating to cinema in Indochina, now held at the Archives d'Outre Mer in Aix-en-Provence. The topic requires archival study in far more detail than has been possible to date.
7. The full term is *lakhon nang sbaek*. There are three main forms: episodes from the Reamker (Ramayana), a range of traditional stories, and more localised plays using small coloured leather puppets. Although it was an entertainment, it was also believed to have powerful spiritual elements which affected the mood of viewers, making them collectively share feelings such as sadness, happiness, shock or anger (cf. Wille 2009: 18).
8. He made two films in the 1940s, titled *Tarzan among the Kuoy* (Norodom Sihanouk, 1940s) and *Double Crime on the Maginot Line* (Norodom Sihanouk, 1940s) (referred to by Chandler 1991: 344). I am sure I have seen an extract from *Tarzan*, perhaps at Bophana, although I did not realise it was the king's film. The Kuoy are considered one of the 'wild' peoples of the Cambodian jungles.
9. In *Rose of Bokor* (Norodom Sihanouk, 1969) he starred as a Japanese general occupying Cambodia in the Second World War. The coup which ousted him took place before he filmed many important scenes. While living in the palace in North Korea provided by his good friend Kim Il Sung he was given a battalion of North Korean army personnel with their equipment and transports to act as Japanese occupation troops so he could finish the film, which he dedicated to Kim.
10. In fact there is no accurate record of the number of films made. Some previously unknown seem to be turning up on YouTube even today. Wille estimates 400 films were made between 1960 and 1975 (2009: 31).
11. I have not been able to establish which directors these were. Most of the famous popular directors claim to have been self-taught. <https://www.youtube.com/watch?v=tXwUMRV6EGE> (last accessed 25 November 2018).
12. Kong Sam Oeun often co-starred with Vichara Dany, who, like Saksi Sbong, was a more overtly glamorous star than Dy Saveth.
13. Mythologies of the Naga Snake vary in framework and emphasis. See Przyluski 1925, Porée-Maspéro 1950; Goloubev 1924; Pavie 1969; Gaudes 1993.
14. I would like to thank Ms Kim Tia, daughter of the late Tea Lim Koun, for her discussion and advice about the titling of the film. Ms Kim is the executor of her father's film estate and has her own collection of materials relating to his work. The most literal translation of the Khmer title is 'The Giant Snake'; however Ms Kim states the original 1970 film should be referred to as 'The Snake Man'. Confusion arose from publicity in other Asian markets, and alternative titles appeared on pirated DVDs, some composed of parts of different films. Ms Kim has been involved in efforts to curb the pirated distribution of her father's films, with commendable success.
15. These singers appear in several of Norodom Sihanouk's films and had an overwhelming star presence in the 1960s. Recordings of many of their songs survive and remain popular today on YouTube.

16. See <https://www.youtube.com/watch?v=GN8JSW3fL6E> (last accessed 25 November 2018).
17. *Shadow of Darkness* directed by Yvon Hem (1987) is credited as the first film of the post-Khmer Rouge era and tells the story of a family's struggle to survive.
18. There are many accounts of Dy Saveth's career in online newspapers and journals. See for instance 'Interview with Dy Saveth' (2007).
19. *Shadow Over Angkor* is based on an historical event in 1959, when General 'Dap' Chhuon Mchulpich (Governor and Commander of the Cambodian armed forces in the Angkor region) plotted with the CIA to overthrow Sihanouk.
20. My deepest thanks to Davy Chou for making a DVD of his film available to me and for his delightful company and discussions in Phnom Penh around his experience of making the film. For a stimulating discussion of Davy Chou's postcolonial project see Barnes (2018).
21. This is a real place, once the Hemakcheat Cinema, where many homeless people and visitors from the countryside have found temporary refuge. It also features in Davy Chou's film *Golden Slumbers*.

Chapter 2

P. Ramlee, the *star*: Malay stardom and society in the 1950s–60s

Jonathan Driskell

Although P. Ramlee died in 1973, he has attained legendary status in modern day Malaysia. His songs are still played on the radio, his films are still shown on television, he has streets named after him and two memorial museums devoted to him: one in Penang where he was born and one in Kuala Lumpur in the house where he spent the final years of his life. There is even a stage musical devoted to his life called *P. Ramlee: The Musical*. While his lasting fame in modern day Malaysia presents a somewhat distorted picture of the period's Malay stardom, with Ramlee almost completely eclipsing its other performers, many of whom also attained huge levels of fame during the 'golden age' of Malay cinema (1950s–60s), he was nevertheless its biggest star. He appeared in over sixty films, most in the lead role, and he was the highest paid performer at Malay Film Productions (Sulong 1990: 130), albeit in part because he took on multiple roles in the filmmaking process: he was actor, writer, director, composer and musician. He also appeared ubiquitously in newspaper articles and the period's fan magazines, some of which I discuss in this chapter.

While Ramlee made his most famous films in Singapore, it is Malaysia that has mainly claimed him as its own. This stems in part from the fact that he was born in Penang and died in Kuala Lumpur, after moving there from Singapore. It is also related to issues of race: while Malaysia is multi-ethnic, consisting of Malays, Chinese, Indians and Orang Asli, Malays are the largest group and this has shaped the nation's politics, including its attitude to culture and the arts. There have been many national efforts over the years to promote the Malay filmmaker Ramlee, which Ahmad and Lee (2015) see as part of a broader agenda relating to the

'Malaynisation' of Malaysian society. For instance, he was posthumously awarded the Darjah Panglima Setia Mahkota in 1990 (a prestigious title in the Malaysian honours system), having already been made the rank of Ahli Mangku Negara in 1962, and in order to fund the creation of a P. Ramlee memorial library, a 'P. Ramlee Week' was held from 20 to 28 October 1984, which included, according to a list of events published in the *New Sunday Times* ('Events lined up' 1984), a charity dinner that was to be attended by Prime Minister Mahathir Mohamad. At the same time, Ramlee was also a Singaporean star: he lived there from 1948 to 1964, and Singapore is where he made many of his most famous films, including *Hang Tuah* (Phani Majumdar, 1956), *Penarek Becha* (Trishaw Puller, P. Ramlee, 1955), the *Bujang Lapok* (Ne'er Do Well Bachelors) series, *Antara Dua Darjat* (Between Two Classes, P. Ramlee, 1960) and *Ibu Mertuaku* (My Mother-in-law, P. Ramlee, 1962), and it has been argued that the quality of his films declined when he started working at Merdeka Film Productions in Kuala Lumpur (Van der Heide 2002: 146). Books on Singaporean cinema usually include sections or chapters devoted to him (Uhde and Uhde 2010; Khiun and Teo 2017; Lim 2018) and the question of whether Ramlee should be considered a Malaysian or a Singaporean star is occasionally discussed in the press (Hardi 2009).

Ramlee, then, was a major figure, who has had a broad and lasting impact in Malaysia and beyond. And yet, while a significant body of scholarship on Ramlee has developed, little has focused on his contributions as a *star*. In part this is because he was talented in a multitude of ways, taking on many roles in the filmmaking process. As Uhde and Uhde (2010: 30) point out, it has been joked that the P in P. Ramlee stands for 'pengarah (director), pelakon (actor), penyanyi (singer), pelawak (comedian), and penulis (writer)' (it actually stands for 'Puteh', taken from his full name Teuku Zakaria bin Teuku Nyak Puteh). Academic studies on Ramlee have tended to focus on his creative roles, particularly his work as a director (Barnard and Barnard 2002; Van der Heide 2002; Hassan 2013) and as a musician (McGraw 2009; Adil 2018), both important directions of inquiry, given Ramlee's accomplishments in these areas. Barnard (Barnard and Barnard 2002; Barnard 2005, 2009) has also asked how Ramlee's exploration of the themes of tradition and modernity can help us better understand his perspective on the changing times, an issue that has been investigated further by Adil (2018) in his writing on Ramlee's music and cosmopolitanism. Ramlee's identity as director, musician and star intersect and overlap: as a director he would skilfully deploy his music and established persona through star vehicles; as a star, his identities as a director and musician were central to his persona. However, while Ramlee is frequently referred to as a *star*, there is little work that questions what this means or how it contributed to the Malay cinema.

The first Malay films were made in the 1930s, but it was in the post-Second World War period that the Malay cinema really took off, with two dominant studios emerging: Malay Film Productions (MFP), owned by the Shaw Brothers, and Cathay-Keris Studio, owned by Loke Wan Tho and Ho Ah Loke. While it catered primarily to the significant Malay populations of Malaya and Borneo, this was (and still is) an ethnically diverse region and we can see some of this diversity in the cinema. The studios were owned by Chinese businessmen and most of the first wave of directors were Indians imported from the Bombay film industry (as well as Filipino directors such as Lamberto V. Avellana and Ramon Estella) – it was not until the mid-1950s that Malays began directing some of these films, with Ramlee himself being one of the first (for details on this transition see Barnard 2009). Also, many of these films' technicians, such as editors, camera operators and sound people, came from outside the Malay community. As William Van der Heide (2002) has argued, the films themselves contained a range of multi-cultural influences. Owing to the influence of their directors, the earliest releases were based on Indian stories and – like the Bombay cinema – included musical numbers, components that persisted even when Malays took over the writing and directing. It is referred to as a Malay cinema though because it was mostly in the Malay language, focused on Malay characters, had predominantly Malay casts and increasingly told Malay stories – sometimes based on Malay history, culture and folktales.

This was a golden age for a few reasons. First, there was a significant degree of industrial organisation, with MFP and Cathay-Keris operating as vertically integrated studios with production facilities in Singapore and distribution and exhibition networks across Malaya and Borneo. Such conditions enabled large quantities of films to be made, with over 360 being released between 1948 and 1973. This was also a golden age, however, because of the role stars played within it (Van der Heide 2002: 135) – they were central to the Malay cinema, evident from the films, in which they are treated as stars by the camera and the narratives, but also from the marketing. They appeared prominently on posters and were discussed extensively in film magazines, such as *Bintang* and *Majallah Filem*. Their stardom was in part influenced by Hollywood, owing to the role the studios played in managing and promoting their performers: both MFP and Cathay-Keris had their own actors and personnel contracted to them, as well as their own marketing wings. Malay stardom was also shaped by local influences and culture, particularly the *bangsawan* theatre, or 'Malay opera', which had emerged from the Parsee theatre in Penang in the early twentieth century (Tan 1997). Many actors who had worked in *bangsawan* began to work in the cinema, often bringing with them the 'larger' acting styles they had developed on stage.

In this chapter, then, I examine P. Ramlee's stardom, looking mainly at the period from the mid-1950s to around 1964, during which he was at the height of his fame (for this reason, I do not discuss his time at Merdeka Film Productions in Kuala Lumpur, where he worked from 1964 until his death in 1973, though a study of his stardom during this phase of his career would be a productive area for further research). This was also a historically significant moment, which witnessed independence (1957), the Malayan Emergency (1948–60) and the formation of Malaysia (1963). Although writers have already offered insightful analyses of Ramlee's significance during this time, particularly as a historical agent who contributed to the period's culture, in this chapter I discuss Ramlee primarily in terms of his 'star persona'. While I consider his appearances in films, I am mainly concerned with how they establish and use his image, and the contributions of his performance. I am also interested in his presence in extra-filmic materials, namely newspaper and fan magazine articles, as these also play a role in shaping his identity. I draw on several ideas derived from the work of Richard Dyer, especially his discussions of ordinariness and extraordinariness (1998), and his ideas about stardom and the individual (2004). In doing so my aim is not so much to understand the 'real' P. Ramlee or his perspective on his historical circumstances, but instead to examine the nature of his profoundly popular star persona and consider what this can tell us about the era in which he attained his fame.

Performance, talent and celebrity

P. Ramlee, who was born in 1929 in Penang, had taken an interest in music as a youth during the Japanese occupation and began performing in bands around the island (see *P. Ramlee: The Bright Star* (Harding and Sarji 2002: 9–11) for images of Ramlee in some of these groups). The story of his rise to fame is often mentioned in popular accounts of his career, especially his 'discovery' (a common preoccupation in discussions of stardom), which is even dramatised in *P. Ramlee: The Musical*. He was spotted by B.S. Rajhans, a film director working for MFP, on 1 June 1948 at a performance in Bukit Mertajam, Penang, where he apparently sang one of his most famous songs, 'Azizah', which he would later include in his directorial debut *Penarek Becha*. He was persuaded to move to Singapore to work for MFP, where he was initially employed as an extra and playback singer, before taking on supporting roles in such films as *Chinta* (Love, B. S. Rajhans, 1948), appearing alongside major stars of the period, S. Roomai Noor and Siput Sarawak. It was in 1950, however, that he got his big break, taking his first starring role in *Bakti* (Devotion, L. Krishnan). He continued to appear in MFP films directed by other filmmakers until the mid-1950s, when he was given the opportunity to direct *Penarek Becha*, and from this point on he would take on the dual role of director-star in most of the films he made.

We can explain several aspects of Ramlee's stardom through reference to his discovery, particularly as this involved him entering the cinema from a musical background, rather than via the *bangsawan* theatre. This was not uncommon, with stars entering the cinema in a variety of ways: Maria Menado, Mariani and Latifah Omar were spotted in beauty contests, the Indonesian Osman Gumanti began as a dancer, and several others went directly into the cinema, such as Saadiah, Nordin Ahmad, Jins Shamsuddin, M. Amin and Ahmad Mahmud, among others. By contrast, stars like Siput Sarawak, Udo Omar, Ahmad Nisfu, Siti Tanjung Perak, Mak Dara, S. Kadarisman and Dollah Sarawak all began their careers in *bangsawan*.

By starting out as a musical performer, Ramlee possessed a different kind of performance style to those who had started on stage. While his films contain moments of melodramatic or comedic acting involving large gestures and movements, which may appear theatrical to a modern viewer, Ramlee's performances tended towards a more spontaneous and naturalistic style, which contained nuances of expression as well as moments of sudden excitement and energy. According to L. Krishnan (in Harding and Sarji 2002: 27), this was why he gave Ramlee the starring role in *Bakti*:

> I never really favoured the typical *bangsawan* actor for the simple reason that he would overact. And this did not go down well on film. As a result I began to look for more versatile talent and this is how I chanced upon P. Ramlee. In 1950 I was working on a film entitled *Bakti* (1950) and was sourcing a lead actor for the role of the hero. At that time Roomai Noor was everyone's favourite choice but I decided to go for Ramlee.

This turned out to be a good decision, as Harding and Sarji (28) comment:

> The camera loved him. Everything he did and said in front of it appeared fresh and spontaneous. There was no suggestion of the staginess associated with *bangsawan* or the artificiality that actors used to the stage often display on film. Indeed, his lack of theatrical experience was a positive advantage, for he approached the cinema with a mind completely free from preconceived notions.

The nature of Ramlee's discovery also indicated that *talent* would be central to his fame. This was demonstrated through his ability to perform in a range of genres (comedy, drama, historical, horror), to sing as well as act (other stars relied on playback singers) and from his musical abilities (he composed songs and played several instruments, including the piano, violin and trumpet). His talents were narrativised in 'stardom films' like *Ibu* (Mother, S. Ramanathan, 1953), *Anakku Sazali* (Sazali My Son, Phani Majumdar, 1956) and *Ibu Mertuaku*, in which he played musicians, a premise that provided narrative motivation for diegetic performances. He even won an award at the 1963 Asia Film Festival as 'Most Versatile Talent' for his work on *Ibu Mertuaku*. There were other examples of Malay actors who went on to become director-stars, including A. R. Tompel, S. Roomai Noor, M. Amin and Mat Sentol – as a small industry the Malay cinema clearly benefitted from individuals who could perform multiple roles in the filmmaking process. Ramlee though was the most well-known example. He appeared in over thirty films that he himself directed, which has invited comparisons with other famous director-stars such as Charlie Chaplin, Noel Coward and Raj Kapoor. This emphasis on his range of abilities has continued to define his persona, right up to the present day, with Ramlee nowadays commonly being referred to as more than just talented, but as a 'genius'.

However, Ramlee's persona was not just based on his professional identity as a musician, performer and filmmaker. A look at the press and fan magazines from the period show that there was also great interest in his off-screen life as a celebrity. He clearly recognised this potential – along with several other MFP stars he created a new fan magazine called *Bintang* (the Malay word for star) in 1953, which he took control of as editor (Teh 2017). Consequently, his stardom was constructed across a range of filmic and extra-filmic materials, where a distinct 'star persona' came to the fore.

Idealised ordinariness

As a performer who took on a variety of roles, Ramlee's persona comprises several features: he is heroic (*Hang Tuah, Sergeant Hassan* (P. Ramlee and Lamberto V. Avellana, 1958)), romantic (*Antara Dua Darjat*), a playboy (*Madu Tiga* (Three Wives, P. Ramlee, 1964)), a suffering, tragic figure (*Ibu Mertuaku*) and a 'nit wit'/buffoon (in many of his comedies, particularly the *Bujang Lapok* and *Labu Labi* films). However, across these characterisations, there are underlying themes relating to tradition and modernity, which intersect with notions of ordinariness and extraordinariness, a tension common in film stardom around the world, where stars are at once identification figures and embodiments of society's ideals (Dyer 1998). Although a simple concept, its application to other contexts, such as Southeast Asia, can offer insight into how stars promote culturally specific notions of normality and idealisation, while also embodying ordinariness in a way that is more direct and relatable for local audiences, owing to their physical and cultural proximity. For instance, in discussing differences between French and Hollywood stardom, Vincendeau (2000: 19) comments: 'They tend to live closer to their audience, at least in Paris – rarely do they have remote Beverley Hills-style suburban villas' (for more on the notion of stardom and proximity see Frymus 2021).

While Hollywood and Indian stars existed far away on the other side of the world and across the Indian ocean, respectively, Ramlee was positioned in his off-screen life as occupying a relatively accessible orbit for his fans in Malaya, Borneo and, especially, Singapore. Articles mention him singing at the Merdeka Stadium in Kuala Lumpur ('Merdeka Day Joy' 1962: 7), visiting Sarawak with other stars of MFP ('Bintang2 Shaws Malay Film Productions' 1962) and honeymooning in Penang with his third wife Saloma ('Singer Saloma, 25, is new wife of film star Ramlee' 1961). However, in most articles he is situated in Singapore, where he performed at concerts and on the radio, attended film premieres and screenings, and where he worked – the MFP studios were situated on Jalan Ampas. His connection with Singapore is stressed in 'Merdeka Day Joy', which refers to him as a star 'from Singapore' and one advert in the *Straits Times* (30 May 1961: 4) for a screening of *Ali Baba Bujang Lapok* (Ne'er Do Well Bachelors Ali Baba, P. Ramlee, 1961) offers a particularly striking example of how potentially accessible Ramlee could be: 'Plus! On stage at Midnight Tonight. Audience Participation. Quiz Contest. Your Quiz Master: P. Ramlee in Person'.

Ramlee was not just in a position of greater physical proximity to his fans, as compared with international stars; he also offered greater possibilities for identification on a cultural level too, especially through his embodiment of traditional Malay identity. He would wear traditional clothing, including *sarongs* and *songkoks* (a type of hat), and in most of his films would live a humble life in the *kampung* (village). His extra-filmic identity also contained such associations. He grew up in a *kampung* in Penang and is still associated with this space, with tourists being able to visit a replica of the wooden house in which he was raised. This aspect of Ramlee's persona is also linked with a working-class identity, which is articulated through its opposition in many of his films to more affluent, but morally compromised, Malay characters. In *Penarek Becha*, *Antara Dua Darjat* and *Ibu Mertuaku*, for example, members of the elite class are presented as dishonest, greedy, snobbish – homicidal even in *Antara Dua Darjat* when Tengku Hassan (Kuswadinata) murders his stepmother, and when Tengku Mukri (S. Kadarisman) tries to kill Tengku Aziz (Yusof Latiff) and Ghazali (Ramlee). In these films the contrast in acting style between Ramlee and former *bangsawan* actors, such as Ahmad Nisfu, S. Kadarisman, Kuswadinata, Udo Omar and Mak Dara, is loaded with meaning: while the *bangsawan* actors use their heightened gestures and mannerisms to suggest dishonesty and inauthenticity, Ramlee's nuanced, low-key acting reveals working-class characters who are honest, unaffected, genuine.

In his films from this period Ramlee is often also defined through his connections to a wider community. In many of these he belongs to a *kampung* and/or a group of friends. *Antara Dua Darjat*, for example, includes an early scene in which Ghazali and his friends play 'keepie uppie' with a *takraw* (a woven rattan ball) in the centre of their *kampung*. In addition, while family is a key theme in stardom in many national contexts, it was particularly important to the Malay cinema, with almost all articles about stars in *Majallah Filem* including discussion of their family lives. Ramlee's characters are frequently represented through a familial role – for instance, as a devoted son in *Ibu* and *Penarek Becha*, and as a criminal son and concerned father in *Anakku Sazali* (he played both roles). His real-life family was also often mentioned in newspapers and magazines, and appeared with him in photographs (for example, page 41 of the July 1962 issue of *Majallah Filem* shows Ramlee, his wife Saloma and their children at the airport). In this respect he embodied what Peletz (1996: 202–3) has described as 'relational identity': 'In Malay culture the person is most fully realised in social relationships, not autonomously or in privacy or isolation, as occurs in Western societies'.

Although Ramlee's embodiment of Malay tradition stresses his ordinariness and relatability, it is clear that he also, as a film star, offers an idealisation of this. While he did not possess 'perfect' looks, owing to his pockmarked face, from acne as a youth, and his body shape, which went from being skinny in his early films to a chubbier build later on, he was nevertheless handsome, particularly when appearing in glossy studio photography. His performance style also brought charisma to his films, especially owing to his energy, confidence and spontaneity, not to mention his broad, charming smile, which he would flash in close-ups and while performing musical numbers (Figure 2.1).

Ramlee would also stand out from the crowd, as a heroic warrior in films like *Hang Tuah* or *Sergeant Hassan*, or as the 'musician hero', as Adil (2018: 140) puts it, in films about music and performance. Even in comedies in which he forms part of an ensemble, such as the *Bujang Lapok* series, he is still the main figure, often standing in the centre of the frame as the leader of the group. However, one of the main ways in which he idealises his ordinary working-class characters is through his

Figure 2.1 P. Ramlee sings 'Selamat Panjang Umur' in *Antara dua Darjat*.

romanticism: his films usually contain romance narratives, often taking place in the *kampung* and depicting some form of 'forbidden love' (often between classes); his real-life romances were often discussed in the press; he was also well known for his romantic songs, such as 'Azizah' and 'Getaran Jiwa', and his performance of these, with his 'silky' baritone being one of the most distinctive features of his work. In short, while Ramlee's persona emphasises his traditional, working-class identity, his stardom idealised this in several ways. But while this aspect of his persona foregrounded a 'relational' identity, he was in many respects also a modern individual, which formed another key part of his image.

A modern individual

Existing work on Malay cinema has already noted the presence of themes relating to modernity, with Barnard, for example, arguing that Ramlee's films offer insight into his perspective on these changing times (Barnard and Barnard 2002; Barnard 2005, 2009). Ideas connected with these changes were also perpetuated through the period's stardom, where stars were icons of individualism and agents of consumption (Driskell 2019: 118–20). Here Ramlee is significant, representing the modern not just through the themes of his films but through his star persona more generally. This is immediately apparent from his physical appearance. His youthfulness (he was in his twenties to early thirties during this time) helped him represent a younger generation, embodying the period's new ideas and styles, in contrast to older characters portrayed by the former *bangsawan* stars he acted alongside. He would also wear 'Western' clothing, such as suits and dinner jackets, as well as sunglasses, an accessory commonly associated with the film star, and was also well-known for his thin moustache, which was part of his modern and distinctive 'look'. An article in the *Straits Times* ('Minister Jokes and Moustaches Go': 9) about the minister for education advising some students at a school in Johor to shave off their moustaches made reference to Ramlee: 'In his address later he said there was nothing wrong in youths sporting moustaches providing they were not blindly copying film stars such as P. Ramlee.' In addition, Ramlee was associated with the modern city and its spaces. By shifting attention to his stardom, and thus towards a consideration of his off-screen as well as his on-screen persona, it becomes apparent that while his films depict him in both the *kampung* and the city, his off-screen life is more firmly rooted in the city, and, as we have seen, Singapore in particular.

We have already considered how Ramlee's traditional persona included an emphasis on a 'relational' form of identity, which Peletz sees as central to Malay notions of personhood. However, Ramlee's stardom also speaks of a parallel emphasis on the individual and here his identity is more in keeping with ideas outlined by Dyer (2004: 7): 'Stars articulate what it is to be a human being in contemporary society; that is, they express the particular notion we hold of the person, of the "individual."' Central to this is the idea that stars represent the public self, based on the world of work and production, as well as the private self, often seen as their authentic, true identity. Through engagement with the star's filmic and extra-filmic appearances fans can believe they are gaining some insight into who the star 'really' is, all of which underscores the idea that there is a 'real' person – an individual – behind the image. We can see many aspects of Ramlee's stardom gesturing towards this real person, and this was undoubtedly a big part of his appeal.

For instance, discussion of Ramlee's off-screen life placed emphasis on his lifestyle as a film star: he is shown in glamorously lit studio photography or at exciting locations, such as concerts, airports and film festivals. At the same time, there was interest in his 'private' self, as indicated by newspaper and fan magazine articles about him, particularly his love life. Many focused on his marriage to his third wife, Saloma, such as one which appeared in *Majallah Filem* discussing a party she had arranged for him (Saloma 1962: 26–31). It included photographs of the party, which had apparently been taken from their own private photo album, further emphasising the idea of an intimate connection with the star. This interest in Ramlee's private life continues into the present day, as is evident from *P. Ramlee: The Musical*, which focuses more on 'The life, the loves and the inspiration', as the tagline for the show's initial run puts it, than on his professional career.

However, while extra-filmic materials would sometimes give glimpses into his private life, they tended to focus mainly on his public engagements, meaning that if fans wanted to get closer to him one of the best ways to do this was to watch one of his films. A star's films are key sites for fans to look for hints of – and possible connections with – the star's true self. As Dyer (1998: 20) has written: 'the roles and/or the performance of a star in a film were taken as revealing the personality of the star'. As we have seen, Ramlee would often play similar roles in film after film, which hints to audiences that they can look to these to learn about the 'real' Ramlee below the surface. This is especially the case with films like *Ibu Mertuaku*, which contain obvious biographical elements: he plays a famous musician and the two main locations are key places in his life – Singapore and Penang. In other films too, it is easy to interpret Ramlee's character as revealing something of his true self, particularly as his pared down performance style allowed him to give naturalistic and authentic performances, and while access to Ramlee's private space in extra-filmic materials may have been scarce, it was more common in his films. We can see this in *Ibu Mertuaku* when he is alone in a room in a *kampung* house, overwhelmed by sadness after being told that his wife has died (Figure 2.2). In contrast to his many public performances, scenes like this offer privileged views of Ramlee in a private setting.

In discussing Ramlee's embodiment of tradition, we saw he possessed sincerity and moral goodness. In some respects, his modern dimensions conflicted with this. For instance, in the minister's comments that youths shouldn't 'blindly copy film stars such as P. Ramlee' we can see hints of concern about the kind of influence stars, such as Ramlee, represented. Similarly, the *Straits Times* published comments from his second wife,

Figure 2.2 P. Ramlee in *Ibu Mertuaku*.

Norisan, who claimed he was a bad husband who never had time for her, owing to his work schedule and parties ('Ramlee and Norisan Part in Divorce' 1961: 9). The report described Ramlee as 'sweating under the glare of arc lights at Shaws' Singapore studios' (9) when asked for comments by reporters, to whom he vigorously denied the accusations. Depicting Ramlee in terms of workaholic and hedonistic values presented a risk to the communal values espoused in other aspects of his persona. Yet, while Norisan's comments cast Ramlee's extreme attitude to work as a potential threat to traditional married life, his stardom often explores the idea that as a musician and performer he brings value and meaning to people's lives, owing to the considerable talent he possesses, an idea that is narrativised in films like *Ibu Mertuaku*, in which he (as Kassim Selamat/Osman Jailani) performs to packed-out venues. In addition, the foregrounding of Ramlee's individualism leads us back to his traditional persona. As we have seen, his films bring the audience close to the star, allowing us to share his private space and stories, often in the *kampung* setting. The implication of these moments is that beneath his modern lifestyle and attire, which is represented extensively in his extra-filmic persona, he is still, underneath it all, the ordinary man from the *kampung*. This has continued to be a key theme in the Ramlee story, as demonstrated by the title of a 2009 *New Sunday Times* article about him: 'A superstar who remained a simple man' (Megan 2009).

Conclusion

An idea central to star studies is that the *popularity* of film stars can help us understand their social significance. To some extent Ramlee's appeal stemmed from the kind of fame he possessed, based on talent as well as on the cultivation of interest in his off-screen life. It was also related to his persona, which centred on both traditional and modern notions of Malay identity. As we have seen, this frequently involved an idealisation of Malay tradition, with the actor consistently playing romantic, heroic characters, who occupy a charismatic place at the centre of the community. As for his modernity, this was not just evident in his films' themes, but also in his physical appearance, in newspaper and magazine articles about him, as well as in his spontaneous and energetic performance style.

This persona was significant during this period of change, during which Malaya achieved independence from British rule (in 1957).

Although this was a negotiated transition of power, rather than a revolutionary war, of the kind experienced in Indochina and Indonesia, it took place against a background of social upheaval – the years leading up to independence witnessed intensified political activity, in the form of industrial action, the emergence of political groups seeking power in the coming independence, and the outbreak of the Malayan Emergency (1948–60), the name given to a twelve-year armed conflict between the Malayan Communist Party and the Malayan and British forces. Ramlee was an important historical agent, who as a creative artist commented on his historical circumstances and offered a valuable perspective on the lived experience of these times. Yet, his importance also stems from his role as a star, and ultimately the tensions within his persona between the traditional and the modern areas of his identity demonstrate a common feature of film stardom: its capacity to reconcile opposing ideological viewpoints (Dyer 1998). From this perspective Ramlee's persona serves an important function, putting forward the paradoxical, but ideologically powerful proposition that change is possible without anything changing, an idea that could be both exciting and comforting to audiences navigating these uncertain times.

References

Adil Johan (2018), *Cosmopolitan Intimacies: Malay Film Music of the Independence Era*, Singapore: National University of Singapore Press.

Ahmad, Mahyuddin and Lee Yuen Beng (2015), 'Negotiating class, ethnicity and modernity: the "Malaynisation" of P. Ramlee and his films', *Asian Journal of Communication* 25:4, pp. 408–21.

Barnard, Rohayati Paseng and Timothy P. Barnard (2002), 'The ambivalence of P. Ramlee: *Penarek Beca* and *Bujang Lapok* in perspective', *Asian Cinema* 13:2, pp. 9–23.

Barnard, Timothy P. (2005), 'Sedih sampai buta: blindness, modernity and tradition in Malay films of the 1950s and 1960s', *Bijdragen Tot De Taal-, Land- En Volkenkunde* 161:4, pp. 433–53.

Barnard, Timothy P. (2009), 'Decolonization and the nation in Malay film, 1955–1965', *South East Asia Research* 17:1, pp. 65–86.

'Bintang2 M. F. P. Berhari Raya' (1962), *Majallah Filem* 25, April, pp. 14–15.

Driskell, Jonathan (2019), 'Majallah Filem and stardom in the golden age of Malay cinema', in Tamar Jeffers McDonald and Lies Lanckman (eds), *Star Attractions: Twentieth-Century Movie Magazines and Global Fandom*, Iowa: University of Iowa Press, pp. 111–22.

Dyer, Richard (1998), *Stars*, new edition with supplementary chapter by Paul McDonald, London: BFI Publishing.

Dyer, Richard (2004), *Heavenly Bodies: Film Stars and Society*, 2nd edn, London: Routledge.
'Events lined up' (1984), *New Sunday Times*, 21 October.
Frymus, Agata (2021), 'Evelyn Preer and Black female stardom in the silent film era', *Feminist Media Studies* 21:2, pp. 1–17.
Hardi Effendi Yaacob (2009), 'Kontroversi P. Ramlee milik Malaysia atau Singapura', *Berita Minggu*, 14 June, p. 21.
Harding, James and Ahmad Sarji (2002), *P. Ramlee: The Bright Star*, Subang Jaya: Pelanduk Publications.
Hassan Muthalib (2013), *Malaysian Cinema in a Bottle: A Century (and a Bit More) of Wayang*, Petaling Jaya: Merpati Jingga.
Kahn, Joel S. (2006), *Other Malays: Nationalism and Cosmopolitanism in the Modern Malay World*, Singapore: National University of Singapore Press.
Khiun, Liew Kai and Stephen Teo (eds) (2017), *Singapore Cinema: New Perspectives*, London, New York: Routledge.
Lim, Edna (2018), *Celluloid Singapore: Cinema, Performance and the National*, Edinburgh: Edinburgh University Press.
McGraw, Andrew Clay and Azti Nezia Suriyanti Azmi (2009), 'Music and meaning in the independence-era Malaysian films of P. Ramlee', *Asian Cinema* 20:1, pp. 35–59.
Megan, M. K. (2009), 'A superstar who remained a simple man', *New Sunday Times*, 9 August, p. 25.
'Merdeka Day Joy: the accent is on youth' (1962), *Straits Times*, 22 August, p. 7.
'Minister jokes and moustaches go', *Straits Times*, 4 March 1959, p. 9.
Peletz, Michael G. (1996), *Reason and Passion: Representations of Gender in a Malay Society*, Berkeley: University of California Press.
'Ramlee and Norisan part in divorce' (1961), *Straits Times*, 20 October, p. 9.
Saloma (1962), 'Kesah Saya dengan Suami Saya', *Majallah Filem* 33, December, pp. 26–31.
'Singer Saloma, 25, is new wife of film star Ramlee' (1961), *Straits Times*, 21 November, p. 5.
Sulong, Jamil (1990), *Kaca Permata: Memoir Seorang Pengarah* [Glass Gems: A Director's Memoir], Kuala Lumpur: Dewan Bahasa dan Pustaka.
Tan Sooi Beng (1997), *Bangsawan: A Social and Stylistic History of Popular Malay Opera*, Penang: Asian Centre.
Teh Leam Seng, Alan (2017). 'Star pull of Bintang magazine', *New Straits Times*, <https://www.nst.com.my/lifestyle/sunday-vibes/2017/09/278314/star-pull-bintang-magazine> (last accessed 20 May 2021).
Uhde, Jan and Yvonne Ng Uhde (2010), *Latent Images: Film in Singapore*, 2nd edn, Singapore: Ridge Books.
Van der Heide, William (2002), *Malaysian Cinema, Asian Film: Border Crossings and National Culture*, Amsterdam: Amsterdam University Press.
Vincendeau, Ginette (2000), *Stars and Stardom in French Cinema*, London, New York: Continuum.

Chapter 3

Shake it like Elvis: Win Oo, the culturally appropriate heart-throb of the Burmese socialist years

Jane M. Ferguson

From their admiration for the charming piano player crooning a dreamy love song in *Hmone Shwe Yee* (Glimmering Gold, Win Oo, 1970) to the sexy guitar-strumming heartthrob in *Hnit Yauk Te Nay Kyin Tay* (Let's Stay Together, U Tin Yu, 1962), Burmese audiences have compared Win Oo to both Elvis Presley and James Dean. Win Oo's active filmmaking career coincided with the years of Ne Win's repressive military governments: 1962–88. For those outside the country, much of what is written about the decades of the military regime has tended to focus on repression, conflict, and economic stagnation. For the Burmese public living during those years, the cinema offered a much needed escape, a chance to laugh and a space to fantasise. In addition to the movie screenings themselves, numerous fan magazines – their covers graced with posters and screen shots from the latest movies – enabled the public to follow the industry and their beloved stars. For many, Win Oo was a renaissance man of the Burmese socialist years: he starred in films, directed films, wrote screenplays, produced films, sang hit songs, and even wrote short stories and entire novels. Few in the history of popular entertainment could ever match his calibre of artistic talent and versatility.

Win Oo's notoriety and fame during those years is undeniable. However, it is essential to consider the ways in which the motion picture industry was constrained by both the economic as well as the ideological imperatives of the Ne Win government and its so-called 'Burmese way to Socialism'. In the 1960s, the military government nationalised cinemas and instituted a stringent censor board. It sought to use the mimetic power of film to push its ideological agenda, emphasising Buddhist philosophical concepts, national unity, and what has been called Burmese-style socialist realism. But for Burmese audiences, it would be misleading to suggest that Win Oo embodied this government agenda. In one film history book, the period 1962–88 is described as 'The Win Oo Era' (တက္ကသိုလ်ခင်မောင်ဇော် 2012: 77). Interestingly, the same twenty-six-year span directly coincides with the years in which General Ne Win was in power. But unlike the military regime, Win Oo's stardom and his aura represent something different: an art, an attractiveness that is cosmopolitan, yet expressed through a cinematic language which is distinctly Burmese. By studying Win Oo, as a romantic male lead during these years of strict censorship and authoritarian militarism, one can find a useful angle and a nuanced, complex insight to the popular scene in Burma. This chapter will offer detail and reflection on how Win Oo represents both cosmopolitan sophistication and masculine bravado, but in a way which does not deviate from Burmese Buddhist values and aesthetics.

Following an introduction and summary of Win Oo's biography, this chapter will discuss what his stardom represented in the 1960s and 1970s, the decades following General Ne Win's coup and the military regimes of the Revolutionary Council and the Burmese Socialist Programme Party government. Then, it will offer plot synopses of two of Win Oo's emblematic movies: *Tein Hlwa Moe Moe Lwin* (Cloudy Sky, San Shwe Maung, 1968) and *Hmone Shwe Yee*. Emphasis will be placed on some of the stylistic expressions of Burmese cinema and the ways in which the political and cultural context created a unique Burmese cinematic language. Since their early years Burmese films frequently incorporate Theravada Buddhist notions of *thila* (precepts/morality), *tukka* (suffering) and *metta* (loving kindness) as part of their thematic patterning. How Win Oo's performances speak to these themes remains to be seen. For many fans of Burmese cinema, Win Oo's continued fame is testament to his own skill and natural good looks and charm. Ultimately, Win Oo's stardom demonstrates that within the ostensibly all-encompassing state ideology of the Burmese Way to Socialism, there is still space for the figure of a romantic lead with international style and charisma, all the while with a stylistic incorporation of Buddhist themes within the government-sanctioned ideological imperatives of Burmese socialist realism.

Win Oo's early years: a biographical sketch

Win Oo was born on 13 March 1935 to a middle-class family; he was the third child out of a total of five. His parents named him Maung Hla Myint. His father, U Ba Nyunt, was a history professor at Rangoon University. Following the Second World War, the young teenage Maung Hla Myint attended Practicing High School (then known as TTC) and finished his tenth standard exams in 1949 at the very young age of fourteen. From there, he entered Rangoon University, studying mathematics, economics and French. While still a university student, under the pen name Nyo Min Lwin he published short stories in the magazine *Thwe Thauk* (Comrade). The name was crafted using the first letter of each of his siblings' names.

But, after three years in University, in 1952 he left to join the army. After a period stationed in the town of Pyin Oo Lwin in Mandalay Division, he was transferred to Meiktila; there he bought a Jawa motorcycle, which he rented out. It was during this period that he started to grow the moustache which would later be his trademark, as it were. In 1959, he went for nine months' training in Australia, but upon returning to the army in Burma, pursued his literary interests more fully (ကျော်သန်းမြင့် 2007: 239–40). The following year, 1960, was an extraordinary year for the writer Nyo Min Lwin: he published nineteen stories in *Shumuwa Magazine*, including the novel, *Takkatho Kyaung Tha Tit Oo* (A University Student) (တက္ကသိုလ်ခင်မောင်ဇော် 2012: 77–8; ကျော်သန်းမြင့် 2007: 240).

The arts scene in Burma in the 1950s was closely intertwined, and by that time the popularity of film had already eclipsed that of theatre (Douglas 2005: 199). Multiple studios cranked out dozens of films to the few hundred cinemas nationwide. Win Oo left the army and entered the film industry in 1961, working with writer/director U Tin Yu on his film *Hnit Yauk Te Nay Kyin Tay*, which was edited by Aung Lwin. The film's release in 1962 launched Win Oo's acting career. His singing, dancing and guitar playing quickly led the Burmese public to start comparing him to Elvis Presley (တက္ကသိုလ်ခင်မောင်ဇော် 2012: 24, 78; ညိုမောင် 1964: 9). Although many actors at the time were also singers for many films, vocal tracks were performed by studio musicians – professional playback singers – and therefore just a handful of performers were recording the vocal tracks for many different films (Douglas 2005: 199).

Win Oo was exceptional in that he performed his own songs, and his recordings endure. Title tracks from movies, released on LP records, became Win Oo music smash hits, adding momentum to the popularity of the films. Win Oo's performance of the songs, and the close shot of him with his short haircut, moustache, and mole on his jaw enhanced his signature appearance; in this sense, regardless of the role he played, these personal attributes would appear in the movies, creating what James Naremore describes as the 'doubling effect of actor and role' (Naremore 2012: 37). Win Oo's film career was so productive, that while working on one production, he was often already lining up another.

A revolutionary pause

Although 1962 marked the year of Ne Win's military coup of the civilian government, and the beginning of the state's iron-fisted grip on the entertainment industry, it also represented the peak of total film outputs. Whereas all broadcast media had been under state control since the early days of colonial independence (Than 2002: 146), the post-1962 clampdown was decidedly more severe. Four months after Ne Win's March coup, the government banned any film, local or foreign, which was deemed to impinge on national unity, character or the morale of the population (Charney 2009: 114). This was consistent with the government's stance towards the culture industries in general. And in the case of the press, which had been one of the most vibrant in Asia in the post-war years, the freedom of expression and right to criticise were eventually completely suppressed (Allott 1993: 3). As part of the Burmese notion of socialist realism, only orthodox Buddhist practices would be allowed to be shown. The government wanted there to be modern revolutionary socialist films (တက္ကသိုလ်နေဝင်း 1972: 27).

In 1963, the government established the Union of Burma Cinematograph Law, which stipulated government control over every aspect of the industry, from economic, to form to content. The new law established the film Censor Board as a branch within the Ministry of Information. Film depictions of the supernatural, *nats* (lingering ghosts of people who die violent deaths), ghosts and witchcraft were banned (တက္ကသိုလ်ခင်မောင်ဇော် 2012: 21). The justification for these ideological changes was that prior to the Revolutionary Council, for-profit films were made for sheer entertainment, but were not 'true' entertainment but instead were poison for the masses. Since the installation of the new regime, one editorial – of course heavily censored itself – argues that since the installation of the Motion Picture Council, the old social, political, educational and cultural systems are gone, and instead the Council strives for the production of 'Films for the People'. Such films include those that focus on rural and village life, news and documentary films; film artists make films to improve the level of art and knowledge. The purpose of filmmaking, as part of the march to socialism, is to stimulate change and educate, and as such, the editorial argues that ideas about social reality, politics and education are taking root and flourishing because of the new government (ရုပ်ရှင်မဂ္ဂဇင်း 1972: 2).

To monitor content, the Censor Board required film producers to submit scripts prior to production, and pay a reading fee. Upon acquisition of approval to shoot, the film company would then be granted reels of unexposed film. Following production and post-production, the film would once again have to be submitted for censor approval before being allowed to be shown in the cinemas. In spite of all of this pre-scrutiny, the Film Council still reserved the right to pull any film from the cinemas, should there be any controversy after release. In one case, ethnic Shan people protested the unsympathetic presentation of a revered eleventh-century Shan princess in the film *Shwezayan* (Khin Maung Nyunt, 1962), and because of the audience responses, the government forbade further screening of the film (Ferguson 2012a: 36). It was because of experiences like these that film producers became more conservative in their content, and learned through experience with the censor board what kinds of scenes would be more likely to end up on the cutting room floor. As a result, there was a genre shift towards *thone pwint saing* 'Love Triangle' movies, as these were considered more benign, and therefore acquired censor board approval more quickly than other kinds of motion pictures (Ferguson 2012b: 34).

Studying the film career of a star such as Win Oo offers a useful insight into what kinds of performances *were* acceptable to the stringent Censor Board, and what this might have signified within and beyond the ideological goals of Ne Win's Ministry of Information.

Win Oo's way to socialism

Despite these structural constraints, within the Burmese creative industries, Win Oo's stardom continued to flourish. July 1963 saw the release of Mandalay Film Company's feature *Maung Toe Cherry Myay* (Our Favourite Land of Cherry, Win Oo, 1963) which was an adaptation of the 1957 American film *April Love* (Harry Levin), starring Pat Boone and Shirley Jones (တက္ကသိုလ်ခင်မောင်ဇော် 2012: 28). As a handsome lead opposite Khin Than Nu, his crooning title love song was a hit single.

In a 1964 article published in the popular film magazine *Yokshin Thit* ('New Film'), one contemporary film critic, Nyo Maung, offers an insightful analysis of Win Oo's stardom in the 1960s (ညို့မောင် 1964). Nyo Maung considers what Win Oo represents to Burmese audiences in the context of the Burmese Way to Socialism. It should be kept in mind that this article was also written during the years of the Press Scrutiny Board, so would also have had to pass through the censors in order to be published. Nyo Maung acknowledges that it was Win Oo's performance in *Hnit Yauk Te Nay Kyin Tay* which catapulted him to film stardom, but which also inspired Burmese audiences to start comparing him with the American star, Elvis Presley. The author points out the similarities to Elvis in Win Oo's style of singing and guitar playing, as well as his *pin hlok* 'butt shake'. As an aside, it became trendy for Burmese young men wearing collared shirts to flip the collar up; that was called a Win Oo style, even though it was clearly connected with Elvis's fashion too.

As a matter of juxtaposition, Nyo Maung lists the ways in which Elvis Presley and Win Oo are similar: they are both handsome; they have a similar allure/aura; they are both popular among their audiences. On a bit of a competitive note, the author adds that Win Oo's acting is more versatile: he has starred in a greater variety of film genres, including comedy, romance, musicals and historical films.

Following the active comparison of Win Oo and Elvis Presley, the author then reflects on Win Oo as a *Burmese* star; whether his style is one which is consistent with Burmese cultural values and whether audiences would be turning away from their traditions in their fandom of Win Oo. In particular, the author discusses Win Oo's *pin hlok* (butt shake), which in *Hnit Yauk Te Nay Kyin Tay* he performs while playing the guitar. Win Oo wears internationally fashionable clothing and adopts these styles and ways to perform, argues Nyo Maung, but he does so in a way that is appropriate to the Burmese context. He understands the situation of the Burmese audiences, and it is not his goal to make people abandon their styles in favour of international styles. As almost a jest/tease, at the end of the comparison, the author reminds readers that Win Oo is still a bachelor (ညို့မောင် 1964: 10–11).

While the author attributes the 'appropriateness' of Win Oo's performances in the Burmese context to Win Oo's savvy, he neglects to mention that not every performance or representation would necessarily be allowed by the motion picture censor board; audiences can only judge the performances which have been allowed through. As Nyo Maung points out, the Burmese cultural context is not receptive to all aspects of Elvis and his character (neither were US broadcasters, for that matter), and Win Oo is sensitive to this, only incorporating some aspects of it into his own work. The motion picture censor board would have been keen on making sure that Win Oo's *pin hlok* action was still within their bounds of respectable propriety for the Burmese cultural context. Although the author does not say so explicitly, the government's increasingly stringent censor board would also have played a key role in framing the content of Win Oo's performance, the extent to which they would have been tagged as 'international' and therefore unacceptable, or appropriate for Burmese audiences (in the eyes of the censors, of course). The socialist government's agenda for promoting national unity would increasingly push for a preservation of certain elements of Burmese culture, often vis-à-vis Western infiltration (Douglas 2005: 199).

Implicit, however, is the compatibility between Burmese masculinity and international styles. For many, there was a double standard for men and women as to who could adopt international fashions. As Chie Ikeya (2008) points out in her article 'The Modern Burmese Woman and the Politics of Fashion in Colonial Burma', in popular media presentations, when women adopted foreign-tagged habits, fashions and hairstyles they were depicted as 'immoral and unpatriotic' whereas Burmese men were the opposite (Ikeya 2008: 1277). This double standard for the sexes during the colonial era in Burma was selectively carried through to the years of independence, particularly once the Ne Win coup declared the Burmese Way to Socialism – a political and economic project of isolation which would have repercussions in the popular media as well. Women in Burmese film during the socialist years were seldom (if ever) depicted drinking alcohol, but on the other hand, there are examples of films in which women would drive cars.

Win Oo's continued success spanned subsequent decades. Like various other successful Burmese film stars, Win Oo made use of his fame, notoriety – and wealth – to establish his own film company: Sanda Film Co. In one film in particular, we start to see a distinct move away from the melodrama, or light entertainment. *Saung Eik Met* (Death is a Dream, Tun Tun, 1967) is one such film, written by and starring Win Oo. It is directed by Tun Tun and also features Bo Ba Ko, Tin Tin Aye and Aye Aye Thin. The protagonist is an engineer with a painting hobby, Kyaw Min, who, because of a childhood bicycle accident suffers recurring apparitions and nightmares. The apparition is a split personality of sorts, a figure of his own evil identical twin or alter ego by the name of Zaw Min, who repeatedly encourages Kyaw Min to commit evil acts. During the initial sequence when Kyaw Min is a child of ten or eleven, Zaw Min appears, and instructs the boy to grab a hammer and smash the windows of his home. Other sinister tasks include strangling a cat and setting fire to his own bed. Following these deeds, Kyaw Min's parents take the boy to see a psychiatrist, who confirms that the boy has schizophrenia. As an adult, these nightmares and apparitions never quite go away, and Kyaw Min continues to be tormented by his alter ego. The film is dark and creepy, a certain departure from the *thone pwint saing* love story formula. The film would win a Burmese Academy Award for Best Script (တက္ကသိုလ်ခင်မောင်ဇော် 2012: 79). Win Oo also received the Academy Award for Best Actor for his performance in this film.

Win Oo for two: synopses of two of Win Oo's iconic films

Tein Hlwa Moe Moe Lwin (1968)

The film *Tein Hlwa Moe Moe Lwin* was directed by San Shwe Maung and produced by Nyunt Myanmar Film Studio. The film is a Burmese adaptation of the 1966 American suspense thriller *Moment to Moment* (Mervyn LeRoy), and stars Win Oo, Aung Lwin, Phoe Par Kyi, Myint Myint Khin and Khin Lay Sway (တက္ကသိုလ်ခင်မောင်ဇော် 2012: 24). It features a married couple, Dr Than Sin (Aung Lwin), Kay Thi (Myint Myint Khin) and their young son. They are currently staying in a luxurious and modern home in the coastal town of Sittwe. Dr Than Sin is a psychiatrist in the army.

Dr Than Sin receives a telegram from the army, calling him away to serve (his letter mentions Mawlamyane in the Mon State as well as Taunggyi in Shan State), and although Kay Thi would like to join him, it is not possible; she must stay in Sittwe and look after their child. One afternoon, during a leisurely stroll at the shore, Kay Thi is chatting with a neighbour woman, Mya Mya Khin (Khin Lay Sway). Her little boy wanders off to let his pet rabbit play on the beach. The rabbit escapes, and is picked up by a handsome naval shipman in uniform, Kyaw Soe Moe (played by Win Oo, Figure 3.1). The film's medium shot shows his snug-fitting uniform, and the side angle shows his bicep as he holds the little bunny; a shot which serves to present Win Oo's character as handsome, strong, but also tender.

Kyaw Soe Moe and the boy have a fun and pleasant interaction and the boy takes him to meet his mother. There is a touch of romantic expectation in the air at the initial meeting, as noted in their glances, and not long afterwards they spend more time together, sightseeing in Sittwe

Figure 3.1 Win Oo in a publicity still for *Tein Hlwa Moe Moe Lwin*.

and the environs, including the ancient Shitthaung temple complex in Mrauk U. After this leisurely time together, he also pays an unexpected visit to her home, and hears her singing a romantic tune, 'Tein Hlwa Moe Moe Lwin' (Cloudy Sky). As she tells Kyaw Soe Moe, it is a song to sing when longing for a lover.

Inspired, Kyaw Soe Moe visits the gift shop at the Sittwe airport, acquires a copy of the record, and enjoys some drinks with the shop owner. That evening, he once again visits Kay Thi, drunk and hiccupping, gives her the disk, and subsequently declares his love for her. She resists his advances, and in a mad fit, he pulls out a gun and points it at himself, threatening suicide. They quarrel and in the tussle he is accidentally shot, and collapses on the floor. Kay Thi is beside herself, and sits in panic on the stairs with the gun in her hand. Later, Mya Mya Khin comes by and is shocked to see Kyaw Soe Moe dead on the floor. They decide they will make it look like a suicide. Mya Mya Khin swipes Kyaw Soe Moe's hand on the gun to place his fingerprints on it, puts the gun in his jacket pocket and the two women take the body away and dump it in the forest. The following day, they check the newspaper, looking for news of his death, but don't find it. The police come by to question Kay Thi and Mya Mya Khin to no avail.

Kay Thi's husband, Dr Than Sin returns to town: he has been called to help with a special project for memory recall. As we learn, Kyaw Soe Moe survived the gunshot wounds but has no memory of what led to the injuries and Dr Than Sin, the psychiatrist, employs hypnosis and other recall techniques to try to stoke his memories. Unable to get Kyaw Soe Moe to recall the events or name a perpetrator for his shooting, they send him off on a plane to Yangon. Before his departure, however, we learn that Kyaw Soe Moe had remembered the events, his memory was jogged by seeing a white rabbit, but then did not want to implicate Kay Thi. The movie ends with Kay Thi and Dr Than Sin standing on the shore watching Kyaw Soe Moe's aircraft fly away. Then, aboard the plane, a little boy approaches Kyaw Soe Moe, striking up a conversation, very much like the way that Kay Thi's son had done in the beginning of the movie.

The film, *Tein Hlwa Moe Moe Lwin*, as a remake of a Hollywood movie, is an indirect nod to a cosmopolitan prestige, but because it is produced by the Burmese film industry, starring Burmese actors, and located on recognisably Burmese sites, the Hollywood film is appropriated, even vernacularised for local audiences. This form of Burmese adaptation was also well-established within the country's popular music industry, where international popular songs were fitted with new Burmese lyrics by famous Burmese poets, then performed by popular Burmese musicians. An entire Burmese musical genre emerged, known as *copy thachin*, copy from English and *thachin*, Burmese for song (Ferguson 2013, 2016).

Hmone Shwe Yee (1970)

Win Oo wrote, directed and starred in *Hmone Shwe Yee*. The story of love, jealousy, and grudges is set in the context of a *zat pwe* or traditional Myanmar travelling musical variety show. A *zat pwe* is comparable to a vaudeville show, with actors, singers, dancers and an accompanying musical ensemble. The members of the troupe comprise the main characters in the film, and the show's performance tent and participants' dressing rooms are the central locations.

Win Oo stars as Myint Thu, the songwriter, pianist and director of the travelling show. Opposite Myint Thu is Khin Hmone, the beautiful and talented singer and dancer. She is clearly the most alluring star of the *zat pwe* showcase. Khin Hmone is played by Khin Than Nu, one of the most famous and prolific Burmese actresses of the twentieth century.

In the opening sequence, an actor in the troupe sneaks away from rehearsal to drink whisky. One of the stage managers runs off to fetch him and upon returning to the stage, the drunkard flubs his lines, stumbles and other members of the troupe laugh at him. Myint Thu, conducting the rehearsal, takes the lush to the side to reprimand him. He sternly admonishes the man, telling him that such drinking is not appropriate and can ruin his career.

Next, a guest pulls up: it is Captain Ye Aung, an old friend of Myint Thu's from his elementary school days. Ye Aung is played by Aung Lwin, the same actor who played Dr Than Sin in *Tein Hlwa Moe Moe Lwin*, and indeed the man who starred opposite Win Oo in dozens of films. Captain Ye Aung has come to visit the travelling troupe, since they are currently in Pyay (Prome). In their happy reunion, Myint Thu teases Ye Aung a bit about still being a bachelor and both sheepishly admit to each other they are single. After their friendly handshake, the opening credits begin. The initial sequences, the admonishment of the drunkard and the introduction of Ye Aung, we will learn, foreshadow some of the main tensions of the plot.

Khin Hmone, the lead performer and star of the travelling show is as talented as she is beautiful. Her singing and dance performances attract the attention of many potential suitors, and there are repeated shots of enthralled audiences admiring her as she performs on stage. Her most persistent audience admirer, we soon see, becomes Captain Ye Aung. We see him watching her perform, and the musicians in the band take notice of his adoring gazes at Hmone. Her fellow band members even tease Hmone about her new suitor. It is clear that the captain has fallen in love with her, and he even writes a letter, but decides that with his job in the army, if they are to be together, she would have to give up her art as a performer.

Myint Thu, feeling sidelined by this budding romance, acts quickly, and proposes to Khin Hmone and they are soon married. In the coming months, Hmone gives birth to a son. Myint Thu, however, overhears some women gossiping about the boy, speculating that the child seems to resemble Ye Aung. This gossip stirs up jealousy in Myint Thu, and in his jealousy, he becomes convinced that the child is not his son. When Hmone gives birth to a baby girl a few years later, Myint Thu accepts that the second child is his daughter. But, jealousy and suspicion about the paternity of the boy get the better of him, cause arguments and the couple splits. Myint Thu becomes depressed and starts to drink excessively.

However, the divided family is still part of the *zat pwe* troupe, and the two growing children take an interest in music and performance. Myint Thu trains his little girl in singing and dancing, and the adorable young performer quickly gains a spot on stage in the variety show. The little boy requests to study music performance, but Myint Thu initially refuses to teach him, saying he will not teach the child because he is not his genuine son. The owner of the troupe chides Myint Thu for this, admonishing him for holding a grudge against an innocent child. The older man announces that he will adopt the boy, and then by status, Myint Thu (as an employee) must instruct the boy. We see the boy then learning to play the traditional Burmese instruments, and later the piano. As the boy becomes more skilled, Myint Thu, sunk in jealousy and resentment, is increasingly a slave to the bottle. He becomes too drunk and incompetent and can neither play the piano nor direct the orchestra. For the shows to continue, the young boy must step in, replacing Myint Thu at the piano.

At this stage, there is a confrontation between Hmone, Captain Ye Aung and Myint Thu regarding the parentage of the boy. Captain Ye Aung reveals that he never touched Hmone, and Myint Thu realises and admits his mistake. Myint Thu's health has deteriorated to the extent that he is in a wheelchair. The final scene is of the boy playing piano while singers and dancers perform on the stage. From the side, Myint Thu calls the boy his son – Hmone repeats this declaration, 'Son! Your daddy is calling you "son!"'; in the scene there is an extended close shot of Myint Thu, showing his loving, teary-eyed glance to his son. The boy responds with a bright, wide smile, and Myint Thu, satisfied, collapses dead, to the sorrow of those around him.

The film *Hmone Shwe Yee* won two Burmese Academy Awards: Best Film, and Best Actor (Win Oo). This film was the fifth top earning film of 1970, commanding a six week run in the cinemas, with a total gross of 173,113 kyat (မောင်မောင် 1971: 15).

Burmese Buddhist cinematic language

In close analysis of these films, we can see how the recurring thematic incorporation of *metta* (loving kindness) is presented as the way to eternal beauty and peace, and centres on love for the family; this is not just for romantic or *thone pwint saing* films, but also ones in which family members are in conflict or holding grudges. It is often through the reunion of those carrying grudges that their problems are resolved by praying to the Buddha and earning merit (*kutho*) together. Resolution involves letting go of a grudge or particular jealousy which caused the tension of the plot; it is through restoration of harmony through *metta* that many Burmese films are brought to a close. Particularly following the increasing emphasis on Burmese notions of socialist realism, *metta* is not just a component for a simple love film, but a part of national moral development (မြန်မာ့ရုပ်ရှင်စိန်ရတုသဘင်ကျင်းပရေးသူတေသန 1996: 78). In many cases, we can see *metta* as an ideal set at the end and in opposition to transgressions such as alcoholism, adultery and jealousy. As such, *thila* or moral precepts, serve the guidelines for the rules that are transgressed by characters in the plot. For many Burmese films involving alcohol, there is no such thing as casual social drinking: it is rarely portrayed and hitting the bottle will almost certainly put the drinker on the path to ruin. As with the example of Myint Thu in *Hmone Shwe Yee*, his grudge combined with alcohol may have killed him, but the conflict is resolved by his acceptance of his own jealous misunderstanding. *Metta* is restored. Similarly, Kyaw Soe Moe in *Tein Hlwa Moe Moe Lwin*, despite recalling the circumstances in which he was shot, refuses to implicate Kay Thi; he must accept his fate and by doing so, expresses *metta* towards Kay Thi.

Conclusion

Although there might be the assumption that cinema under an authoritarian regime would be strictly propagandistic and hardly entertaining, let alone fun, in Burma (as elsewhere) there are examples of the popular culture industries finding creative ways to play to and skirt certain government regulations. In Taiwan, for example, during the martial law years 1949–87 (Roy 2003: 104), popular artists adapted Mandarin lyrics to Japanese songs as a way to record and distribute international songs which had been banned (Ta 2009: 29). The transnational Taiwanese diva Teresa Teng (Deng Lijun) struck a chord with audiences in Mainland China, despite the government's condemnation of her songs as capitalist trash. For some in the PRC, Teng's songs represented nostalgia for a bygone era, yet for others, they represented the notion that love and desire could be acceptable (Moskowitz 2010: 21).

We can look at popular music and film during the socialist years as examples of this kind of adaptation in both theme and performance; like genres of music that adapted international melodies and fitted them with Burmese lyrics, Win Oo played the part of cosmopolitan masculinity, but in a vernacular Burmese cinematic language. Although many examples of Burmese films (and popular songs) for that matter, are adaptations and covers of international films, it is hardly accurate to use the conventions of international genres and directly apply them to these Burmese cultural productions. As Krishna Sen also reminds scholars, the extent to which melodramatic aesthetics can be extended to non-Western cultures is debated (Sen 1993: 205). Similarly, given the paucity of international scholarly research on film in Burma, it is important to be wary of the tendency for scholarship generally to analyse Western film through film theories whereas non-Western films are looked at as products of their national industries (Gray 2010: xi).

Although the Ne Win years are known for strict censorship and economic mismanagement, the very fact that Win Oo was – and continues to be – such a well-known and beloved figure offers insight into the cultural aesthetics of those years, and what he continues to represent. Cinema offers a window into the styles of a time (though they may be the styles of the most privileged) and can give insight to some of the ideas and prejudices of the culture-producing class (Gray 2010: x). Some of these strategies and representations are also made explicit in film magazines, thus providing an ideological roadmap for understanding what is presented on the silver screen. Win Oo lost his life to colon cancer on 14 December 1988, the year of the massive 8 August uprising, known shorthand as 8888. The movement spurned Ne Win to step down and the military to force a coup. While the timing of both Win Oo's ascent to stardom and his premature death share an uncanny coincidence with the years of Ne Win's autocratic rule, Win Oo's enduring contributions to Burma's popular entertainment offer a glimpse into what audiences wanted both because of (and in spite of) military rule and economic stagnation. Win Oo's cultural durability among Myanmar fans has to do with his evident talent, charm, and hard work. What is also noted by his many admirers is that he had spent time in the West, but rather than be perceived to ape Western styles, developed his own blend of Burmese-ness. For Burmese audiences, Win Oo is charismatic, cosmopolitan and worldly, but truly 'one of ours'.

References

Allott, Anna J. (1993), *Inked Over, Ripped Out: Burmese Storytellers and the Censors*, New York: PEN American Center.

Charney, Michael W. (2009), *A History of Modern Burma*, Cambridge: Cambridge University Press.

Douglas, Gavin D. (2005), 'Myanmar (Burma)', in John Shepherd, David Horn and Dave Laing (eds), *Continuum Encyclopedia of Popular Music of the World, vol. V, Asia and Oceania*, London: Continuum, pp. 196–202.

Ferguson, Jane M. (2012a), 'From contested histories to ethnic tourism: cinematic representations of Shans and Shanland on the Burmese Silver Screen', in David Lim and Hiroyuki Yamamoto (eds), *Film in Contemporary Southeast Asia: Cultural Interpretation and Social Intervention*, London: Routledge, pp. 23–40.

Ferguson, Jane M. (2012b), 'Le grand ecran en terre dorée: histoire du cinéma Birman', in Gaëtan Margirier and Jean-Pierre Giminez (eds), *Le Cinéma d'Asie du Sud-Est/ Southeast Asian Cinema*, Lyons: Asia-Expo, pp. 15–37.

Ferguson, Jane M. (2013), 'Burmese super trouper: how Burmese poets and musicians turn global popular music into *copy thachin*', *Asia Pacific Journal of Anthropology* 14:3, pp. 221–39.

Ferguson, Jane M. (2016), 'Yesterday Once More: tracking unpopular music in contemporary Myanmar', *Journal of Burma Studies* 20:2, pp. 229–57.

Gray, Gordon (2010), *Cinema: A Visual Anthropology*, Oxford: Berg.

Ikeya, Chie (2008), 'The modern Burmese woman and the politics of fashion in colonial Burma', *Journal of Asian Studies* 67:4, pp. 1277–308.

Moskowitz, Marc L. (2010), *Cries of Joy, Songs of Sorrow: Chinese Pop Music and Its Cultural Connotations*, Honolulu: University of Hawai'i Press.

Naremore, James (2012), 'Film acting and the arts of imitation', *Film Quarterly* 65:4, pp. 34–42.

Roy, Denny (2003), *Taiwan: A Political History*, Ithaca, NY: Cornell University Press.

Sen, Krishna (1993), 'Politics of melodrama in Indonesian cinema', in Wimal Dissayanake (ed.), *Melodrama and Asian Cinema*, Cambridge: Cambridge University Press, pp. 205–17.

Ta, Trong Shawn (2009), 'Becoming Teresa Teng, becoming-Taiwanese', unpublished MA thesis, University of Southern California.

Than, Tin Maung Maung (2002), 'Myanmar media: meeting market challenges in the shadow of the state', in Russell Hiang-Khng Heng (ed.), *Media Fortunes, Changing Times: ASEAN States in Transition*, Singapore: Institute of Southeast Asian Studies, pp. 139–72.

Works in Burmese

ကျော်သန်းမြင့် (2007) မြန်မာ့ရုပ်ရှင်ငွေကြယ်ပွင့်တို့ရှပ်ပုံလွှာများရန်ကုန် အလင်းသစ်စာပေ.

မောင်မောင် (1970) နှစ် ၅၀ မြန်မာ့ရုပ်ရှင်ခရီး ရုပ်ရှင်မဂ္ဂဇင် 7 March, pp. 18–22.

မြန်မာ့ရုပ်ရှင်စိန်ရတုသဘင်ကျင်း (1996) ရုပ်ရှင်စာတမ်းငယ်တစ်ဆယ် ရန်ကုန် မြန်မာ့ရုပ်ရှင်စိန်ရတုသဘင်ကျင်းပရေးသုတေသန.

ညိုမောင် (1964) ဝင်းဦးချစ်ခင်မှုကိုတမ်းဖိုတသူ ရုပ်ရှင်သစ် March, pp. 9–12.

စံရွှေးမောင် တိမ်လွှာမှိမှိ့လွင် ညွှန်မြန်မာ

တက္ကသိုလ်ခင်မောင်ဇော်. (2012) မြန်မာ့ဂန္ထဝင်ရုပ်ရှင်အနုပညာရှင် (၂၀) ရန်ကုန် ရွှေစာပေးတိုက်

တက္ကသိုလ်နေဝင်း (1973) နိုင်ငံခြားရောက်မြန်မာရှ ရုပ်ရှင်မဂ္ဂဇင်းရေပြသ နာကိုစေတနာရှိ January, pp. 34–6.

တက္ကသိုလ်နေဝင်း (1975) တိမ်မြှပ်နေသောရာဇဝင်သမိုင်းကားရုပ်ရှင်မဂ္ဂဇင် သူတိုင်းစိတ်ဝင်စားကြသည် ရုပ်ရှင်မဂ္ဂဇင် February, pp. 14–16.

ရုပ်ရှင်မဂ္ဂဇင် (1972) တော်လှန်ရေးဆယ်နှစ်ပြည့်အထိမ်းအမှတ်နှင့်ရုပ်ရှင်ပြော င်းလဲချက်များရုပ်ရှင်မဂ္ဂဇင်း March, p. 2.

Chapter 4

Trà Giang's stardom in wartime Vietnam: simple glamour, socialist modernity and acting agency

Qui-Ha Hoang Nguyen

A 1975 Jane Fonda article in *Cineaste* includes a photo of the actor-activist-star and her family, along with another woman and a little girl (Georgakas and Rubenstein 1975). The photo is framed tightly in between the article's headline '"I prefer films that strengthen people", an interview with Jane Fonda', which is written in an extremely large font. A smaller subheading at the end of the page reads, 'Vietnamese actress Trà Giang and daughter, Jane Fonda and son, and Tom Hayden in a scene from *Introduction to the Enemy*'. The interview centres entirely on the already famous Fonda and her infamous trip to North Vietnam in 1973; no further information about Trà Giang and her daughter is provided. Trà Giang predictably yielded little attention from the US media in the context of the Cold War, given that Vietnamese socialist cinema was largely condemned as a mere propaganda tool, a view that has continued into the present (Healy 2006, 2010; Hamilton 2009).

Yet Trà Giang (Figure 4.1) is considered a legendary actor of the Vietnamese socialist cinema, associated with the iconic mother-fighter character in wartime Vietnam. A photo of her offering flowers to President Hồ Chí Minh at the 1962 National Festival of Arts (Figure 4.2) was widely circulated by the government, underscoring its cultivation of a close relationship between the arts and politics. Until the present, Trà Giang's name still invokes strong sentiments and positive public memories about the golden age of Vietnamese cinema (1954–75), even though socialist films have fallen out of favour in modern Vietnam, following the economic changes of 1986, known as the Reform. Although she was the first star of the Vietnamese revolutionary cinema

Figure 4.1 Trà Giang. Photo courtesy of Trà Giang.

to win an international award – she won the best actress prize at the 1974 Moscow Film Festival for her appearance in *The Seventeenth Parallel: Day and Night* (*Vĩ tuyến 17: Ngày và Đêm*, Hải Ninh, 1972) – Trà Giang has received little scholarly attention in Western film studies or in research in Vietnam.

Figure 4.2 Trà Giang and President Hồ Chí Minh. Photo courtesy of Trà Giang.

Drawing on my interviews with Trà Giang (2016; 2019), archival research and textual analysis, this chapter examines the dynamics of star-making in Vietnam, looking in particular at Trà Giang's stardom and her artistic interventions in socialist filmmaking culture. I discuss her beauty, talent and persona and the role they played in shaping her stardom, while also considering how she found ways to express herself and develop professionally in a state-governed film industry in wartime Vietnam. By shifting the focus to Trà Giang's artistic interventions within socialist film culture and her experiences of war, this chapter points to the diversity of stars' experiences within socialist stardom. I contend that while Trà Giang's modest persona was conveniently created to embody various layers of socialist culture, an aesthetic of simplicity and an emphasis on specific female virtues, her stardom gives insight into the complex notion of socialist modernity, which at once regulated and carved out space for gender equality in professional development. Through acting, Trà Giang incorporated her sentimental persona and articulated her traumatic experiences of war, putting forward an image that counters the common communist stereotypes based on the cult of spiritual heroism and strong-mindedness. As I will show, socialist stars had a space for providing creative and personal input on and off-screen.

As an analytical lens, socialist stardom is in need of further definition. Unlike the image of luxury associated with Hollywood stars, based on material excess and glamour, the ordinariness of socialist stars points towards their status as *workers*: hardworking, devoted to the nation and dedicated to the building of socialism. In Lu's view, as a worker, the socialist star 'reconceptualize[s] the relation between the star and the spectator: encouraging intimate camaraderie between the star and the spectator rather than spectators' craze for the star' (2008: 115). Jessica Ka Yee Chan (2019: 119–20), on the other hand, highlights through her discussion of glamour certain similarities between capitalist and socialist forms of stardom. I would like to explore this characterisation further, particularly through discussion of how the simplicity of socialist stars contrasts with the abundance found in more commercial forms of stardom. This simplicity is central to socialist stardom's particular inflection of glamour, which I would call 'simple glamour'.

As a burgeoning field that emerged in the 1980s with Richard Dyer's *Stars* (1979), star studies gradually entered film studies and has offered a lens through which to view stardom in relation to social, political and institutional issues. In the research that followed, there has been a great emphasis on Hollywood stardom, the glamorous images of its stars and their empowerment in capitalist societies. This view provides insight into the economic and social significance of film stars in a Western context but has limitations when it comes to understanding stardom regulated by authoritarian regimes. Scholarship on socialist stars of the Maoist era demonstrates the vulnerability of stars and the constraints they faced during this time (Lu 2008; Zhang 2010; Yu 2012). Operating within the framework of the 'worker-model' mentioned above, socialist stars are perceived as objects of the state apparatus whose on- and off-screen images align with propagandistic ideas relating to the idealised socialist subject (Lu 2008; Yu 2012).

While literature on Chinese socialist stardom provides insight into some of the ways in which it is distinct from Hollywood stardom, this scholarship often places emphasis on the state's monolithic power, ignoring the agency that stars possess. Current work in academia has challenged this tendency to reduce the star to 'an object being remodeled by the socialist ideology' (Lu 2008: 122). In examining early Maoist cinematic standards of expression, Jonh Zou (2010) offers a more nuanced discussion of socialist stardom, explaining how Mei Lanfang's theatrical facial expressions destabilise the norms of political performance in the Chinese opera film. In a similar vein, Antje Ascheid (2003) investigates stars whose personas and acting styles exceed the constraints defined by Nazi gender ideologies. This scholarship has shown a dynamic relationship between stardom and the state, rather than a deterministic top-down model. This chapter follows this established scholarship and offers an account of Trà Giang's artistic autonomy, which counters assumptions about the artist's subordination to the state in Vietnamese socialist cinema.

Stardom in Vietnam: a brief history

Stardom was not a new phenomenon in socialist Vietnam when Trà Giang became famous. It had already been embedded in colonial Vietnam's film culture and was mainly associated with ideas relating to the foreign, rather than the domestic. The French imported cinema to the country only a couple of years after the first film screening in France in 1895, and the Vietnamese became familiar with film stars through print media in the late 1920s and early 1930s. Hollywood movies were regularly screened in theatres throughout the urban centres of Hanoi, Saigon, Hue, Haiphong, Danang and others. Many popular papers such as *New Women* (Đàn bà mới), *Women's New Literature Review* (Phụ nữ Tân Văn) and *Ha Thanh Mid-noon Newspaper* (Hà Thành Ngọ Báo) ran columns about movie stars not only to generate advertising revenue but also to appeal to and maintain their readership. A business with considerable financial potential, cinema was mainly under the control of French companies and two in particular – Société Indochine Films et Cinémas (IEFC) and Société des Ciné-Théâtres d'Indochine (SCTI) – controlled most of the cinema business in Indochina (Hoàng Thanh 2003: 17). Later, some movies were made with Vietnamese casts, but very few records about the domestic stars of this period exist.

After the defeat of the French in 1954, Vietnam was partitioned into two. In contrast to the rise of stardom in the commercial film industry in the south,[1] stars and stardom were viewed more negatively in the socialist culture in the north. Revolutionary cinema in the north was officially founded in 1953 – the year President Hồ Chí Minh signed the 147/SL Decree to establish the Vietnam Movie and Photography Enterprise – and consciously built up its socialist values in opposition to the colonial and commercial cinemas in the south, setting its ultimate goal as serving the nation (for further insight into the South Vietnamese stardom of this period see Guha's discussion of Kiều Chinh in Chapter 5 of this volume). Within this cinema, actors served as labourers or cultural cadres whose role was to support national independence and the masses on the cultural front.[2]

Like other film crew members, socialist actors received salaries that afforded them and their families modest working-class lives. My interviews of actors and their children of the period shows that actors lived in 'khu tập thể' (communal apartments) in Hoàng Hoa Thám and had a space of around fifteen to twenty square metres depending on the number of family members.[3] They experienced the same shortage of material comforts as other people in wartime Vietnam. Maintaining such a simple life fitted with communist officers' ideas relating to the artist in at least two senses. First, the image of a simple life helped reinforce the equal position of artists and the traditional working class, thus preventing them from existing as a petty-bourgeois class separate from the masses. Second, experiencing the same simple and financially harsh life as the masses would help actors authentically portray this experience in films, particularly through the use of the realistic acting style created by the Stanislavski system.[4]

Trà Giang's biography

Trà Giang (b. 1942) was among the first generation of students who graduated from acting classes at the School of Theatre and Cinema that was established in North Vietnam in 1959. Compared to her contemporaries who also became famous actors of the period – such as Tuệ Minh, Đức Hoàn, and Mai Châu – Trà Giang did not have ostentatious beauty. Yet, no one possessed the ideal socialist female beauty and persona like Trà Giang. Her very long, spring-like and subtly wavy hair, and round, innocent face embody the Vietnamese traditional ideal of femininity. In particular, her dark eyes have been called 'the eyes that can say anything'.

Trà Giang's most successful typecasting involves her playing a heroic southern mother-fighter.[5] Her fame was established in two revolutionary classics, *Sister Tư Hậu* (Phạm Kỳ Nam, 1964) and *The Seventeenth Parallel*. In *Sister Tư Hậu*, Trà Giang plays a woman in a seaside village who transforms from being a rape victim and insecure mother and widow into a heroic guerrilla fighter. In *The Seventeenth Parallel* her character, Dịu, a communist, rises to a leadership position in the long-haired army which defeats the Southern soldiers. When she plays the lead role of a mother, her traditional femininity is an essential quality of the film's narrative and aesthetics.

Trà Giang's modest beauty is employed for a dual and paradoxical purpose in both *Sister Tư Hậu* and *The Seventeenth Parallel*. On the one hand, her good-looking but not overtly sexy appearance and physicality is ideal for her roles as an underground guerrilla and as a communist leader, which she plays in *Sister Tư Hậu* and *The Seventeenth Parallel*, respectively. On the other hand, to highlight the male enemies' immorality and sexual brutality, Trà Giang's charming beauty is visualised as a desired sexual object in these films. Tư Hậu is raped by a Frenchman and is also a target of a captain's sexual harassment, and in *The Seventeenth Parallel* her character experiences sexual harassment from Trần Sùng, the captain of a troop of soldiers. Her chaste beauty preserves her characters' morality as her beauty is a natural trait embedded in her nature, not something she tries to show off in order to seduce men.

Not only does her beauty play a role in relation to her films' narratives, Vietnamese socialist films also needed female actors who conformed to the nation's idealised beauty standards in order to meet the audience's visual expectations. Director Hải Ninh noted his consideration of Trà Giang's physicality when casting her for the lead in *The Seventeenth Parallel*. In his imagination, the revolutionary heroine Dịu possesses a 'gentle and unrevealing beauty' and a 'firm well-proportioned body' that cover a 'hidden power' (2006: 72). Trà Giang was cast over Phi Nga, an established actress who had appeared in the first Vietnamese feature film, *On the Same River* (Nguyễn Hồng Nghi and Phạm Hiếu Dân, 1959), because of Trà Giang's youth and beauty (2006: 71). Hải Ninh emphasised that Dịu's beauty needed to 'appeal' to audiences in order to engage them for the full duration of a three-hour film (2006: 72).[6]

Simplicity: the nation's imagination of socialist ethics and aesthetics

A 1974 article about Trà Giang, written shortly after she won the best actress award for *The Seventeenth Parallel* at the Moscow Film Festival, notes the author's first impression of her simplicity when he met her. The first paragraph describes Trà Giang's charm and her identity as an ideal socialist figure, an ordinary woman whose simplicity helps erase the psychological barriers between her as the host and him as the guest. The author then describes her modest living space, which is just twenty square meters and contains only a few pieces of furniture: a bed behind a curtain, but no chairs, no table and no pictures on the wall. The guest and host sit on a 'simple and very clean mat' (Trương 1974: 22). Through the refined lens of the socialist ideology, Trà Giang's image appears relatable to a wide range of readers and her simplicity helps erase class boundaries between her and the masses.

Trà Giang's simplicity was promoted in line with the lifestyle that the nation state encouraged its citizens to adopt. Simplicity was regarded as a key ethical value associated with patriotism in wartime Vietnam. The above-mentioned article was published in 1974, coinciding with a time when the Hanoi regime faced financial and cultural tensions. The long war, especially the bombing experienced in the early 1970s, depleted the nation's finances and everyone was required to devote themselves to the nation under the slogan 'All for the South' (Tất cả cho miền Nam). To love the nation usually involved adopting a selfless life and sacrificing material comfort to save money for the war effort and nation-building. In this regard, simplicity as an essential quality of revolutionary virtue influenced the portrayals of public figures such as movie stars.

The treatment of Trà Giang's simplicity also served as a culturally powerful image for the younger generation, especially for young girls in the city in the early 1970s. Parallel to the economic decline experienced in the north in the mid-1960s, society witnessed a change in the lifestyle of young people in urban centres. Unlike the older generations who embraced socialist values while experiencing the hardships of war, many members of the younger generation growing up in cities started to depart from this modest lifestyle, opting for a more pro-Western attitude (Pettus 2004: 56). This received criticism in some quarters, with newspapers such as *Phụ nữ Việt Nam* (*Vietnamese Women*) expressing concern. The critiques of the 'new girl/new woman' in this era are similar to those of the 'new woman' in colonial Vietnam in the late 1920s and 1930s, as both expressed anxiety towards women embracing the Western styles and consumerism that departed from traditional values. However, there were also differences in these critiques. While the colonial new girl/new woman was mainly dismissed because her Westernised lifestyle was seen as posing a threat to traditional values and Vietnamese notions of idealised femininity, the new girls/new women in socialist Vietnam were criticised because of their perceived self-centeredness, which was seen as conflicting with established socialist ethics.

Against this social backdrop, Trà Giang's simplicity is canonised at the nexus of socialist authenticity and the ideals of traditional femininity. A newspaper article by Trương Quân (1974: 23) describes Trà Giang as possessing 'spring-like' hair and as an embodiment of national and traditional beauty. Furthermore, this idealised image frames her as at once a film star and a cultural ambassador of the nation:

> Trà Giang was walking on the pavement in Moscow, and the people respected her like a queen. *The best actress* in a modest style with a traditional hat, strolled in the capital; she did not look sparkling like a star, but was sauntering, simple, confident and proud for she successfully played a role that could represent her people, her nation, so that the world could understand the Vietnamese and Vietnam. (Trương 1974: 23)

Centring on her ordinariness – albeit in an exaggerated manner – the newspaper emphasises the power of simplicity as a national quality, which made Trà Giang stand out and helped generate the respect of international audiences. It is the star's talent (Trà Giang was awarded the prize for best actress) and her ordinariness that make her sparkling, not outfits and an extravagant style.

But the features of Trà Giang's star image, as an embodiment of natural and simple qualities, are by no means unique to constructions of socialist stardom. In a manner similar to star-making in Vietnam, Ascheid (2003: 49) highlights Kristina Soderbaum's ordinariness as a significant aspect of her persona in Nazi star culture, which enabled 'audiences to identify with the star on a more immediate level'. Simplicity also applied to promotional strategies in wartime Hollywood with Gene Tierney being a case in point. In its effort to create an 'all American woman' for the public and soldiers, Fox Studios reframed Tierney's star image so that it centred upon simple fashion and the absence of make-up and ornamentation (Scheibel 2018).

In the socialist worldview, ornamentalism refers to material excess and bourgeois formalism. Hans Gunther (2011: 97) notes that socialist realism was founded on a new aesthetic doctrine which made the education of the masses its utmost priority. Accessibility was therefore a key characteristic of socialist arts and to be accessible, socialist arts needed to be simple. Simplicity in Hans Gunther's interpretation is the opposite of ambiguity; art must be transparent to avoid potential misunderstandings.

More importantly, simplicity acted as one of the Party's 'weapons' in the fight against naturalism, formalism, and other 'deviations', which were regarded as individualistic ornamentalism, as expressions of capitalism and, therefore, as unhealthy to the masses (Gunther 2011: 104).[7]

As a standard of socialist realist aesthetics, simplicity also found a way to regulate acting. Many writings pointed out that it was Trà Giang's modest persona that helped her authentically express her characters. In this sense, simplicity is placed in contrast to exaggeration, which is associated with artifice. Trà Giang's simplicity is central to her becoming a successful actress because of the unique characteristics of the cinematic medium. One article highlighted that 'cinema is the type of art that depends on authenticity. Artifice is easily exposed on screen, for cinema is capable of zooming into small details' (Trương 1974).

This discourse on Trà Giang's simplicity emphasises the need to resist a selfish lifestyle in order to restore lost socialist values in wartime Vietnam. The press does this by highlighting her simple lifestyle, but also by making a connection with her maternal role. The article mentioned above was included in a newspaper which featured an image of Trà Giang holding her daughter Bích Trà on the cover. Another photo in the article also features Trà Giang and her daughter, where the author highlights Trà Giang's dismissal of ornamentalism, while identifying the daughter as her real source of happiness. Amidst the emergence of foreign commodities in urban north Vietnam, the depiction of Trà Giang in a simple living space is significant because the author uses it to celebrate motherhood. While he observes that her room doesn't have a doll, a decorative object often found in the houses of those who travelled abroad, he highlights that Trà Giang's eight-month-old daughter is as adorable as a doll, which reduces the need for any other decorative objects (Trương 1974: 22). This points to the idea in socialist aesthetics that decoration is 'senseless' or 'cheap beauty'. Furthermore, by locating Trà Giang's source of happiness in her daughter over her material possessions, the article prompts its readers to see a woman's value as residing in her maternity, a 'natural responsibility', rather than in seeking leisure among materialist objects.

Yet, although Trà Giang's motherly image is employed to convey a propagandistic purpose, her motherhood also illustrates the complexities and dynamics of socialist modernity, which also encouraged women's professional development. The author presents Trà Giang as a star who can balance her domestic social role with the nationalist idea of modern femininity. At one point the article positions her as a socialist new woman through her act of leaving her six-month-old daughter at home to participate at the Film Festival in Moscow. Her husband, music professor Đỗ Ngọc, helped take care of the daughter as Trà Giang went on business, reversing the gender roles of a traditional Vietnamese family.[8] It is important to note that Đỗ Ngọc took care of Trà Giang when she was pregnant, following the film crew of *The Seventeenth Parallel* to Quảng Trị (Trà Giang 2019). The ideas of socialist womanhood and motherhood, while constructed to serve a nationalist discursive agenda, also involved an emphasis on gender equality in everyday life, which is often ignored in feminist writings.

Acting agency and socialist filmmaking culture

Trà Giang's modest persona, talent and labour have occupied central positions in Vietnamese media. However, few writings have paid sufficient attention to her subjectivity as a creative artist, which in order to be investigated requires a look at what went on behind the scenes in her filmmaking. Two reasons may explain this absence in Vietnamese socialist filmmaking culture. First, although the role of individuals in film crews is recognised, a film is usually considered a product of the collective, where the focus on the group surpasses that of any individual's efforts. The second reason stems from the first one: individuals within film crews usually attribute the success of the film to the entire crew, rather than their own work and talents. In many cases, artists mention their own contributions, but ultimately they point towards the role of the collective. In a certain sense, this is what historian Wang Zheng (2016: 18) calls the practice of 'self-effacement', which formed part of 'the politics of concealment' that was frequently adopted during the Maoist era. Wang argues that socialist feminists, including those who worked in the film industry, hide their subjectivities by adopting socialist coded languages, working hard for the collective and even disavowing their own power. Therefore, it is difficult to recognise feminist endeavours operating in many fields inside China including in film production.

Trà Giang did not uniformly adopt the practice of 'self-effacement'. Compared to mainstream writings about her success, which stressed her significance as a cultural symbol, Trà Giang presented herself as a creative artist actively engaging in the filmmaking process. The 1972 newspaper *Vietnamese Screen* (*Màn ảnh Việt Nam*) included an article by Trà Giang

(1972: 5–6) in which she wrote about her experience of playing Dịu in *The Seventeenth Parallel*:

> During the process of doing research for the film script, actors have to contribute their thoughts and suggest their opinions to the director to decide the best and most logical acting expression. Sometimes I only suggested a minimal idea, but the director had to spend three to four days thinking about it and then meet up with actors to discuss again and add more … I liked this way of working … sometimes I faced disagreements to the extent that I burst into tears; the director was not happy either. But after that, we discussed again.

What is striking about this statement is that Trà Giang would respond emotionally in public. Tears, which are discursively associated with femininity, reveal her expressive sensitivity. Trà Giang's tears likely also speak of the oppressive system and hierarchal culture. However, such an intensely emotional response also illuminates Trà Giang's strong will to defend her view to a male director, whom she called older-brother ('anh') Hải Ninh.

Trà Giang's sharing also opens a space to rethink the culture of collectivism in a socialist regime. This emphasis on the collective has received numerous critiques because of the belief that such a tendency prevents individual freedom. Thus, Trà Giang's perspective as a professional actor and her voicing of her opinions highlights the gap between the policies and practices of filmmaking. Despite such uncomfortable work experiences, Trà Giang said that she liked the cooperation that brought about collective thinking (1972: 6). Her view stems from the socialist idea that individualism is 'one-sided' and 'limited' (Trà Giang 1972), for it only reflects a subjective perspective. Her point, resonating with socialist ideology, may be easily interpreted as the condemnation of individualism. At the same time, it contains the belief that the individual's contributions can thrive as part of the collective. As Ban Wang (1997: 151) suggests, 'the individual can be made to feel more authentically his own self and experience an ecstatic self-enforcement precisely at the moment when he is at the bidding of the party-state, when he is designated a "communal subject"'.

Animating presumptions that socialist artists were regulated by the government, scholarship on socialist stars usually looks at them through a political lens while neglecting their artistry. A careful examination of Vietnamese revolutionary cinema provides an alternative account. Evidence of Trà Giang's acting agency can be found in her diary written in 1972 in which she reflects day by day on her acting. After finishing one day's work she confesses to feeling that she has given a poor performance: 'I had a sense that I illustrated the script without creativity in many scenes. If I am creative and active in some scenes, I feel confident immediately' (cited in Như Hoàng 2010: 40). Moreover, Hải Ninh cast Trà Giang over the famous actor Phi Nga for *The Seventeenth Parallel* in part because of her creativity.[9] In his view, an actor should be a 'creator' (*người sáng tạo*) who holds an independent position, as a 'conscious member of the creative process (of a film)' rather than being a 'means' to illustrate the director's ideas (2006: 69).

Hải Ninh also notes that Trà Giang strongly committed to developing her acting skills, avoiding 'repeating' herself when playing different characters. According to Hải Ninh, Trà Giang 'demanded' that the director analyse the character's psychology, that she be given the opportunity to rehearse significant scenes with the director, and that the director be present during the shooting of every scene (2006: 137). Trà Giang's language, as recalled by Hải Ninh, presents her as an active participant in the filmmaking process and gives new insight into the socialist culture of filmmaking by showing how the voices of individuals were heard.

During the interview I conducted with Trà Giang (2016), she reminded me of a scene in *The Seventeenth Parallel* in which her character Dịu leads the long-haired army. Holding a dead child in her arms, she calls for the southern soldiers to put down their rifles since they, as the allies of the US Army, helped cause the death of innocent Vietnamese people. The deployment of the dead body was Trà Giang's original idea. She learned this story from the female captain of a guerrilla group and was profoundly moved by it. When the time came for her to act in this scene, Trà Giang recalled the story and suggested to the director Hải Ninh that they represent this real-life event. By depicting a guerrilla leader holding a dead child, Trà Giang helped to relive and archive a woman's experience of the traditionally masculine culture of war.

Trà Giang's acting agency transformed the cinematic stereotype of the communist mother, enriching it with pathos in order to create an emotional identification with the trauma that women had experienced. In the scene in which Dịu carries the child across the Bến Hải river to give him to her husband, a communist soldier guarding the free zone on the north side (Dịu and her husband live apart because of their revolutionary responsibilities), Trà Giang needed to express the emotional complexities of her character by portraying her as both an emotionally suppressed wife and mother as well as a spiritually strong communist leader. According to Trà Giang, Hải Ninh and she spent a couple of days discussing and rehearsing this scene. They carefully considered which behaviour would work: Dịu opens her eyes and looks at her husband or closes her eyes and leans her head on her husband's shoulder (Trà Giang 1972: 5). In taking into account this detail, Trà Giang draws the readers' attention to her artistic intervention, professionalism, and the collective cooperation and negotiation that socialist artists went through. Moreover, she shows her sensitivity in creating a mother-fighter character who counters the common image of the statue-like portrayal of communists on screen.

Conclusion

The last film Trà Giang appeared in was *White Flower River* (*Dòng sông hoa trắng*, Trần Phương, 1989), following which she ended her acting career at the age of forty-seven. It was said that Trà Giang wanted to stop at the peak of the profession, but she herself stated that she could not find a 'fitting' role for herself in the market-oriented economy (Trần 2012). In 1986, eleven years after the national unification in 1975, the Vietnamese government switched from a socialist economic system to a market-oriented economy, a shift known as the Reform. Accordingly, the Vietnamese film industry witnessed a quick rejuvenation in the early 1990s due to the success of private companies, which were competing with the state-owned studios. The latter, which had produced films to assist the war effort during wartime, continued to deal with subjects relating to the war and its consequences. Such conservative and narrowly focused production hardly attracted audiences in the post-war period. Meanwhile, the Reform opened the door for private studios to produce films reflecting modern life, with a focus on youth, consumerism and middle-class life. The instant noodle films (*phim mì ăn liền*) a commercially popular set of films recorded on video that successfully exploited those new subjects, mushroomed in the 1990s and dominated theatres nationwide. This pushed the artistically styled cinema coming out of the state studios into a deep crisis.

This sharp turn in film culture explains Trà Giang's withdrawal from the cinema. But as a symbol of the golden age of Vietnamese cinema, her stardom and values remained relevant within mainstream discourses on womanhood in the globalised era. To maintain traditional values and construct an appropriate idea of modern womanhood in the face of globalisation, the media persistently held beauty pageants. Trà Giang participated as a judge nine times from 1994 to 2006. The presence of Trà Giang and her role in selecting a representative of Vietnamese beauty demonstrates her significance as a transmitter of socialist ideals relating to femininity. Trà Giang's fame and glamour as an icon of Vietnamese socialist cinema still receives acclaim and recognition from today's audiences, who enjoy her nostalgic opposition to consumerist notions of stardom in modern Vietnam.

References

Ascheid, Antje (2003), *Hitler's Heroines: Stardom and Womanhood in Nazi Cinema*, Philadelphia: Temple University Press.

Chan, Jessica Ka Yee (2019), *Chinese Revolutionary Cinema: Propaganda, Aesthetics and Internationalism, 1949–1966*, London: I. B. Tauris.

Dyer, Richard (1979), *Stars*, London: British Film Institute.

Dyer, Richard (2004), *Heavenly Bodies: Film Stars and Society*, 2nd edn, London: Routledge.

Georgakas, Dan and Lenny Rubenstein (1975), '"I prefer films that strengthen people": an interview with Jane Fonda', *Cineaste* 6:4, pp. 2–9.

Günther, Hans (2011), 'Soviet literary criticism and the formulation of the aesthetics of socialist realism, 1932–1940', in Evgeny Dobrenko and Galin Tihanov (eds), *A History of Russian Literary Theory and Criticism: The Soviet Age and Beyond*, Pittsburgh, Pennsylvania: University of Pittsburgh Press, pp. 90–108.

Hải Ninh (2006), *Điện ảnh – Những dấu ấn thời gian* [*Cinema – The Imprints of Time*], Hà Nội: Nhà xuất bản văn hóa thông tin [Information Culture Publisher].

Hamilton, Annette (2009), 'Renovated: gender and cinema in contemporary Vietnam', *Visual Anthropology* 22:2–3, pp. 141–54.

Healy, Dana (2006), 'Laments of warriors' wives: re-gendering the war in Vietnamese cinema', *South East Asia Research* 14:2, pp. 231–59.

Healy, Dana (2010), 'From triumph to tragedy: visualizing war in Vietnamese film and fiction', *South East Asia Research* 18:2, pp. 325–47.

Hoàng Thanh et al. (eds) (2003), *Lịch sử điện ảnh Việt Nam Quyển 1* [*The History of Vietnamese Cinema, vol. 1.2*], Hanoi: Department of Cinema.

Lân (1973), 'Vĩ tuyến mười bảy ngày và đêm' [*The Seventeenth Parallel*], 3, pp. 9–12.

Lu, Xiaoning (2008), 'Zhang Ruifang: modelling the socialist red star', *Journal of Chinese Cinemas* 2:2, pp. 113–22.

Mai Châu (2018), personal interview, conducted by Qui-Ha Hoang Nguyen, July.

Nguyễn Phương Hoa (2016), personal interview, conducted by Qui-Ha Hoang Nguyen, July.

Như Hoàng (2010), 'Trà Giang', in *Trà Giang: Nghệ sĩ nhân dân, diễn viên điện ảnh* [*Trà Giang: A People's Artist, a Cinema Actress*], Hà Nội: Viện phim Việt Nam [Hanoi: Film Institute], pp 23–44.

Như Quỳnh (2019), personal interview, conducted by Qui-Ha Hoang Nguyen, June.

Pettus, Ashley (2004), *Between Sacrifice and Desire: National Identity and the Governing of Femininity in Vietnam*, New York: Routledge.

Scheibel, Will (2018), 'Working it: Gene Tierney, Laura, and wartime beautification', *Camera Obscura: Feminism, Culture, and Media Studies* 33:2 (98), pp. 161–95.

Thanh Tú (2019), personal interview, conducted by Qui-Ha Hoang Nguyen, June.

Trà Giang (1972). 'Nhân vật Dịu là một thử thách mới đối với tôi' [Dịu character is a New Challenge to me], *Vietnamese Screen* 2, pp. 3–9.

Trà Giang (2016), personal interview, conducted by Qui-Ha Hoang Nguyen, July.

Trà Giang (2019), personal interview, conducted by Qui-Ha Hoang Nguyen, July.

Trần, Thanh Hạnh (2012), 'NSND Trà Giang: Mối tình đầu tiên và mối tình cuối cùng' ['NSND Trà Giang: The First Love and The Last Love'], *Dân trí*, October 31, <https://dantri.com.vn/van-hoa/nsnd-tra-giang-moi-tinh-dau-tien-va-moi-tinh-cuoi-cung-1352061427.htm> (last accessed 26 March 2021).

Trương Quân (1974). 'Gặp Trà Giang' [Meeting Trà Giang], *Hanoi Screen* 1, pp. 22–3, 36.

Wang, Ban (1997), *The Sublime Figure of History: Aesthetics and Politics in Twentieth-Century China*, Stanford, CA: Stanford University Press.

Wang, Zheng (2016), *Finding Women in the State: A Socialist Feminist Revolution in the People's Republic of China, 1949–1964*, Oakland, CA: University of California Press.

Yu, Sabrina Qiong (2012), 'Vulnerable Chinese stars', in Yingjin Zhang (ed.), *A Companion to Chinese Cinema*, Somerset: Wiley-Blackwell, pp. 218–38.

Zhang, Yingjin (2010), 'Zhao Dan: spectrality of martyrdom and stardom', in Mary Farquhar and Yingjin Zhang (eds), *Chinese Film Stars*, London and New York: Routledge, pp. 86–96.

Zou, John (2010), 'Mei Lanfang: facial signature and political performance in opera film', in Mary Farquhar and Yingjin Zhang (eds), *Chinese Film Stars*, London and New York: Routledge, pp. 69–85.

Notes

1. Many stars of the South Vietnamese cinema gained high social status and economic empowerment, such as Kim Cương, Kiều Chinh, Thanh Nga, among others.
2. While some artists working in cinema in the colonial period were recruited, I cannot find any big name actors from this time who appeared in revolutionary films. It is worth noting here that the first films of revolutionary cinema are newsreel-like documentaries without actors. The first feature film, *On the Same River* (Nguyễn Hồng Nghi and Hiếu Dân, 1959) cast Mạnh Linh and Phi Nga, two theatre actors who were not very popular with the public. When film initially became popular, the media only referred to them as 'actors' rather than 'stars' (*diễn viên*, literally meaning the person who plays a role).
3. In my interviews with the famous socialist actor Mai Châu (2018) and with the cartoon director Nguyễn Phương Hoa (2018), daughter of film star Đức Hoàn, they shared their nostalgic memories about material shortages when living in a communal house.
4. The Stanislavski system includes rules to guide performers to reach the inner depth of their characters. Konstantin Stanislavski, the creator of the system, stressed both

the psychological and physical dimensions of performing. This system dismisses formalist acting, regarding it as imitative and unreal as opposed to realistic acting, which, for him, is genuinely artistic. As I have illustrated, Stanislavki's acting theory could be challenged, as the boundary between realism and formalism is not a hard line. Actors like Trà Giang would usually exaggerate to communicate their feelings transparently to the masses in an affective mode. For a detailed discussion on the Stanislavski system see Chan (2019: 134–5) and Lu (2008: 119–20).

5. Beside the well-known mother-fighter role, Trà Giang's on-screen image is diverse. In *Floating Village* (*Làng nổi*, Huy Thành, 1965), Trà Giang plays Cốm, a young and active woman who helps her friend develop the irrigation system for farms. In *Forest Fire* (*Lửa rừng*, Phạm Văn Khoa, 1966), Trà Giang plays an ethnic minority woman persuading her husband, who works for the enemy, to become a supporter of the revolution. As Việt Hà in *The Fighting Continues* (*Cuộc chiến đấu vẫn còn tiếp diễn*, Khắc Lợi and Hoàng Thái, 1969), she plays an underground officer. In *Holy Day* (*Ngày Lễ Thánh*, Bạch Diệp, 1976) she plays Nhàn, a Catholic woman – her most popular anti-protagonist – who forbids her younger sister's romantic relationship with a communist soldier.

6. Trà Giang told me that she never thought she was beautiful. When enrolling in film school, she usually felt unconfident about her beauty because her classmates' good looks stood out. Two other socialist film stars Thanh Tú and Như Quỳnh who I interviewed in June 2019 also asserted that being good-looking was very important for a film acting career. Như Quỳnh said that although *We Will Meet Again* (*Đến hẹn lại lên*, Trần Vũ, 1974) brought her fame, the role of Mai, a young warm-hearted nurse in *Road to the Front* (Trần Đắc, 1973) interested audiences much more. Audiences responded to the character's fresh beauty. She received a large number of letters from audiences around the country after the film's screening. Pocket-sized portraits of her were circulated widely; many soldiers told her that they kept the portrait with them.

7. Nhân Văn Giai Phẩm (1955–6), a literary movement against the Party's control over the arts, is a fine case in point. Many artists were imprisoned or suffered strict punishments because they explicitly requested the party to loosen its power to allow for diversity in content and form in the arts, rather than just adopting socialist realist methodology.

8. Trà Giang was not an exception. Cartoon artist Phương Hoa, the daughter of Đức Hoàn and well-known director Trần Vũ, told me that her father usually took care of her when her mother went away with film crews for film shoots in rural locations.

9. Another famous actor, Lâm Tới, who plays the antagonist role of Trần Sùng in *The Seventeenth Parallel*, also talks about his creativity as a performer.

Chapter 5

Seeking a passport: the transnational career of Kiều Chinh

Pujita Guha

Robert Wise, the Hollywood director, best known for *The Sound of Music* (1965), had met Kiều Chinh[1] (one of South Vietnam's most prominent actresses) in Taipei before the fall of Saigon. Chinh was all set to work with him in a film that ultimately did not materialise (Chinh 2017). After Saigon's fall and the reunification of North and South Vietnam,[2] Kiều Chinh, fleeing the nascent communist Vietnam, found herself a penniless refugee, in Vancouver, Canada, from where she later moved to Sacramento, California. As she reached out to her Hollywood contacts, Robert Wise, among others, came forward to help her, writing recommendation letters to major studios and directors. One director who took an interest was Francis Ford Coppola, then casting for a small part in *Apocalypse Now* (1979). Chinh was cast as the wife of Colonel Walter E. Kurtz, the enigmatic rogue soldier turned cult leader who would be immortalised by Marlon Brando. However, when shooting in the Philippines was to begin, Chinh was unable to join the set. As she was not a permanent resident of California at that time, the Department of Immigration barred her from leaving the United States, leading to the role being removed from the film. Ironically, if her Vietnamese and/or her Asian identity made it possible for her to land a role in *Apocalypse Now*, the same identity as a Vietnamese immigrant proved to be a bureaucratic barrier for her as well. Nevertheless, Kiều Chinh would soon find her first Hollywood paycheck opposite Alan Alda in the television series *M*A*S*H*, portraying a Korean princess fleeing the war. Her career in America, thus, began by straddling a series of racially stereotyped Asian parts with those of war-afflicted migrant Asian-(American) characters.

Kiều Chinh's career span of fifty years has been intricately bound up with the fate of Vietnam and the turbulent national and racial politics that marked the Cold War decades. Chinh's stardom and her capacity to manoeuvre within such volatile socio-political contexts cannot, therefore, be seen outside her own biography. Born after the Second World War into a gentrified Buddhist family from northern Vietnam, Kiều Chinh migrated from Hanoi to Saigon in 1954 under Operation Passage to Freedom.[3] After Vietnam was split into two, a 300 day window allowed families to migrate from North to South Vietnam after the North's communist takeover and South's passage to French-American control. Chinh was separated from her family during the passage. Fortunately, she found her feet in the cinema, debuting with minor roles in *The Quiet American* (Joseph Mankiewicz, 1958) and *Hồi Chuông Thiên Mụ* (The Bells of Thiên Mụ Temple, Dân Lê, 1957) until she became a major film star in the fledgling cinema industry of Saigon (Chinh 2019: 165–70). Alongside Thẩm Thúy Hằng, Chinh became one of Saigon's most prominent actresses, with the two starring together in *Từ Sài Gòn Đến Điện Biên Phủ* (From Saigon to Dien Bien Phu, Ying Chang, 1967). Like the Saigonese film industry, which reflected the South's anti-communist agenda, *Dien Bien Phu* bolstered war politics through its commercial genre cinema (Duong 2014; Wilson 2007).

As the heart of French Indochina, cinema began in Saigon with travelling Pathé and Lumière filmmakers, and swiftly crystallised into a modern (elite) public sphere with its art-deco theatres, jazz bars, pools, clubs, and cafes (Chinh 2019). After 1955, Saigon's film industry tried to produce local films, while meeting the demand for films through imports of popular Hong Kong, Taiwanese, Indian and American films. However, in a war-torn land, the industry moved in fits and starts, relying substantially on private donors and American capital for local productions. South Vietnam's production companies included the Republic's Army Film Service, the USIS (United States Information Service), the National Motion Pictures Center, and private players like Freedom Films, Alpha Studio, and Giao Chỉ Film (Duong 2014; Chinh 2019). While Chinh recollects that approximately thirty studios operated at the time, scholars find it difficult to write any comprehensive history of South Vietnamese cinema because of the systematic neglect, erasure and oblivion cast on it by the post-reunification Vietnam state (Duong 2014; Chinh 2019). The archivist's lore is that members of the Saigonese film industry fled with copies of films to wherever they migrated, saving precious cultural heritage under historic and political duress. As one Vietnamese art historian told me, if one wants to research South Vietnamese cinema, one should forage the VCD stores in Orange County, California. Saigon has next to nothing! Chinh's own films were saved similarly and are easily found in Orange County's video stalls. Some have since been uploaded to YouTube and enjoy a modicum of internet following. Chinh's career in a sense follows the larger arcs within the Saigonese film industry, which was sustained with occasional Hollywood support. Her career took off at light speed when she starred in two major Hollywood films emerging out of the Vietnam War context, shot on location in mainland Southeast Asia: *A Yank in Vietnam* (Marshall Thompson, 1964), and *Operation C.I.A.* (Christian Nyby, 1965). By the late 1960s, Kiều Chinh had entered Hollywood through the Southeast Asian fringes. She starred in two films produced by the Manila-based American producer Rolf Bayer and directed by Lamberto V. Avellana, *Destination Vietnam* (1968) and *The Evil Within* (1970), and at the same time also liaised between the Vietnamese entertainment industry and Hollywood stars who flew down to entertain the American soldiers in Vietnam (Chinh 2017). Twice displaced – first, from Hanoi to Saigon, and then from Saigon to Sacramento, California – Chinh's career emerged with the ebbs and flows of the Vietnam War. While Chinh has been acknowledged as a South Vietnamese star, with her career from the mid-1950s to the mid-1970s bookending the biography of a nascent nation, and later still as an Asian American diaspora star, I follow her career and life through the rubric of 'passportlessness': figuring her stardom as one of continuous spatial and identitarian displacement, war and exile.

The passportless person, Derrida has argued, is a paperless person, an 'outlaw, a non-subject legally', 'a noncitizen or the citizen of a foreign country [who has been] refused the right conferred, *on paper*, by a temporary or permanent visa, a rubber stamp' (Derrida 2005: 61). To be passportless and stateless means that one is 'unprotected by any specific law or political convention' (Bernstein 2005: 50). Decidedly a political concept, passportlessness, I believe, reconfigures some of the questions of capital and stardom inherent to transnational stardom studies. Transnational stardom scholarship focuses on stars as sites of cultural articulations; transnational mobility allows them to 'dialogue between geopolitical contexts, social relations and cultural assumptions' (Marino 2015: 112). Shifting focus from the cosmopolitan global star who confidently navigates the routes of transnational media and global capitalism, often crossing over and straddling multiple industries, 'passportless' stardom situates the star on the very margins of the state and capital, as an outsider

(Meeuf and Raphael 2005: 1–18). The passportless star responds to the precarious, insecure conditions of her statehood, in contrast to the aspirational, upward mobility associated with transnational stardom at present. Passportlessness highlights the precarity of a refugee's exile, rather than the transnational star's surfing of the waves of global capital. Stars (within market contexts) are often considered the epitomes of capitalist agency, figurations that produce desire that could be monetised from the audiences (King 2006: 153–4). And while stars are industrial forces around which capital and power concretises, passportlessness as an analytic category helps see the star as a fragile body and symbol who mutates as she moves through turbulent, cramped political contexts (which, in Chinh's case, is a volatile mid-twentieth-century Vietnam). If on the one hand, Derrida has configured passportlessness as a condition of political subjectivity, scholars like Hamid Naficy, on the other, have written about exilic cinema from the loci of independent cinema (Naficy 2001). For Naficy, exilic cinema factors in the doubleness of exile – from one's host country/place of belonging, a spatial dislocation, and concomitantly, from the mainstream industry of a place. My work, thus, looks at the condition of a star in exile, accruing capital, wealth and value yet also being displaced from the same in time. Passportless stardom thus is a paradoxical construct – of stardom from the margins of the industry – and of industries and nations themselves caught in flux.

Chinh's stardom, as I look at it, has traversed through a perpetual state of losing her home, occupation, family, work and 'the everyday life-world of one's language' (Bernstein 2005: 50). It is a stardom borne out of the necessity to assimilate and to adjust, of the false optimism of hybrid identities and the eagerness to blend into surroundings (50). Therefore, if the bearing of a passport is a juridical guarantee of the self, a paper that responds with a 'here am I' to state interpellation, I look into how Chinh's 'passportless' stardom navigates between worlds: embodying a sublime, inviolable aura at the same time as it negotiates the legal standing of a 'non-subject'. Aside from her quite diminutive presence, and the central position she occupies in her films, Chinh's aura partly emanates from her status as a 1960s Saigonese style icon. She popularised Saigon modernist fashion, a mashup of long flowing *áo dàis* and the latest Parisian style of the day: beehive hairdos, capri pants, tartan skirts and shift dresses.[4] And yet even in this auratic domination of the screen, Chinh was rendered fragile and precarious, her passportlessness haunting her cinematic presence throughout her Southeast Asian career as well. I argue that passportlessness is not only a constraint that Chinh bears throughout her Hollywood career – a straightjacketing of the diasporic star – but also a trope that undergirds her prolific if brief career in Saigon and Southeast Asia. In her Vietnamese films, I show how Chinh repeatedly acts as a non-subject in becoming, perpetually experiencing loss, derision and passportlessness. I figure Chinh's passportlessness both in her portrayal of women caught in war-afflicted landscapes in South Vietnamese films, and in her performances in transnational productions where she often has to masquerade her Vietnamese identity in lieu of playing any substitutable Asian/East Asian characters. I consider this substitution, or Oriental masquerading, as a form of passportlessness too, where Asian stars are denied their cultural and national identity. This chapter, therefore, asks that for an eternally stateless star, what does being displaced from one's national–cultural identity mean? And how might her career and life be intricately bound with the turmoil of Cold War geopolitics, with endless migrations and a perpetual state of passportlessness?

Performing passportlessness

A little into *Người Tình Không Chân Dung* (Warrior, Who are You?, Hoàng Vĩnh Lộc, 1971),[5] the film suddenly switches from a quasi-desolate, war-torn landscape of South Vietnam to the dynamic war theatre itself. Soldiers trek up a mountain, bombs, grenades and bullets are loaded into airplanes, and fighter jets noisily take off from the runway, almost piercing through the frame. My-Lan (Chinh) arrives at the air force base, her ashen, dreamy face standing in stark contrast to the speeding frenetic action behind her. A radio announcer, she is thrown violently into the war, trying to find a soldier named Thuần, whose letters to her radio show move her enough to embark on this unforeseen quest through a battle-scarred Vietnam. Though she is a radio announcer by profession, the 'voice of the nation', Chinh emerges instead as the film's mute witness (Duong 2014: 267). She witnesses and archives an undocumentable history – the everyday silent aftermath of war – the countless mass graves, deaths, bodily disfiguration, poverty, chaos and the earth's desecration. When the audience first encounters My-Lan, with her pallid face and measured steps, her svelte body in the flowing golden *áo dài*, appearing as a distinctly outlined feminine figure traversing the war-ravaged landscapes, she becomes the nation's allure, a 'walking enigma' caught in the throes of war.

As she wearily ponders about the inherent cruelty of war, she finally finds Thuần amidst a ward of half corpses in a hospital. Bandaged from head to toe, Thuần remains unrevealed to her, speaking in half-finished sentences until his sudden death (Figure 5.1). With his physical face obliterated, Thuần is no longer recognisable to both Chinh and us, his new bandaged 'face', reveals an opaque, impenetrable presence that does not return our gaze. If the face is the bodily site where we perceive the world, it is also the site through which the world perceives us, conferring upon us our identity. Thuần's faceless condition produces a non-identity, no longer a 'face' we could relate to. He becomes pure landscape, a corrugated irregular surface that renders his body to us as without singularity or subjectivity (Deleuze and Guattari 1987: 167–92). No longer recognised by the state, his anonymity, or non-identity, induces in My-Lan a similar affliction. Beginning to lose her sanity, she wanders barefoot around the countryside like someone possessed, running into the forest and becoming imperceptible in its midst. My-Lan's dissolution into madness, insensate without a stable identity or self, pushes the self so far beyond the subjective human that she is neither recognisable, nor desirable to the state. She embodies

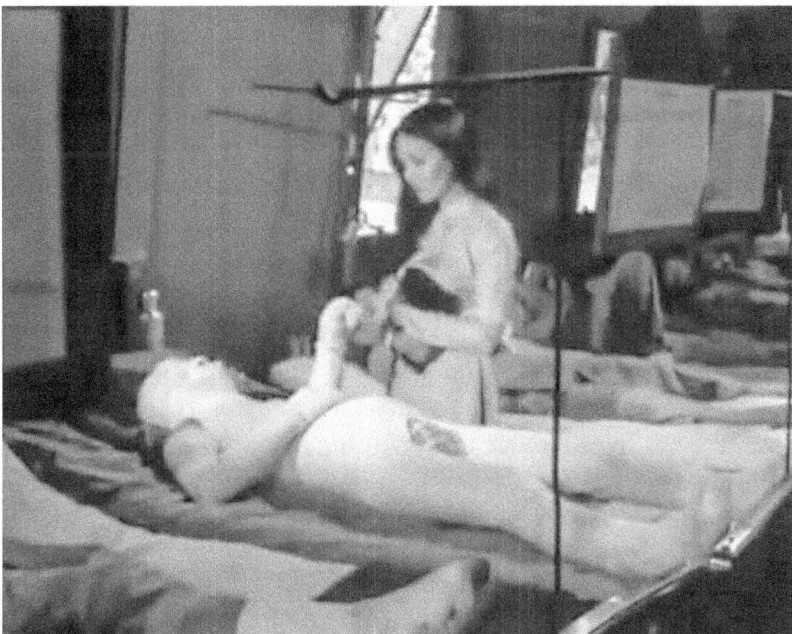

Figure 5.1. My-Lan meets Thuần at the hospital ward. Screenshot from *Người Tình Không Chân Dung*.

madness, a passportlessness, a loci from where she is no longer a part of a civil polity (Foucault 2006), nor can she return to it, having experienced the horrors of war up front. By her entropic dissolution into madness, she becomes an undocumented figure, an unidentifiable anonymous object like the broken upturned helmet in the middle of a battlefield that bookends the film as its first and last image.

Kiều Chinh's stardom is then intricately bound to the war-torn landscape of Vietnam. It is here that the forested highlands of Vietnam become an oft-repeated site in her films; setting her passportlessness against the landscape. In the opening scene of *Chiếc Bóng Bên Đường* (Roadside Shadow, Van Tuong Nguyen, 1973) a valley surrounded by such forested highlands turns out to be a threatening place teeming with land mines. Off to rescue a child caught in its midst, the army officer Tuấn (the male protagonist played by Thành Được) not only saves the child but gradually falls in love with the mother, Mai (Kim Cương). Halfway into the film, when Tuấn's wife, Loan (Chinh), decides to visit the camp, she learns of his marital infidelities. The same valley returns this time heaving with emotion and affect, an intimacy familiar to the audience. The camera not only frames them against a harrowing, difficult environment, but the winds engulf them – their *áo dài*s fluttering – almost devouring their terse throw of words. While the camera intermittently frames them in close-ups (to maintain the sanctity of the star image) (Barthes 1991: 56–7), it increasingly captures them against extreme wide shots, steadfastly moving away from both actresses, turning our attention to the landscape (Figure 5.2). The camera thereby graphically enjoins the star's fate to the fate of the land. Towards the end of the film, what was once a fecund piece of land is destroyed by landmines, and in the process also tears apart Loan when Tuấn dies in an explosion. Now a widow, Chinh appears dressed in white, running deep into the cemetery with its white marble plaques, a land inscribed with many more such deaths that haunt the frame. As long as she is the army officer's wife, the film guarantees her star presence by organising the *mise-en-scène* around her instantly recognisable face. Consequently, her becoming a widow renders her a stateless non-subject indistinguishable from the landscape. The film concludes with the camera pulling back as she walks away from the frame, her black laced gown blending into the road upon which she walks. Chinh's gradual disintegration into the traumatised landscape marks her own passportlessness, her own falling through the cracks, the abysses of the state. She emerges as a star notionally embodying South Vietnam's own precarity, its own war-torn, bereaving landscape.

Figure 5.2 Mai and Loan talking against the war-torn landscape. Notice the video maker Thuy Nga's logo on top. Screenshot from *Chiếc Bóng Bên Đường*.

Richard Dyer argues that film stars are 'personas constituted by on-screen and off-screen narratives' (Dyer 1979). The star image is made not only of on-screen performances, but from a heady concoction of off-screen promotion (in newspapers, film magazines, television and now the internet), scandals, gossip and rumours, with an effusive portrayal of ordinary domesticity thrown in. While it is generally believed that audiences recognise stars' characteristic tropes quite easily, and find these tropes circulating across films (Mazumdar 2012: 833), I argue that the nature of a star's persona is linked to the very material circulations that the films embody. A star's life is equally enmeshed in the life its film takes, moulded by the exhibition circles, legal/illegal circuits, film festival presences, franchise histories, or even censorship debates that touch upon it. Working in a nascent and fragile film industry, Kiều Chinh's stardom, I believe, cannot be seen outside the sphere of circulation within which her films exist. *Chiếc Bóng Bên Đường*, for example, which was uploaded on YouTube by a popular channel MrVietphim, has the imprint of its video days – the video label Thuy Nga Video marks both the beginning and the end of the copy and the watermark runs throughout its entire length. This pirated copy of *Chiếc Bóng* typically reveals lost resolution from multiple generations of duplication – its transfer from celluloid film to analogue video to digital video to digital file – so that the colour looks washed out, the sound distorted, the subtitles dislocated and snipped off on the left and right side edges. These imprints, however, place *Chiếc Bóng*'s bootlegging within a specific political and technological moment. While it is largely argued that bootlegging became prevalent with the 'pervasiveness of personal VCRs' through the late 1970s and 1980s (Hilderbrand 2004: 53), a similar time-frame marked the exile of many South Vietnamese families from Vietnam after the war. In the context of South Vietnam's capitulation to the communist North and the state's subsequent erasure of its traumatic histories, these films were caught in a specific narrative of dislocation and passportlessness. These films, smuggled out of the nation by a refugee people and then continually pirated via digital and video technologies, are embodiments of the need to preserve a cultural memory of South Vietnam in the face of state apathies. Kiều Chinh in an interview recollects how she personally travelled with the print of *Người Tình* while fleeing during Saigon's fall to North Vietnam. Since the South Vietnamese community dispersed and survived as anguished migrants across continents, the films transferred across many hands and generations of people and media formats came to bear the imprint of their decades-long passage. With scratches, grains, black lines and video aberrations of a community that now found itself in an aberrant wretched condition, the images began to suggest both a nostalgic, decayed quality, and their rough passage in time, their precarious existence outside state sanctioned archives (Steyerl 2009). Kiều Chinh's face, the star's beloved close-up, and her body survives here only in a fragmentary and dispersed form – cut up by many blotchy lines and staggered edges. The repeated reproduction of the bootleg videotapes compound this effect, so that the image loss with each successive copy and each new duplication aesthetically reflects Chinh's subjective and 'bodily wasting: her disappearing body becomes manifest in the material information loss' (Hilderbrand 2004: 57).

Countless friends and scholars mention how Chinh's work before 1975 can easily be found in DVD stores. These films have now been re-digitised by major Vietnamese American production companies such as Thúy Nga Asia and repackaged with colourful titles, with 'pre-1975' tags and alluring images of the major star of the period. While DVD companies bank on Chinh's glamour and allure, the periodisation of 'before 1975' speaks of a perpetual sense of passportlessness against which such 'diasporic' performances can be invoked. The year 1975 is a clear signifier, marking Saigon's fall to North Vietnam and the subsequent reunification of Vietnam, the period in which substantial numbers of the South Vietnamese population fled to America or elsewhere for refuge. This passportlessness is more than symbolic, as there prevails an implicit ban on films from this era and region within Vietnam (my own ethnographic research in Saigon yielded little for this very reason). As Lan Duong (2014) notes,

> understood in a context of institutionalized state censure, these 'pre-1975' films extra-textually represent a love for a time past and a love for the 'past-time' of film-going before the end of the war, a film culture that was once vibrant and alive for many in the diaspora.[6]

And the duplication degeneration that appears within these films presents a material inscription often read nostalgically by the Vietnamese community which treasures and consumes these films.

In such a milieu, the internet becomes an 'imperfect repository' of a disappearing history, virtually constructed and kept alive in images, including those of the stars who embodied this film history. As the communist state of Vietnam rushes headlong to erase South Vietnam's history, while simultaneously wooing an affluent diasporic community to return, the internet expresses the deep trauma that was experienced by the refugees of Vietnam with countless websites providing the screening of Vietnamese films, and YouTube comments filled with nostalgic comments about having seen particular films in the past (Carruthers and Huynh-Beattie 2011: 148). A YouTube search on Kiều Chinh throws up not only the films that she acted in but also snippets from *Kiều Chinh: A Journey Back Home*, a film that documented her return to Vietnam in 1996 (for the first time since she fled Vietnam in 1975). Interviews in which she anguishes over her passportless condition after the fall of South Vietnam are also available on the internet. In an hour-long interview with the Vietnamese America Diaspora Association, she not only records her painful journey in Hollywood, surviving off Tippi Hedren and others, but also her harrowing experience working with the Vietnamese refugees arriving in boats during the late 1970s, and her philanthropic work with the Vietnam Children's Fund (a non-profit organisation that establishes schools in the war afflicted areas of Vietnam). Passportlessness is constantly remembered, signalling both a silent dream for a lost nation state (South Vietnam) and the difficulties of belonging elsewhere in the USA. Chinh's later films *The Joy Luck Club* (Wayne Wang, 1993) and *Journey from the Fall* (Ham Tran, 2006) recount such passportlessness in detail (the latter made with an entirely South Vietnamese crew) through narratives of arduous transcontinental journeys and splintered war-torn families much like her own. I contend, then, that Chinh's biography seeps into and defines her transnational career, speaking in low tones from the silences, gaps, and fissures of history.

Masquerading and reclaiming a passport

In her first major role in Hollywood, Kiều Chinh was cast in 'In Love and War' (Alan Alda, 1977), a sixth season episode of the hit television show *M*A*S*H*. A fleeting love interest for the show's lead character Hawkeye (played by Alan Alda), Chinh played an aristocratic woman Kyung Soon, whose mother Hawkeye tends to in the episode. In an early, flirtatious encounter between the two, Soon divulges that in this deserted forlorn, war-ravaged landscape, she pines to hear French, a language she learned during her well-spent youth in France. She confesses how French reminds her of her former lover with whom she spoke in French, and the high art, literature and poetry that was the subject of the conversations between them. In an attempt to win her over, Hawkeye gawkishly mutters, 'je suis poulet a la poetry' (he means to say, 'I am pulled [attracted] to poetry'). Soon bursts forth in laughter, revealing that he instead said 'I am chicken'.[7] Hawkeye's gaffe reveals his failing command of French (and thus his true status as a pure Anglophone American), as well as the hyperbolic tropes of masquerading – the comic stuttering is accompanied by Hawkeye's gestures of pulling something vigorously (Chung 2006: 42). All the while, though, the joke is on him, since the scene gestures towards the real masquerading at play – Kiều Chinh passing herself off as a French-speaking Korean. Even as the episode narrativises Soon's aristocratic upbringing in France, it hides Chinh's real upbringing in colonial French Indochina, where its gentrified subjects often learned the language of the coloniser (Chinh 2017). From the very outset then, Chinh's career, much like those of other Asian American actors who preceded her in Hollywood, is rendered into an elaborate exercise in Oriental masquerading: her career unfolding as a composite of multiple Asian ethnicities (Chung 2006: 32).

Despite being cast in a number of Vietnam-related films and television series of the day – *My Husband is Missing* (Richard Michaels, 1978), *The Children of An Lac* (John Moxey, 1980) and later *Catfish in Black Bean*

Sauce (Chi Muoi Lo, 1999) and *What's Cooking?* (Gurinder Chadha, 2000) – she appears as a Burmese heir-princess in *The Evil Within* (1970), a Chinese character in *The Lucifer Complex* (Kenneth Hartford and David L. Hewitt, 1978) and *The Letter* (John Erman, 1982), a Singaporean in multiple episodes of *Dynasty* (Richard and Esther Shapiro, 1983), and often just an unspecified Oriental woman in *Fantasy Island* (George McCowan, 1981). One might read this masquerading as yet another way of becoming passportless, performing multiple roles that do not acknowledge her Vietnamese origins. Conforming to Hollywood's (mis) casting norms when it comes to Asian and Asian American actors, her star persona is as if without a fixed passport, able to essay any character from a large pool of 'Asian' identities. Both in her Vietnamese and pan-Asian roles then, Kiều Chinh's Hollywood career reflects her own status as a passportless refugee. This, I maintain, is both an acknowledgement of her Vietnamese origins and yet also an erasure of a singular difference – her status as a 'Vietnamese' refugee in the wake of the war – into a blinding homogeneity that imagines Eastern and Southeast Asian faces as easily substitutable.

In *Operation C.I.A.* (1965), Kiều Chinh plays an undercover secret agent who aids Mark Andrews (Burt Reynolds), a CIA operative sent to Saigon on an undercover mission to save the American Embassy there from an impending attack by the communist forces. Mark Andrews emerges as a James Bond prototype – suave, cosmopolitan, witty and worldly wise. Like Bond, Andrews relishes women galore, who firmly establish his heterosexual masculinity (Funnell 2015: 1–5). The first of these women, who intermittently keeps appearing, is the Southeast Asia expert Denise, played by Danielle Aubry, with whom Andrews has a playful, flirtatious relationship. Through most of the film though, he is aided by Kim Chinh (Kiều Chinh), his native informant, an undercover agent who doubles up as a clerk at the tourism department. Though the two share a highly professional relationship, it sometimes seems to teeter dangerously close to a romantic liaison. Ferrying Russell, who is clearly out of his depths both in learning about the tropics as well as the intricate communist networks across the city, Chinh emerges as the Bond girl – at once everyday and ordinary on the one hand, and intelligent and agile enough to accompany Russell on his adventures on the other (Hines 2018: 132). In a crucial action/reconnaissance scene in the film, Russell and Chinh find themselves in the river, and it is Chinh who familiarises Russell with the closely interwoven waterways of the city, the student demonstrations across the river and the villain's purported hideout amidst the rows of wooden houses on stilts (Funnell and Dodds 2017: 109-35). This claim to Saigonese nativity is however complicated by the film's own production history. *Operation C.I.A.* was slated to be shot in Saigon, following on the heels of another Kiều Chinh Hollywood film *A Yank in Vietnam*. Worsening political conditions in Saigon however forced the shooting to be shifted to Bangkok. While the film's opening shot declares the setting as Saigon, *Operation C.I.A.* passes off Bangkok as Saigon with nonchalance (Mark Andrews greets Thai-speaking locals with the quintessentially Thai 'Sawadee', while famous landmarks like Wat Arun and Wat Pho jostle with Thai public signages in the film's cityscape). This circumstantial Oriental masquerading similarly complicates Chinh's character onscreen. Chinh's background is never confirmed, but between Vietnamese conversations with her servant, wearing svelte silken dresses typical of 1960s Saigonese fashion and intimate familiarity with the Chao Phraya river (as befits a native informant), she emerges as a Saigonese native passing off her knowledge of what is Bangkok in reality. Oriental masquerading might have been a common phenomenon in Hollywood owing to white America's inability to perceive ethnic and racial difference (Chung 2006: 47). However, when seen against Chinh's career in Vietnam in which she so often plays a wasted subject, Oriental masquerading reinforces her passportlessness on screen. The film neither confirms nor denies her character a Vietnamese identity and what remains in its stead is a passportless Asian identity that refuses to acknowledge Asian cultural ethnic specificities and differences, where every character or attribute is merely Oriental and indifferent to the white spectatorial gaze.

In one of the most expansive, transnational films of her career, Kiều Chinh appeared in *The Evil Within* (also known as *The Passport to Danger*)[8] opposite the Indian matinee idol Dev Anand. The film is a Cold War espionage thriller around drug trade in southern and south-eastern Asia, and was shot across Hong Kong, Vietnam, the Philippines and in Udaipur Palace in Rajasthan, India. From the very moment of her arrival at Bombay airport, Chinh caused a media sensation ('Film Folk-us!' 1970: 49). A certain officialdom always marked her presence – from a formal photo with the Air India Maharaja (MacDonald, 'The Evil Within') to formal dinners at the Jaipur Maharaja's palace (Bhatia 2011: 49), to even planning a South Vietnam-Indo film festival ('Miscellanea' 1971: 13). Chinh was both an enigmatic object for the Indian public, and a visible currency of cross-cultural exchange. Her public performances were always laced with a performance of cultural diplomacy. Even in her interviews, Chinh kept emphasising that her presence in India was in fact part of a larger flow of personnel who were training in India to set up a vibrant 'industry' back in Vietnam ('Miscellanea' 1971: 13). In an interview with *Times of India*, she pointed out that, not only had the cameraman of her film *Từ Sài Gòn Đến Điện Biên Phủ* been trained under Fali Mistry (a close associate of Dev Anand and director of photography of *The Evil Within*), but that she was in talks with P. V. Prabhu (the India head of 20th Century Fox) to organise a South Vietnamese film festival in the country. In fact, photos of Chinh (often alongside producer Rolf Bayer and Dev Anand) featured in many news snippets detailing industrial and infrastructural flows between Bombay and Hollywood unrelated to *The Evil Within*, thus contextualising her presence in India within a larger genealogy of co-productions emerging in Bombay cinema at that point in time ('Dubbers Brotherhood' 1970: 17).

Despite Chinh's status as a cultural diplomat, questions of masquerading and passportlessness always seem to haunt the picture. In the film, Chinh plays the role of the primary antagonist, Kumar Souraiya, a Burmese princess who is heir to a drug empire. This masquerading corresponds with the fact that the film itself is shot in Udaipur, India, and references Indian cultures, in a desert topography far away from Burma. But more subliminally, passportlessness seeps into the film's promotional life. Panning out against India's own officially non-aligned political climate, which even criticised the American presence in Vietnam (Thakur 1979: 958), Chinh's personal life was largely kept a secret, masqueraded over by official scripts and regularised attendances ('A Touch of Pageantry' 1971: 11–17). Chinh's poignant separation from her family in Hanoi and her resettlement in Saigon elicited questions from journalists, which Chinh glossed over as best as possible ('Miscellanea' 1971: 13). It was an unutterable, too intimate a horror, that could be performed during vulnerable moments in private interviews only.[9] Her public appearances (the cherry on the cake being her attendance as guest of honour at the Filmfare Awards Night, 1971) were marked by official photo-ops, guest appearances and short scripted speeches. What stuck out in this melee was that Chinh was asked to present the Best International Film Award to Richard Attenborough's *Oh! What a Lovely War!* (1969), an epic anti-war drama that narrativised the disillusionment of soldiers in the First World War. While the award itself could be allegorised as India's own feeble effort at de-escalating the Vietnam War, Chinh's presence in this equation was far more ambiguous. In a political milieu that largely favoured North Vietnam, her public appearances masked her personal trajectory which had been jeopardised in the North. Chinh's belonging to the state could only be made possible by papering over her passportlessness as she migrated from North to South Vietnam, losing her family in the exilic process. Kiều Chinh's passportlessness came to be enmeshed within Cold War global geopolitics and could only creep about in silent uneasiness, lying dormant under the mask of cultural diplomacy that marked her brief transnational career in Southeast Asia. Passportlessness governed her transnational activities even within Asia: narratively reduced to essaying generic non-specific Asian women on-screen, but off-screen, as a cultural diplomat having to paper over her complicated upbringing in South Vietnam. Chinh's status as a passportless star then situates her in a paradoxical relation to the state. She at one end is caught between the state and not, its diplomat but unable to acknowledge its tumultuous and recent origins. And at the other, she is a transnational southeast Asian star, whose very transnational presence effaces her national identity, each performance exemplifying a forgetting and uprooting from her situatedness.

Conclusion

Kiều Chinh was a national star, representing South Vietnam's film industry elsewhere, always embodying the nation as one of its primary voices and witnesses. Chinh's career in South Vietnam was mapped onto South Vietnam's situation itself, its tumultuous existence from 1955 to 1975. Chinh was also a transnational star in Asia at that time, moving between Taipei, Hong Kong, Bangkok, Manila and Bombay, navigating the Southeast Asian region, its South Asian and East Asian extensions, and all its interwoven industrial circuits. And yet, caught between the nation and the region, Chinh was always passportless – always falling off the seams of the state – always ceasing to be an identifiable subject. If masquerading effaced her national identity in the transnational arena, then her domestic appearances in melodramas (as a widow or a schizophrenic woman) cast her aside, with no place in the polity. Passportlessness expresses a degree of precarity – of being fragile, of unravelling, of being cast away. Passports are state-sanctioned documents after all, and as Lisa Gitleman argues, perform a know and show function. That is, documents gain power only when shown, or demonstrated in public spaces; their validity coming from showing and being seen (and acknowledged) by the viewer/spectator (Gitelman 2014: 1). Passportlessness is then the condition of no-show, the inability to present documents, to be accounted for and acknowledged by the viewer (Gitelman 2014: 1). But passportlessness in stardom pronounces an inconsistency. On the one hand, stardom exists in the realm of visibility – stars are often heavily documented off- and on-screen, hypervisibilised, and it is this visibility that is then capitalised upon (in terms of public appearance fees, brand endorsements, etc.). On the other hand, passportlessness produces the conditions of invisibility, of effacement and erasure, of masquerading, and becoming imperceptible within the landscape as it were. Passportless stardom then is a paradox, of being publicly available *and* being publicly effaced, but one whose entire appearance is structured around unacknowledged subjectivities. Passportless stars are documented and yet remain undocumented, visible yet invisibilised, caught in myriad of contradictions. Chinh's stardom therefore is structured around this perpetual condition of becoming visible as a public figure and then falling through its cracks time and again. Passportlessness acquires multiple valences in Chinh's work and life, being embodied in performances, material circulations of print, international collaborations and her resettlement across countries and continents. Chinh's career documents precarities, difficulties, travails and cultural erasures that come in the wake of being a Vietnamese caught in Cold War geopolitics.

As a result of Chinh's continued portrayal of the passportlessness of the South Vietnamese (and now Vietnamese American) people, she has acquired an iconic persona that undergirds her public performances until today. *Người Tình Không Chân Dung* was featured at the inaugural Vietnamese International Film Festival (VIFF) in 2003 in Orange County, California, where the largest community of Vietnamese Americans (including Chinh) currently reside. Chinh is the star of Little Saigon, Orange County, both as one of its most famous residents, and also as an active participant in all forms of Vietnamese American or Asian American public engagement (in one of her most recent public appearances, she appeared on a Zoom-based discussion on the representation of the Vietnamese in Spike Lee's *Da 5 Bloods* (2020) – a black perspective on the Vietnam War – organised by DVAN (Diasporic Vietnamese Artists Network)) ('ACCENTED' 2020). Chinh is also mentioned in Saigonese public culture, appearing in numerous articles about its fashions in the 1960s, and showing up in an exhibition on Saigonese urban history in the Presidential Palace in 2018. While there is an implicit ban on the reliving of the public life of Saigon before 1975, I came across Kiều Chinh's image along with Kim Cương's (another star of South Vietnamese cinema) at a state-sponsored event to celebrate its history in Saigon. The exhibition, showcased in the premises of the Presidential Palace, memorialised them in the context of Saigon's milieu during its time as the capital of south Vietnam. The room was reconstructed as a bar, with record players, decanters and goblets atop a vintage wooden bar, cane chairs, tables that mimicked a tropical café, and walls with photos of actors and actresses of the period, including Chinh and Cương (Figure 5.3) ('Exhibition on History' 2018). Along with *Saigoneer*, an online news portal of the city, which regularly publishes articles on Saigon's erstwhile public culture, this exhibition points towards the first instances at which such a public memory may be brought back to life, a disappearing history musealised. She is, even now, constantly evoked as a star of a bygone era, of an elite aesthete modern culture never to be fully recuperable, much like the South Vietnam state subsumed into the unified Vietnam in 1975. Chinh's passportlessness is in ways tied to South Vietnam's formation and dissolution, a passport made and unmade in a span of twenty years, and a film culture quickly forgotten in film history.

Figure 5.3 A room in the exhibition commemorating the history of Independence Palace, Saigon. Absolute left – Kiều Chinh, above Kim Cương. Photo by Pujita Guha.

References

'ACCENTED |Vietnamese Representation On-Screen and Behind the Scenes' (2020), *DVAN*, 18 July 2020, <https://www.eventbrite.com/e/accented-vietnamese-representation-on-screen-and-behind-the-scenes-tickets-112504355556#/> (last accessed 18 July 2020).

'April 30, 1975 | Saigon Falls' (2012), *New York Times*, 30 April, <https://learning.blogs.nytimes.com/2012/04/30/april-30-1975-saigon-falls/> (last accessed 5 May 2018).

'A Touch of Pageantry' (1971), *Filmfare*, 7 May, pp. 11–17.

Barthes, Roland (1991), 'The face of Garbo', in *Mythologies*, trans. Annette Levers, New York: Noonday Press, pp. 56–7.

Bernstein, Richard J. (2005), 'Hannah Arendt on the stateless', *Parallax* 11:1, pp. 46–60.

Bhatia, Siddharta (2011), *The Navketan Story: Cinema Modern*, New Delhi: Harper Collins.

Carruthers, Ashley and Boi Tran Huynh-Beattie (2011), 'Dark tourism, diasporic memory and disappeared history: the contested meaning of the former Indochinese refugee camp at Pulau Galang', in Yuk Wah Chan (ed.), *The Chinese-Vietnamese Diaspora: Revisiting the Boatpeople*, London and New York: Routledge, pp. 147–60.

Chinh, Kiều (2017), 'Kiều Chinh Nguyen Oral History | Viet Stories', *YouTube*, 20 December, <https://www.youtube.com/watch?v=Ivj9Pesz1sE> (last accessed 20 February 2020).

Chinh, Kiều (2019), 'The cinema industry', in Tuong Vu and Sean Fear (eds), *The Republic of Vietnam, 1955–1975: Vietnamese Perspectives on Nation Building*, Ithaca, NY: Cornell University Press, pp. 165–72.

Chung, Hye Seung (2006), *Hollywood Asian: Philip Ahn and the Making of Cross-Ethnic Performance*, Philadelphia, PA: Temple University Press.

Deleuze, Gilles and Felix Guattari (1987), 'Faciality', in *A Thousand Plateaus*, trans. and foreword by Brian Massumi, Minneapolis: University of Minnesota Press, pp. 167–82.

Derrida, Jacques (2005), *Paper Machine*, trans. Rachel Bowlby, Stanford, CA: Stanford University Press.

'Dubbers Brotherhood' (1970), *Filmfare*, 7 December, p. 17.

Duong, Lan (2014), 'Gender, affect and landscape: wartime films from North and South Vietnam', *Inter-Asia Cultural Studies* 15:2, pp. 256–73.

Dyer, Richard (1979), *Stars*, London: British Film Institute.

'Exhibition on history of Independence Palace held in Ho Chi Minh City' (1980), *Tuoi Tre News*, 10 March, <https://tuoitrenews.vn/news/lifestyle/20180310/exhibition-on-history-of-independence-palace-held-in-ho-chi-minh-city/44461.html> (last accessed 20 February 2020).

'Film Folk-us!' (1970), *Star and Style*, 25 December, pp. 47–9.

Foucault, Michel (2006), *History of Madness*, trans. Jonathan Murphy and Jean Khalfa, Oxford: Routledge, Taylor and Francis.

Funnell, Lisa (2015), 'Introduction: the women in James Bond', in Lisa Funnell (ed.), *For His Eyes Only: The Women in James Bond*, London and New York: Wallflower Press, pp. 1–4.

Funnell, Lisa and Klaus Dodds (2017), 'The Asian city: modern/vertical vs. pre-modern/horizontal spaces', in Lisa Funnell and Klaus Dodds (eds), *Geographies, Gender and Geopolitics in James Bond*, London: Palgrave Macmillan, pp. 109–35.

Gitelman, Lisa (2014), *Paper Knowledge: Towards a Media History of Documents*. Durham, NC, and London: Duke University Press.

Hilderbrand, Lucas (2004), 'Grainy days and Mondays: superstar and bootleg aesthetics', *Camera Obscura* 57 19:3, pp. 56–91.

Hines, Clair (2018), 'The Bond women', in *The Playboy and James Bond: 007, Ian Fleming and* Playboy *Magazine*, Manchester: Manchester University Press, pp. 122–58.

King, Barry (1985), 'Articulating stardom', *Screen* 26:5, pp. 27–51.

MacDonald, Tammy, "The Evil Within 1970s Still Photos", *Flickr*, <https://www.flickr.com/photos/9078758@N08/sets/72157645636601008/> (last accessed 20 July 2018).

Marino, Sara (2015), 'Transnational stardom: international celebrity in film and popular culture', *Transnational Cinemas* 6:1, pp. 112–13.

Mazumdar, Ranjani (2012), 'Film stardom after liveness', *Continuum: Journal of Media and Cultural Studies* 26:6, pp. 833–44.

Meeuf, Russell and Raphael Raphael (2013), 'Introduction', in Russell Meeuf and Raphael Raphael (eds), *Transnational Stardom: International Celebrity in Film and Popular Culture*, New York: Palgrave Macmillan, pp. 1–18.

'Miscellenea' (1971), *Times of India*, 25 April, p. 13.

Naficy, Hamid (2001), *Accented Cinema: Exilic and Diasporic Filmmaking*, Princeton: Princeton University Press.

Steyerl, Hito (2009), 'In Defense of the Poor Image', *E-Flux journal* 10, November, pp. 1–9.

Thakur, Ramesh (1979), 'India's Vietnam policy', *Asian Survey* 19:10, pp. 957–76.

Wilson, Dean (2007), 'Film controls in colonial Vietnam: 1896–1926', in Philippe Dumont and Kirstie Gormley (eds), *Vietnamese Cinema: Le Cinéma Vietnamien*, Lyon: Asiexpo Edition, pp. 75–85.

Notes

1. Kiều Chinh was born as Nguyễn Thị Chinh, 3 July 1937.
2. This *New York Times* article from 30 April 1975 details the fall of Saigon to North Vietnamese and Viet Cong forces and its immediate socio-political consequences ('April 30, 1975 | Saigon Falls' 2012).
3. One should carefully note that Operation Passage to Freedom was a term coined by the American Navy to assist the transfer of Vietnamese citizens from Hanoi to Saigon as part of the Geneva treaty of 1954 which divided Vietnam into North and South along the 17th parallel.
4. The *áo dài* is a traditional Vietnamese garment, most commonly worn by women. In its current form, it is a tight-fitting silk tunic worn over free-flowing trousers. *Áo* refers to a shirt, and *Dài* is 'long'.
5. The film was produced by Kiều Chinh herself.

6. While there is an implicit ban on the reliving of the public life of Saigon before 1975 (which a quick search at local DVD stores reveals), I came across Kiều Chinh's image along with Kim Cương's at a state-sponsored event in Saigon. An event to celebrate Saigon's history, the exhibition showcased in the Presidential Palace premises, memorialised them within the context of Saigon's milieu during its time as the capital of south Vietnam. The room was reconstructed as a bar with record players, decanters and goblets atop a vintage wooden bar, cane chairs, tables that mimicked a tropical café, and walls of actors and actresses of the period, including Chinh and Duong, with interactive games on computer display screens to boot. Along with *Saigoneer*, an online news portal of the city which regularly publishes articles on Saigon's erstwhile public culture, this exhibition points towards the first instances at which such a public memory may be brought back to life, a disappearing history musealised.
7. The joke plays upon the English verb *to pull* and the French word for chicken, *poulet*.
8. The working title of the film shifted between *Inside Out, Flower of Evil* and its released title was *The Evil Within*. Far from being a mainstream Hindi film, *The Evil Within* was a transnational project spanning the film industries of South and Southeast Asia. Produced by Rolf Bayer, an American settled in the Philippines, directed by the Filipino director Lamberto Avellena, and starring Indian matinee idol Dev Anand in the main role, the film also starred young Indian actress Zeenat Aman, Filipino screen diva Tita Munoz and American Blaxploitation star Rod Perry. This was the second time Chinh was starring in a film produced by Bayer (the first being *Destination Vietnam*). Despite its glamorous international co-production, the film never found a theatrical release in the USA, and only a Japanese poster of the film is found circulating on the internet. Plus a pirate copy of the film that is available on the internet bears the Fox Movie Channel watermark – indicating that the film may have only received a television broadcast in its time.
9. What is very interesting to note is that while most sources claim Kiều Chinh as Vietnamese, thus eliding the specificity of North and South Vietnam, one of the times her nationality is mentioned is when newspapers highlight how she had won the Best Actress Award from President Nguyễn Văn Thiệu (South Vietnam's President from 1965 to 1975).

Chapter 6

Three kinds of stardom in Indonesia

David Hanan

In the 1950s, the first decade of the new nation after the achievement of independence from Dutch colonial rule, the Indonesian film industry produced on average about thirty-five films a year. The 1960s saw a decline in the number of films made, due initially to the political problems of the Guided Democracy period. There was only a total of forty-five feature films produced in the four years immediately following the abortive army purge of 30 September 1965 and the rise to power, via a gradual 'countercoup', of General Suharto's army-led repressive New Order regime. However, in the early 1970s, beginning with the introduction of widescreen and colour, the Indonesian film industry saw unprecedented growth, with on average some seventy films produced each year for nearly the next twenty years. James Siegel has suggested that the early New Order period was also the period in which musical celebrities (pop stars), or celebrities of any kind, first appeared in Indonesia (Siegel 1986: 212).

This chapter explores three kinds of stardom that emerged in Indonesia in the 1970s and were influential for most of the New Order period and later: the songs and films of the Betawi singer and film comedian Benyamin S (1939–95); the songs and films of the *dangdut* singer Rhoma Irama (b. 1946); and three stars who emerged in the framework of Teguh Karya's film and theatre collective, Teater Populer: Christine Hakim (b. 1956), Slamet Rahardjo (b. 1949) and Tuti Indra Malaon (1939–89). The chapter takes these three phenomena as examples of different kinds of stardom. In the case of Benyamin S, I argue that it is Betawi culture, and not just the artist, that is the star. In Rhoma Irama's case, it is the individual as superstar that is the star. Regarding the three actors from Teater Populer, these were professional actors first, who became stars and used their stardom to give themselves other roles in the society.

Discussions of stardom in the USA, Britain and Europe, that is, countries of the First World, have been pioneered by Richard Dyer, initially in his book, *Stars*. Early in this book Dyer argues that although his study is primarily semiotic (he is concerned with 'the specific signification [of stars] in media texts'), that 'the semiotic concern has to be founded in the sociological' (Dyer 1982: 1). At the core of Dyer's book are discussions of stardom in Hollywood films and particularly semiotics in the context of the evolving studio system of Hollywood, where stars were shaped by the industry. The Indonesian stars discussed in this chapter were not shaped by a studio system – indeed the two singing stars emerged as a result of their own musical talent – and my discussion shows how in their films, over which they had some degree of authorial control, they could further relate to the world views and social aspirations of particular social groupings from whom they emerged or to whom they appealed. One important framework for this chapter is therefore the particular social formation in which each of these stars emerges – and seeks to further cultivate – in the course of her/his career.

The Betawi film comedian and singer Benyamin S: a popular culture of the poor

Betawi singer Benyamin S came to prominence in the Indonesian film world in the early 1970s. The Betawi constitute a distinct ethnic group within Indonesia, even though they are a marginal group. They are often referred to as the descendants of the original inhabitants of Jakarta in that they are the descendants of both free servants and slaves, people brought by the Dutch from other parts of the Indonesian archipelago – and elsewhere, from India and the Middle East – to work in the expanding colonial outpost, initially a fortress city, founded in 1619 and known as Batavia (now Jakarta), while the local West Javanese population was excluded (Hanan and Koesasi 2011: 37). Initially the language this servant class used was Portuguese, but by the mid-eighteenth century they had begun to use an evolving local dialect, based on port Malay and known as *bahasa Betawi*, as their lingua franca. *Bahasa Betawi* is known for its frankness, directness and earthy humour. Noted scholar of Southeast Asia, Benedict Anderson, has described *bahasa Betawi* thus: 'It is rough, lower-class urban speech, totally without "high" moral or status pretensions. It is virtually impossible to be pompous in bahasa Jakarta,

Figure 6.1 Betawi singer and comedian Benyamin S, seen here in a film comedy about stardom in radio broadcasting and in the popular music industry, *Ambisi* (Ambition, 1973), written and directed by Nya Abbas Akup. Image courtesy of Sinematek Indonesia.

so brutally earthy and humorous is its feel' (Anderson 1990: 142). In the early twentieth century, the Betawi evolved their own form of drama, *lenong Betawi*, noted for its comic, repetitive exchanges in Betawi dialect, and for its lilting, lyrical music, *gambang kromong*, a musical form that evolved in conjunction with the music of local Chinese communities.

The Betawi, although historically a marginalised group, are known for their friendliness, solidarity and reciprocity, as well as their extraversion and earthy humour, kinds of resourcefulness they evolved as a mutually supportive, marginalised community. It is these kinds of resourcefulness that are popularised in the movies of Benyamin S. Indeed, he embodies in his personality and performances all the qualities of the Betawi outlined above (Figure 6.1).

Benyamin S first came to attention as a singer producing popular songs using Betawi language and modified *gambang kromong*, known as *gambang moderen*. Ben was born into a Betawi family in 1939 in Kemayoran, a suburb of North Jakarta with a large Betawi population. As a teenager Benyamin Sueb sang American light music. In 1963 President Sukarno denounced American music and its influence in Indonesia. Ben's interest in Indonesian musical forms, and particularly *gambang kromong*, arose as a result of Sukarno's 1963 prohibition (Cahyana and Suhaeri 2005: 147).

Between 1970 and 1995 Benyamin S appeared in some fifty-eight films, the majority being cheaply made B-movie comedies, starring himself. These B-movies mostly create comedy out of ordinary situations that might occur within communities of poor Betawi. In doing so these films sometimes spoofed superheroes of international popular culture. For example, in *Zorro Kemayoran* (A Zorro of Kemayoran, Lilik Sudjio, 1976), Ben wears a mask as though he were Zorro. As in the American films, he defends the vulnerable from exploitation, among his exploits rescuing a widow who has mortgaged her house and land to desperadoes to pay for her son's circumcision ceremony. Ben's B-movies highlight Betawi culture at the same time as they depict the actual situations of many citizens. In *Benyamin Raja Lenong* (Benyamin, King of Lenong, Syamsul Fuad, 1975), Benyamin plays a laundryman, who doubles as a *lenong* performer on Saturday nights. The film concludes with a *lenong* performance to celebrate a wedding, in which Ben, accompanied by a *gambang kromong* orchestra, sings a song, 'Bang Jabrik', about a mythical Betawi trickster hero with magical powers. He then performs in a *lenong* play, 'The King from the Kingdom of Nowhere'. But elsewhere in the film Ben's social position is very different. He is unmarried, lives with his mother, a laundress, and helps her with the washing she takes in, washing it in a nearby fast-flowing river. Ben's position is not as a patriarch, but as a sort of inadvertent anarchist, constantly in trouble. In one scene he chases clothing he is washing down the river after it has floated away, the river lined with improvised bamboo platforms used by local people as toilets, a phenomenon still present in Jakarta a decade after the film was made. In *Pinangan* (A Proposal, Sjuman Djaya, 1976), set in a fishing village near Jakarta, Ben plays an upwardly socially mobile Betawi keen to marry the daughter of a pretentious local Javanese aristocrat. This film contains lengthy scenes of conversations in a *warung* (small sidewalk café), designed to show the highly interactive aspects of Betawi social life, as though communication is a value in itself, and the use of Betawi performance traditions as a source of carnivalesque enjoyment in people's lives. In other films the emphasis is on social critique. *Benyamin Jatuh Cinta* (Benyamin Falls in Love, Syamsul Fuad, 1976), shows Betawi community life in Jakarta being squeezed out by unrestrained development in the Suharto era, and by the increasingly pervasive values of a new, impersonal business world, which destroys community. Indeed, some of the films overtly critique the increasing corruption of the period. *Raja Copet* (King of Thieves, Syamsul Fuad, 1977) begins with Ben, the leader of a group of pickpockets, entering a five-star hotel to pick the pockets of those attending a business conference, at a time when hotel-based business conferences were becoming an increasing trend. By the end of the film he is himself holding a conference in a hotel, the hotel auditorium emblazoned with a banner displaying the slogan 'Lifting Revenue in Pickpocketing'.[1]

But there is a second stream to Benyamin's B-movies, the films where within a Betawi context Benyamin spoofs well-known superheroes of global popular culture, in comic, genre-pastiche movies with such titles as *Benyamin Spion 025* (Benyamin Spy 025, H. Tjut Djalil, 1974), *Koboi Ngungsi* (Refugee Cowboy, Nawi Ismail, 1975), *Tarsan Pensiunan* (A Retired Tarzan, Lilik Sudjio, 1976) and *Zorro Kemayoran*. The films draw upon, celebrate and spoof the popular culture of Hollywood, often showing the absurdity of first world popular culture in a Third World context, a phenomenon found in some of Benyamin's songs, notably in his song 'Superman', sung partly in English.[2]

If one asks why Benyamin was a star, there are a number of explanations. First are his qualities as a singer of humorous but also subtly moving songs, most using Betawi language and modernised Betawi musical idioms. Second, his films have clearly been written and directed to exploit a sense of familiarity that audiences have with their own environments, which are so poor and so under-resourced that this in itself becomes a source of absurdist comedy. Third is his play with iconic superheroes of international popular culture, which give his films a global topicality even while affirming different perceptions and values compared with those found in the films they spoof. Fourth, what Benyamin presents in the majority of his songs and films are perspectives derived from Betawi culture, a culture of the poor.

It may be suggested that, along with the talented Benyamin, the star of these songs and films is Betawi culture itself, as projected by Benyamin. At the time of Ben's death in 1995, in a tribute paid by the weekly *Gatra*, a journalist argued that Betawi culture was important to Indonesia because it was democratic, despite being increasingly marginalised by the growth of modern Jakarta: 'Bang Ben did us the service of lifting Betawi culture, which is egalitarian, into a national focus' (Massardi 1995: 21). Loven summarises discourses among the Betawi about what constitutes their culture (Loven 2008: 211–15), concluding by emphasising their humour and resilience – their ability to turn bitter experiences into a joke. This is further confirmed in the biography of Benyamin, which reports the views of the Betawi poet Nadjib Abu Yasser, who speaks of the Betawi tendency towards boisterousness and sarcasm, and attributes their cheerfulness and resilience to shared values and a community spirit that arose as one generation after another confronted years of marginalisation in Batavia under colonialism (Cahyana and Suhaeri 2005: 150–1).

So popular was the Betawi image brought to public attention by Benyamin S, that the Betawi television series, *Si Doel Anak Sekolahan* (Educated Doel, Rano Karno), first aired on television in 1994, became the longest running television series ever produced for Indonesian television, finally concluding in 2003. The title was derived from Sjuman Djaya's 1973 film *Si Doel Anak Betawi* (Doel, Child of Betawi) in which Benyamin appeared as the father of the boy Doel, a film based loosely on a novel from the 1930s. The presence of Benyamin in the television series (for only a year or so before his death) was regarded as so essential that the producer of the series, Rano Karno, said he would not have produced the series if Benyamin had not been prepared to appear in it (Loven 2008: 78).

Rhoma Irama and his *Dangdut* Islamic musical films: a challenge to the West

The second star discussed here is Rhoma Irama, who like Benyamin came to make films after he had established himself as a singing star, in Rhoma's case singing *dangdut*. Rhoma, too, emerged as a star in the early 1970s, at a moment in New Order Indonesia when films and popular music were produced in an increasingly competitive, international environment. Rhoma's response to the challenge posed by Western music was to provide in *dangdut* new sound combinations that could resonate with states of feeling to which Indonesians might be attracted. A substantial account of Rhoma's early work, especially of his music in a social context, has been given by the historian William H. Frederick (1982). The musical evolution of *dangdut*, and Rhoma's role in this, have been explored by ethnomusicologist Andrew Weintraub (Weintraub 2010). Rhoma's music might be seen as Indonesian precisely because it was syncretic – syncretic in that he produced a fusion of Portuguese, Malay, Indian and Middle Eastern music, combined with Western rock. In producing this fusion, he continued the tradition of syncretic combinations of Hindu-Buddhist and Islamic elements, noted by many as characteristic of large areas of Indonesian culture, but now conjoined with rock rhythms that could contest the ground of popular culture in Indonesia with an intensity commensurate with that of his Western 'rivals'. In the early 1980s Rhoma Irama was 'the giant of the Indonesian movie industry' (Frederick 1982: 118).

In my discussion of Rhoma Irama, I concentrate on four key films – made by Rhoma between 1977 and 1980 – to explore how he used these films strategically: firstly, to propound the purposes and relevance of *dangdut* as distinctively Indonesian music, which for him should have a connection with Islam; secondly, to connect with certain audience sectors (whether with teenagers and young people generally, or the poor and the socially marginalised) and to augment his image as a musical star; and thirdly, to justify in a religious context what some described as the commercial use of Islam.

While the songs and films of Benyamin had appeal for people of all ages, Rhoma created music designed to appeal to young people, particularly to young men from poorer classes. And yet again, the relevance of this music to Indonesia is strongly emphasised. This is seen in Rhoma's second film, *Darah Muda* (Young Blood, Maman Firmansjah, 1977), a film which sets out to state the difference between Western rock music, and *dangdut*. Early in the film Rhoma is shown breaking off any association with a band named 'The Apaches', which plays American rock music, and forming his own band that plays *dangdut*. The Apaches are shown to be socially aggressive and irresponsible (the film opens with a scene of them riding their motorbikes dangerously on public roads), addicted to beer and whisky, engaging in fist fights, and frequently treating people with contempt, especially women, whom they harass and abuse. In *Darah Muda* Rhoma's objections to rock music and his reasons for his espousal of *dangdut* are made clear, in an informal speech he makes to a group of young people (actually his own Soneta group) he 'comes across' playing *dangdut* in a public park:

> RHOMA: Good. Very good. I hear one difference in your music.
> I can feel closer to it—and its rhythms are very touching.
> INTERJECTOR: Don't say that, Bang. Our music is *kampungan* (ordinary). It's just *dangdut*.
> RHOMA: No. Your music is a music of the East. Truly, I – indeed all of us – can be closer to one another, as a result, and be more spirited.
> I am fed up with them. They are truly boring. They are too Westernised.
> Yes, we can imitate the West. But, of course, only the best of what it offers.
> For example, its music, its knowledge … But not that which is drunken, and which encourages sexual promiscuity and such things. This we must resist.

> Oh yes! I have an idea. I will form a group. Of course, it must be a *dangdut* group.
> I will prove to them that, in truth, this music is holy. Music is not an instrument of immorality. By means of *dangdut* I will propagate teachings of good deeds. *Amar ma'ruf nahi munkar.* [my translation]

In concluding, Rhoma uses a phrase in Arabic, taken from the *Qu'ran*, meaning 'Do good deeds and avoid those that are bad'. In *Darah Muda*, Indonesian values, their cultural specificity, and Islamic values, are proposed as a way to counter the threat of the perceived vulgarity of Western rock music, and as a basis for the *gravitas* of many of Rhoma's songs. Note that here Rhoma plays his contemporary self, and the film is a statement about the potential role of *dangdut* in Indonesian society. Not only did Rhoma, in his films, usually play his contemporary, evolving self, in some partly fictionalised form, in the context of the music and film industries, but he used some of his films to connect with, and (to use Althusser's term) to 'interpellate' (address or hail) sectors of his potential audience, the *rakyat Indonesia* (Althusser 1971: 170–7).

In a chapter devoted to Rhoma Irama entitled 'Music and *Rakyat*: Constructing "the People" in Dangdut', Weintraub explores three ways in which *dangdut* might be seen to relate to the *rakyat*, the people of Indonesia. Weintraub discusses the claim that *dangdut* 'is the Indonesian people', that it represents their difference from the West and their capacity to resist Western modernisation, quoting from an article by the cultural critic and religious leader Emha Ainun Nadjib, entitled, 'Jiwa Dangdut Kita pada Dasarnya Sangat Besar' ('Fundamentally Our *Dangdut* Soul is Very Big' [my translation]) (Weintraub 2010: 84). Others quoted by Weintraub include critics who refer to Rhoma's capacity, in his love songs and songs about the underclass, to express both honesty and suffering. Secondly, Weintraub's own analysis of Rhoma's songs prefers to see them as 'for the *rakyat*', rather than 'of the *rakyat*' (86–106). He also explicates a third category, citing ways in which journalists writing for the Indonesian upper classes in the 1970s referred to 'dangdut's underclass audience' as 'uneducated, ignorant and irrational' (106). Nevertheless, by the 1990s *dangdut* had been accepted by all classes, with *dangdut* performances obligatory at rallies organised by all political parties at the time of elections.

Rhoma's early positioning of himself in relation to the *rakyat*, and particularly to the Indonesian poor and marginalised, is seen in the film *Begadang* (Stay Up All Night, Maman Firmansjah, 1978). The early scenes of *Begadang* are set in a *warung*, in a poor part of Jakarta, the *warung* clients being unemployed males, including Rhoma who sings there, staying up late with the others. Both the *warung* owner and most of his clients (although not Rhoma) speak in Betawi dialect. Subsequent scenes show wealthy middle-class local residents complaining about the noise made by the unemployed youth and by Rhoma's singing, describing it as *kampungan* (lower-class mentality). Eventually in *Begadang* Rhoma achieves recognition as a talented singer. But he inadvertently becomes involved with a young woman who is murdered, and he is arrested as the killer. In jail Rhoma comes even closer to the marginalised in the society, this expressed through his very moving song 'Narapidana' (Convict), sung from behind prison bars. *Begadang* is clearly designed to express Rhoma's relevance to the very poorest of the *rakyat* both in terms of the milieu in which these people live, and the fates that can befall them. The song 'Narapidana' includes the words 'Now for the first time I experience the life of a convicted person. But am I not a tree, my heart able to endure this?'

A concern with dramatising his relation to his audiences is found also in *Raja Dangdut* (King of Dangdut, Maman Firmansjah, 1978). Here, a wealthier Rhoma, now a rising star with a large following, romances his most loyal fan, Ida, a Muslim teenager at a Jakarta high school, who wears a white Muslim headscarf and has written more than a hundred fan letters to Rhoma. Ida lives with her widowed mother in a bamboo hut. The mother sells snack food from a little street-side *warung*. At the end, Rhoma marries Ida. Earlier on, Rhoma and Ida – before actually meeting – become increasingly entranced with one another, and are depicted, via a split screen, lying in their respective beds in their very different family homes, singing a romantic duet, separated by the frames of the split screen and by class, but united in song. In fact, the fictional Ida is played by Ida Royani (b. 1953), who had emerged earlier in the 1970s as a talented singer frequently performing in improvised duets with Benyamin S. This use of actual first names of well-known stars occurs sometimes in Rhoma Irama films, to both close the gap between stardom and reality, and to create a certain star fascination around the fictional character.

But Rhoma was also concerned with members of his audience devoted to Islam (87 per cent of the Indonesian population is at least nominally Islamic). The struggle for acceptance of the Islamic dimension in his songs is most tangibly present in the film *Perjuangan dan Doa* (Struggle and Prayer, Maman Firmansjah, 1980). Early in the film Rhoma comes across articles in newspapers accusing him of 'Mengkommersialisasi Islam' (the commercialisation of Islam). At the centre of the film is a twenty-minute-long scene of a formal debate at a *pesantren* (Islamic boarding school), chaired by an Islamic teacher, in which Rhoma responds to questions from the students. Initially his answers are rather lightweight. When asked if it is acceptable for a person to dance to lines from the Qu'ran recited at the opening of his song 'La Ilaha Illallah' ('There is no God but Allah'), Rhoma, replies that he does not sing the lines, but recites them to music, and whether to dance or not is up to each individual. Asked why he uses *dangdut* and not *qasidah* (Indonesian pop based on religious poetry) to unite prayer with song, he answers that *dangdut* is closer to the people than is *qasidah*. Eventually Rhoma gets the opportunity to propound his fundamental position. Asked whether he is guilty of commercialising Islam, he responds that music is not simply a form of entertainment, rather music is the most effective way to propagate the faith. After all, most people do not want to spend all their time at assemblies of pious people, and young people, especially, are captivated by music. So, Rhoma claims, he uses something that enthuses them – music – to urge them to the path of Allah. Moreover, people should remember that it was not so long ago that Western values had a tremendous influence on Indonesian people, especially through its music, and this Western music at the time became the very trumpet of Satan ('trompet Setan'). He concludes with the assertion that his Soneta group emerged as a counterpoise to Western music, which was 'on the point of overwhelming us'. In concluding the debate, a presiding Islamic authority takes Rhoma's side, reasoning that if Rhoma's intention was to direct his audiences to Allah, then the song can be a prayer: 'If it is done in the name of Allah it is not commercialisation, for Allah will purify it (menghalalkanya)' [my translation].

Not all of Rhoma's movies are taken up with religious concerns or with Rhoma as a star finding ways of interpellating an audience. In *Pengabdian* (Devotion, Maman Firmansjah, 1984) he engages with the fact that his wife is pining away due to his total preoccupation with his music and his position as a superstar. The spectacular *Satria Bergitar* (The Knight with the Guitar, Nurhadie Irawan, 1983) set in the Middle Ages, is a historical fantasy in which he plays a knight, called Rhoma, who helps restore a king to his rightful position as leader of his country (Figure 6.2). *Kemilau Cinta Langit Jingga* (A Radiant Love in an Orange Sky, Muchlis Raya, 1985) is a complicated melodrama set in the world of film production, with his producer secretly attempting to have him killed. However, one of Rhoma's best films, *Nada dan Dakwah* (A Song and a Sermon, Chaerul Umam, 1991), has him as one of the Muslim establishment, who are defending a

Figure 6.2 Dangdut singer and film star Rhoma Irama (left) in the period adventure-drama/musical set in a 'never-never land', *Satria Bergitar*, written by Nurhadie Irawan and Rhoma Irama, and directed by Nurhadie Irawan. In this film, Rhoma plays a wandering minstrel, who is also a knight, and who helps Raja Wasit Aron (right above) regain his kingdom from the usurper, Abu Garin, who has also kidnapped the Raja's daughter, Tirza, in order to marry her. In the course of doing so, Rhoma converts Raja Wasit and his followers to Islam, and later succeeds in himself marrying Tirza. Image courtesy of Sinematek Indonesia.

pesantren (Islamic boarding-school) threatened by New Order developers with the expropriation of some of its land (Figure 6.3). Nevertheless, while Rhoma was regarded as anti-establishment in the 1980s, in 1997 he supported the Golkar party created by the ruling dictator, Suharto, by singing at its election rallies (Sen and Hill 2000: 181).

Here we may briefly compare Rhoma Irama, as a star, with Benyamin S. Earlier I suggested that the star of Benyamin Sueb's films was not simply Benyamin himself, but Betawi culture, noted for its earthy and realistic humour, its reciprocity, its camaraderie, its egalitarianism and its resilience, the resilience of a long marginalised but spirited people. In other words, the star of his films is also a culture and a community. As I have argued elsewhere in greater detail, even though Rhoma is culturally Indonesian in that his work embodies many kinds of Indonesian syncretism, the image Rhoma himself projects is not so much that of a culture and a community,

Figure 6.3 Rhoma Irama (left, with white stole over his Indonesian batik shirt) commences singing in *Nada dan Dakwah* as he is greeted by teenage students, all dressed in white, at the pesantren (religious boarding-school), Al Hamidiyah, at Depok in South Jakarta. The students will begin singing in response, and male students will perform a group dance. In the right foreground is the charismatic Jakarta-based preacher Zainuddin MZ. Image courtesy of Sinematek Indonesia.

but an individual (Hanan and Koesasi 2011: 75). Indeed, he projects a powerful and simplified image of an individual, whether as a character in a film or on stage, and, in this sense, he also emulates the celebrity image that Western pop stars had begun to fill in popular culture elsewhere. Echoing developments in the West, Rhoma's success is an example of change in the mass media. The cult of the individual develops in a space created by the new mass media. Yet in creating this phenomenon, Rhoma Irama provided an alternative point of identification – other than Western rock stars – for Indonesian people.

Stars of the 'Teater Populer' collective: developing new talents

At this point I turn my attention to three stars of the Indonesian cinema who were members of the film and theatre collective Teater Populer: Tuti Indra Malaon, Slamet Rahardjo and Christine Hakim. Tuti and Slamet were joint founding members of Teater Populer, established by the theatre director Teguh Karya (1937–2001) in October 1968. Teguh had studied and later taught at the Akademi Teater Nasional Indonesia (ATNI), as well as studying at the East-West Center at the University of Hawai'i. He established Teater Populer in response to the closure of ATNI, bringing some of his students with him, including nineteen-year-old Slamet Rahardjo. The group staged their plays in the auditorium of the Hotel Indonesia to increasingly appreciative audiences from the intellectual and creative elite of society (Riantiarno 1993). As a child Tuti was known as a dancer, and eventually became a lecturer in English at the University of Indonesia, a journalist and a translator of plays. So, these Teater Populer actors had experience in live theatre before they came to film, and both Tuti and Teguh had been formally involved in education. Another actor working with Teater Populer was the future satiric playwright and theatre producer Nano Riantiarno, who formed his own group, Teater Koma, in 1977.

In 1971 the Teater Populer group made their first film *Wajah Seorang Laki Laki* (Face of a Man, Teguh Karya), set in early nineteenth century, Dutch-controlled Batavia, with its main character, Amallo, of Portuguese descent, played by Slamet Rahardjo. This film, about conflict between father and son (the father works for the Dutch), established Slamet as a fine screen actor– alert, good looking, highly sensitive, independently minded, idealistic but self-pre-occupied, so certainly misunderstood. Slamet's presence here – reminiscent of James Dean in his three 'generation-gap' films made in the 1950s – might well classify him on the basis of one film, as the rebel type, discussed by Dyer (1982: 59–61). Tuti Indra Malaon played a mature, wise and supportive older woman, a friend of Amallo. Commercial failure of this taut, well-made Indonesian film led Teguh to pause film production for two years, during which he set out to personally study and ascertain what popular cinema is, so that he could make films that were competitive in the market (Soehadi 2015: 90–100).

For his second film, Teguh planned a romantic melodrama set in contemporary Jakarta, entitled *Cinta Pertama* (First Love, Teguh Karya, 1973) (Figure 6.4). Teguh needed to find a female lead who could partner Slamet Rahardjo. It was then that he discovered Christine Hakim, who at that time, aged sixteen, had only done modelling, but who by 1988 had won the award for best actress in the Indonesian cinema six times. In *Cinta Pertama* Teguh deliberately made his central female character, Ade, the daughter of a family living in a luxurious house in the wealthy Jakarta suburb of Menteng. As Teguh stated, audiences at that time wanted to see

Figure 6.4 Image from Teguh Karya's second feature film, *Cinta Pertama* – this second film was not an auteur film, but a prize-winning, popular romantic melodrama, in which, after extensive research and deliberation, Teguh established Christine Hakim and Slamet Rahardjo as major stars within the Indonesian cinema, and hence the viability of his Teater Populer group within the Indonesian film industry. Image courtesy of the Teater Populer collective.

the lifestyles of the rich, so this was part of the commercial formula for his second film, the primary aim of which was to achieve popularity in the market (Soehadi 2015: 92). But Teguh also made Slamet's character, Bastian, from the lower middle-classes, and – although a talented architectural draftsman – someone with an obscure background.

While early on the film is replete with the exchanges of gazes and romantic emotions of a first love, the situation becomes more complex when it is discovered that Bastian is a widower, and his first wife died at his hands in a mysterious shooting accident, for which he has been in prison for manslaughter. So, while the actor, Slamet Rahardjo, is handsome and sensitive, he plays a character about whom one must have doubts, and who must be investigated by the film's audience, thus providing the twists and turns of an absorbing narrative. This approach, where the male is warily observed, is more subtly and fully treated in the last Teater Populer film in which Christine and Slamet appear together, *Dibalik Kelambu* (Behind the Mosquito Net, Teguh Karya, 1982), which won a prize for each of them as best actor/actress of the year at the 1983 Indonesian Film Festival. *Dibalik Kelambu* is about a newly married couple – with young children – for financial reasons living in the home of the wife's father, the husband becoming uneasy, unsettled and even irrational in this situation. This positioning of the male 'hero' as someone to be scrutinised is in contrast to what Mulvey argued is common in Hollywood cinema, especially in key films by Hitchcock (Mulvey 1975). It is a position into which Teguh placed Slamet in at least three of the five films in which Slamet and Christine were paired together between 1973 and 1982. In these films the image of the rebel has modulated into the figure of the romantic but problematic and troubled male.

One of Slamet's most important performances was in Teguh Karya's historical epic *November 1828* (1979), in which he played a tyrannical, officious, brutal *Indo* (Dutch-Indonesian) officer, Captain de Borst, a leader of a Dutch platoon in the Java War (1825–30), largely a war of resistance to the imposition of Dutch colonialism. On the other hand, one of Christine Hakim's most important performances was in *Tjoet Nja' Dhien* (Eros Djarot, 1987) about the heroic female leader of resistance to Dutch forces in the jungle and mountains of Aceh at the beginning of the twentieth century. At the age of thirty-one Christine played a woman in her fifties rapidly ageing due to exigencies of her situation as the leader of itinerant guerrillas harassed by Dutch forces.

If we ask about continuities in Christine Hakim's work, one does find significant patterns. In her first film, *Cinta Pertama*, as we have seen, she plays a teenager, trying to cope with the ambiguous background of a young man in his mid-twenties with whom she has experienced her first love – her distress at this mollified by supportive parents. In her last two films with Teguh Karya as director, *Badai Pasti Berlalu* (When the Storm is Over, Teguh Karya, 1977) and the 1982 *Dibalik Kelambu*, she plays a discerning young woman, mature and responsible, if vulnerable, trying to understand the man she has married, their difficulties arising either due to his unstable character, or due to outside pressures impacting on their domestic situation. In these three films she is a role model for women in relationships. Her image as a strong and resourceful woman is further enhanced with her role in *Tjoet Nja' Dhien*.

But early in her career Christine also proved herself a consummate professional actress in films not made by the Teater Populer group. She showed herself adept at comedy in Sjuman Djaya's *Si Doel Anak Modern* (Si Doel, Child of Modernity, 1976), where she more or less plays herself, as 'Kristin', a much sought-after model, an increasingly celebrated public figure, whom a pretentious, upwardly socially mobile Doel (Benyamin S) pursues. The film contains numerous uniquely humorous conversations between them, where Christine, dialoguing with the hyperactive Benyamin, is vivacious, playful, curious (about Doel-Benyamin), and relaxed and natural, despite her attributed star quality. In Wim Umboh's *Pengemis dan Tukang Becak* (The Beggar and the Rickshaw Driver, 1978), she moves beyond the early romantic melodramas in which Teguh cast her and plays an initially timid and reticent maid – overawed by and sexually harassed by her wealthy master – who eventually comes to protect the small daughter of the family during the subsequent marital crisis, leaving her master's home and travelling with the child from city to city, the two surviving in poor slum areas. In this film, for which she won the best actress prize again at the Indonesian Film Festival, she defined a screen role for herself as a supporter of the weak and socially vulnerable, a role she was to assume more regularly in later films, some produced by her (Figure 6.5).

Figure 6.5 Members of the Teater Populer group in 1985, in the early hours of the morning in Bandung, celebrating via a discussion their successes the previous evening at the Indonesian Film Festival for that year. Teguh Karya is at the left (signalling), with Christine Hakim (centre) and Slamet Rahardjo (not facing camera) just behind her. In 1985 the Teater Populer group won four Citra Awards for Teguh's film *Doea Tanda Mata* (Two Souvenirs, 1985). Best actor 1985, Alex Komang, sits far right. Photo by David Hanan.

Although he has continued to act in films, it is as a writer/director/producer that Slamet Rahardjo excelled in his later career. Slamet wrote and directed his first film in 1979, *Rembulan dan Matahari* (Moon and Sun), an experimental feature which addresses the issue of migration into the capital city of poor village people who find their circumstances in the city worse than in their village. Ten years later Slamet wrote and directed a political allegory, *Langitku Rumahku* (My Sky My Home, 1989). The film is about a friendship between two boys, one from a rich family, the other a street kid, virtually homeless. The film cuts between classroom scenes where cleanly clad, upper-middle-class children learn about the five principles of the *Pancasila*, the national philosophy promulgated by Sukarno in 1945 (including the principle of prosperity for all), and scenes of the shanty town where the poor boy lives. While the Censorship Board had no objections to the film, it met with concern by those in power, and was withdrawn, after only one day, from the cinemas owned by Suharto's stepbrother, Sudwikatmono, on the grounds that it was not doing well at the box office. Slamet challenged this decision in court. In 1993 a decision that went against Slamet's challenge was handed down by the court. On that day Christine Hakim was photographed weeping outside the court at the decision (Chudori 1997: 21).

Unlike Rhoma Irama, the stars that emerged from Teater Populer did not indulge in simplistic political alliances. Every so often one of them would make a film that addressed the social realities of Indonesian society. And their associations were with education and with critical journalism rather than with mainstream political parties. Eros Djarot, the brother of Slamet Rahardjo and writer-director of *Tjoet Nja Dhien*, in the early 1990s founded a polemical weekly tabloid, *Detik*, which ran such outrageous interviews with all sides of the political spectrum, that it was banned by the Suharto government in 1994 (Chudori 1997). Christine Hakim moved from a concentration on acting to a more varied career, at times working as a producer of projects on themes and topics she valued. Films she has produced include a feminist film directed by Nan Achnas, *Pasir Berbisik* (Whispering Sands, Nan Triveni Achnas, 2001), a woman's view of a mother-daughter relationship, and Garin Nugroho's, *Daun di Atas Bantal* (Leaf on a Pillow, Garin Nugroho, 1998), about street kids in Jogjakarta, in which the children were played by actual street kids. This Indonesian 'neorealist' feature was prompted by an earlier documentary by Nugroho on street children in Jogjakarta. Although in this later period, for twenty or so years Christine Hakim only acted in a relatively small number of films, turning more to producing and to social activism, these later roles tend to be of women from poorer classes, aware of the poverty they are surrounded by, and deeply supportive of those they perceive are the most needy. In *Daun di Atas Bantal* for example, she plays Asih, a trader in a Jogjakarta market who, despite her own obvious privations and difficulties, becomes a 'foster mother' for homeless children who hang out there, her solicitousness for the children being one of the few points of stability in their lives.

After ten years of making films together, Teguh lost his two main leads. But Teguh began to work with others, including Tuti Indra Malaon. In *Ibunda* (Mother, Teguh Karya, 1986) Tuti plays a Javanese widow, with a nearly fully grown family, who is aware of deficiencies in the behaviour of her not yet fully mature children, and the social pressures to which they are responding. This film is in part a family drama, with the mother at its centre, as an advisor to her children – but also a stoic spectator of their dramas. In this way *Ibunda* also becomes a political allegory. One strand of the film depicts the youngest daughter upsetting her older, married sister (and *her* racist husband) by becoming involved with a West Papuan student. Another strand of the film depicts a married son, an actor, involved with the female producer of a play in which he is performing, a play about tyranny, and political persecution. Tuti was no stranger to political allegory. In her theatre work she had imitated President Suharto's wife in Riantiarno's comic critique of New Order ethos, *Opera Kecoa* (The Cockroach Opera), first staged in 1985.

Conclusion

Benyamin S and Rhoma Irama were stars of a rather different kind. Benyamin's output was regionally, linguistically and culturally specific, but his local Betawi outlook was adopted widely as one dimension of the experience of the nation. Although Benyamin S played with many of the iconic superheroes of international popular culture (Superman, Tarzan, James Bond), he never amplified the idea of himself as a superstar. Rather, he mocked pretension and was one of 'the people', the 'people' usually being the regionally and culturally specific Betawi. It is for this reason that what is represented in his songs and films is a folk culture, rather than a mass media phenomenon headed by a unique individual. Benyamin did not simply 'act' as a Betawi, he was a Betawi, and it is Betawi culture that is the star of his films. While Rhoma Irama saw his powerful *dangdut* music as a means of resisting Western influence, including its individualism, and saw his music as 'for the people', in fact as a superstar individual he provided an Eastern alternative to a Western contemporary mass culture, led by superstar individuals. In the case of the stars who emerged from Teguh Karya's Teater Populer, Slamet Rahardjo and Christine Hakim, stardom was a preparation for other roles in the community and in the film world. The Teater Populer collective, after six years of success with popular cinema between 1973 and 1978, moved on to make two significant historical films and at least three socially critical films. Overall, the Teater Populer collective was a forum and training ground for the education and dynamic growth of its best talent. Significantly all the stars discussed in this chapter had some control, at some stage, over the films they made, Benyamin S and Rhoma Irama throughout their careers, and Christine and Slamet as they came to produce or direct their own films.

References

Althusser, Louis (1971), 'Ideology and ideological state apparatuses (notes towards an investigation)', in *Lenin and Philosophy and Other Essays*, New York: Monthly Review Press, pp. 127–86.
Anderson, Benedict R. O'G. (1990), *Language and Power: Exploring Political Cultures in Indonesia*, Ithaca, NY, and London: Cornell University Press.
Cahyana Ludhy, and Muhlis Suhaeri (2005), *Benyamin S: Muka Kampung Rezeki Kota*, Jakarta: Yayasan H. Benjamin Sueb.
Chudori, Leila S. (1997), 'Christine Hakim: "Saya Harus Menentukan Arah Hidup Saya . . ." [Interview]', *Media Indonesia*, 1 August, p. 21.
Dyer, Richard (1982), *Stars*, London: British Film Institute.
Frederick, William H. (1982), 'Rhoma Irama and the Dangdut Style: Aspects of Indonesian Popular Culture', *Indonesia* 34 (October), pp. 102–30.
Hanan, David and Basoeki Koesasi (2011), '*Betawi Moderen*: songs and films of Benyamin S from Jakarta in the 1970s – further dimensions of Indonesian popular culture', *Indonesia* 91 (April), pp. 35–76.
Loven, Klarijn (2008), *Watching Si Doel: Television, Language, and Cultural Identity in Contemporary Indonesia*, Leiden: KITLV Press.
Massardi, Yudhistira A. N. M. (1995), 'Si Babe', *Gatra*, 16 September, p. 21.
Mulvey, Laura (1975), 'Visual pleasure and narrative cinema', *Screen* 16:3, pp. 6–18.
Riantiarno, Nano (ed.) (1993), *Teguh Karya dan Teater Populer 1968–1993*, Jakarta: Pustaka Sinar Harapan.
Sen, Krishna and David T. Hill (2000), *Media, Culture and Politics in Indonesia*, Oxford and New York: Oxford University Press.

Siegel, James T. (1986), *Solo in the New Order: Language and Hierarchy in an Indonesian City*, Princeton, NJ: Princeton University Press.

Soehadi, Gaston (2015), 'Teguh Karya: A Film Auteur Working Within A Collective', unpublished PhD thesis, Monash University.

Weintraub, Andrew N. (2010), *Dangdut Stories: A Social and Musical History of Indonesia's Most Popular Music*, Oxford: Oxford University Press.

Notes

1. Synopses for these films and production data (indeed for most Indonesian feature films) can be found at the 'Filmindonesia' website and include English translations. Available at <http://catalogue.filmindonesia.or.id/> (last accessed 2 November 2019).
2. The song 'Superman', including lyrics partially in English, is available at <https://www.youtube.com/watch?v=0UHDwTGleBk> (last accessed 2 November 2019).

Chapter 7

The Indonesian sex bomb: female sexuality in cinema 1970s–90s

Thomas Barker

In Indonesian cinema there is a female star type called the *bom seks* (sex bomb) defined by her *berani*, namely her willingness or boldness to appear in roles that involve sex and seduction and in scenes that require minimal dress. Sometimes described as *artis panas* (hot artist) or *wanita penggoda* (temptress), the *bom seks* were a significant phenomenon during the golden age of Indonesian cinema from the early 1970s to the late 1990s. On-screen she performed in roles that required her to embody a kind of sexuality that was flirtatious, sensual, and provocative. Off-screen she was the subject of tabloid fascination and gossip and featured in magazines and other extra-filmic materials in ways that further accentuated her image of brazen sexuality. Together these roles and materials contributed to her sex bomb star image.

Following a star studies paradigm, this chapter discusses the ways in which the Indonesian sex bomb phenomenon interfaces with broader cultural themes in Indonesian society as it underwent development and modernisation under the New Order regime (1966–98). In part this research is prompted by a renewed popular interest in the sex bomb phenomenon and by the emergence of a new historiography about Indonesian cinema (Paramaditha 2017). Based on detailed research of newspaper and magazine articles from the 1970s onwards, this chapter discusses the sex bomb star type and the women's careers as they negotiated work, fame, morality, and ageing. In nominally 'conservative' Indonesia, sex bombs also provide a means to interpret and understand morality, gender norms, sexuality, and women's media image in Indonesia more broadly and challenge essentialist interpretations of Indonesian sexual and moral history.

What is a sex bomb?

Film industries across the world have featured actresses who come to be defined primarily through their provocative sexuality and bodily display. Apart from their physical beauty and attractiveness, common features include being voluptuous, raunchy, flirtatious, seductive, and sexually charged. A sex bomb is not only created in her on-screen roles and publicity material, but also in her off-screen life which may be characterised by scandal, rumour, and gossip. Apart from the 'sex bomb' moniker, they may be known as 'sex goddesses', 'sex symbols' or 'bombshells' (Jordan 2010). Famous sex bombs include Marilyn Monroe, Brigitte Bardot, Raquel Welch and Ti Na (Tina Leung), but also the voluptuous-but-dangerous heroines of American exploitation such as Pam Grier, Dyanne Thorne and Judith Brown, or Gloria Guida, Edwige Fenech and Laura Antonelli who featured prominently in Italian cinema of the 1970s. Southeast Asian cinemas featured their own roster of sex bombs including Alma Moreno in *bomba* films of the Philippines or *Dao Yua* ('sexy stars') in Thailand such as Malarin Boonnak and Kaenjai Meenakanit.

Sex bombs offer more than simple titillation and sex appeal in their on-screen roles and off-screen personas, even if that is a major drawcard for audiences. Sex bombs can have complex and polysemic star images that can express various iterations of sexuality and gender norms of the time and place in which they operate. As embodiments of sexuality and following the work of Richard Dyer (1986), sex bombs as a star type can be linked to a social type. Social types represent certain cultural ideas or myths with important ideological functions within a particular social context. In his study of Monroe and Jane Fonda, Dyer identifies their type as the 'pin up', not only because they featured in posters and calendars and were 'set up as an object of male sexual gaze' (Dyer 1986: 20) but because their image evoked 'the girl next door' (37). Dyer argues that Monroe's 'image spoke to and articulated the particular ways that sexuality was thought about and felt in that period [1950s America]' (24). At the same time, sex bombs play an important role in character and narrative configurations, such as the femme fatale in film noir who seduces and manipulates the male patsy character whilst often undergoing their own struggle for independence (Grossman 2007).

Similarly, Indonesian cinema features a roster of 'sex bombs' whose meanings are filtered through local morality and presentations of sexuality. As Indonesia underwent modernisation, sex bombs embodied changing sexual mores and gender roles at the intersection of state policy, tradition, religion, commercial forces and global imagery. Women themselves were also active in broadening the definition of womanhood and femininity. Traditional ideas of gender roles came into conflict with newly emerging discourses of the modern woman and official policies such as 'state *ibuism*', which defined women as mother and housewife in support of her husband (Suryakusuma 1996). Likewise, in a country where the cinema screen is seen as a repository of morality (Barker 2014), women's on-screen roles emphasising sexuality and seduction challenged prevailing norms and boundaries of appropriate behaviour. This contradiction is oftentimes overcome in film narratives by taming woman's sexuality through monogamous marriage or by forms of punishment including on-screen death (Sen 1994). Yet the nature of stardom as also extra-filmic meant that she always escapes the confines of the narrative because of her off-screen life and her subsequent roles.

However, much of the existing analysis and coverage of Indonesia's sex bombs typically falls into either the salacious and tabloid or the outraged and moralising. Media scholars such as Ahmad Junaidi (2012) see sexual content as detrimental to women and decry the ways in which such content is morally corrosive. Other sources of information, especially online tabloid portals *Detik.com, Bintang.com* and *Kompasiana*, are more salacious in approach identifying, for example, the 'Top Ten Sex Bombs' of Indonesian cinema and discussing their careers and films. Whereas those articles tend to be brief, providing scant biographical information but an abundance of visual content, they are also driven by a nostalgia for a different era of moral standards. Neither approach, however, reflects on how the sex bomb takes on certain meanings within her social and historical context.

In studying the Indonesian sex bomb, this chapter contributes to a very small body of work looking at stars in Indonesia. The lack of scholarly attention reflects not so much the popularity and significance of the film industry, but rather the way in which stars have not been a serious topic of research. Only a few isolated individuals have received substantive coverage such as singer-actors Rhoma Irama (Weintraub 2010; Hanan, this volume, Chapter 6) and Benyamin S (Hanan, this volume, Chapter 6), gangster-cum-actor Johny Indo (Hangguman 1990), and actress Doris Callebaut, whose life story is fictionalised in a book (Bonnie 1977). For an emerging field of star studies scholarship, there is, however, a wealth of information available to the researcher that includes newspapers, magazines and film posters. Sex bombs warrant a serious study because they have to date been treated with contempt, moral outrage or tabloid fascination.

The Indonesian sex bomb

In Indonesian cinematic history the 1970s and 1980s were a 'golden era' of the sex bomb because of the prominence of actresses, their roles and the extra-filmic material available about their lives. This contrasts with the decades prior to the 1970s when the antecedents to the sex bomb are evident but not fully realised and to the 1990s when the film industry turned to much more explicit sexual content but declined in terms of its cultural relevance and public prominence of its actresses. This coincided with the introduction of private television broadcasting in 1989 and its rapid adoption as the country's main form of entertainment.

Showcasing women as sexual objects predated cinema and can be traced to practices in a range of publications such as magazines and pulp fiction. In film, the first notable incidence is the appearance of actress Nurnaningsih in a scene of undress in *Harimau Tjampa* (Tiger from Tjampa, D. Djajakusuma, 1953). She caused further scandal in mid-1954 when she was photographed in a bikini. These incidents earned her the moniker of Indonesia's 'first sex bomb'. However, she did not consolidate that role and had a patchy acting career afterwards, never becoming a significant star. It was only in the late 1960s that sexual content in cinema became more prominent when import regulations were relaxed, allowing risqué titles from countries such as Japan and Italy. This was meant to normalise cultural life following the coup of 1965–6 that saw General Suharto ascend to the presidency in 1967. Under this new regime and with foreign imports as examples, many local producers turned to sex and exploitation themes in their films.

According to critic Salim Said (1991: 81), Indonesia's first 'daring' film was *Bernafas Dalam Lumpur* (Breathing in Mud, Turino Junaidy, 1971) starring actress Suzzanna. Suzzanna plays Yanti, a housewife who ventures to Jakarta in pursuit of her errant husband only to be preyed upon by a series of men, leading her into prostitution. Suzzanna featured in a number of similar roles throughout the 1970s, including in *Bumi Makin Panas* (Earth Gets Hotter, Ali Shahab, 1973) and a string of mystical-horror films in which she played the witch or queen figure. Many regard Suzzanna as the first sex bomb and she is often included in popular lists, but having been an actress since the 1950s and transcended her 'sex bomb' roles, she is more of a transitionary figure who allowed for a new kind of actress to emerge who was recruited almost solely on her willingness to play in *berani* roles.

Therefore, it is in 1972 with the release of *Tiada Jalan Lain* (No Other Way, Hasmanan, 1972) starring debutant Debbie Cynthia Dewi that the *bom seks* emerges as a distinct star type. Dewi's appearance naked in a bathroom scene caused controversy with reports that the film was subsequently banned in Indonesia and comparisons made between Dewi and the actress Raquel Welch in *100 Rifles* (Tom Gries, 1969). Later in the same year debutant, Yatti Octavia, appeared bare-chested in *Intan Perawan Kubu* (Intan the Kubu Virgin, A. N. Alcaff, 1972) beginning her career as a *berani* actress. Both Dewi and Octavia continued to act in significant sex bomb roles throughout the 1970s and 1980s. They acted together in the 1978 film *Si Genit Poppy* (Poppy the Flirt, Yopie Burnama, 1978) with Dewi playing Dora, the older sister of Poppy (Octavia) (Figure 7.1). *Si Genit Poppy* was said to be a copy of a film starring Edwige Fenech who was at the time a French-Italian sex symbol. Both Octavia and Dewi continued acting until the 1990s appearing in sixty-four and forty-seven films respectively.

By the late 1970s, there was an increase in roles demanding undress, sexual innuendo, and so-called '*ranjang*' (mattress) scenes. Themes of prostitution, extra marital affairs, seduction, and sexual exploitation were common. Partly this was a producer strategy to attract audiences through titillation and exploitation techniques, which simultaneously represented an indictment of the corruption and hypocrisy accompanying Indonesia's rapid development and urbanisation under Suharto (Yngvesson 2014). For example, in the 1977 film *Akibat Pergaulan Bebas* (Consequences of Free Intercourse, Narto Erawan Dalimarta) the 'Big 5' stars of Indonesian cinema (Yatti Octavia, Roy Marten, Jenny Rachman, Robby Sugara and Doris Callebaut) appear in a story about pre-marital sex and its consequences for young people (Figure 7.2). The film contained few sex scenes or nudity, and although moralising about pre-marital sex, it nevertheless brought themes of sex, infidelity, virginity, abortion and sexually transmitted infections into the mainstream.

In this environment, it became possible for producers to create the first sex bomb star in Eva Arnaz. As a teenager, Eva Yanti Arnas won two beauty contests in Jakarta before being recruited for her first film role in 1977 in *Duo Kribo* (Afro Duo, Edward Sirait) aged nineteen. Although acting was not her career intention and despite concerns from her mother (Welly 1980: 5), Arnas continued acting. In her third role, *Napas Perempuan* (Breath of a Woman, Ali Shahab, 1978), director Ali Shahab changed her stage name from Eva Yanti Arnas to Eva Arnaz (Figure 7.3). Justifying

Figure 7.1 Original poster for *Si Genit Poppy* featuring Yati Octavia and Debbie Cynthia Dewi.

Figure 7.2 Original poster for *Akibat Pergaulan Bebas*. Image courtesy of Rapi Films.

Figure 7.3 Original poster for *Napas Perempuan* with Eva Arnaz in supporting role.

the change Ali Shahab said: 'In Hollywood there's Desi Arnaz. Here I will present Eva Arnaz. This is intentional to make her name cooler' (Welly 1980: 5). With a new image, Eva Arnaz became one of the new type of actresses in the 1980s: bold and voluptuous, combining sexiness and bravado, and working across multiple genres (comedy, action, drama). Her defining roles included *Gadis Bionik* (Bionic Girl, Ali Shahab, 1982), *Barang Terlarang* (Forbidden Goods, Maman Firmansjah, 1983) and *Montir-Montir Cantik* (Beautiful Mechanics, BZ Kadaryono, 1984).

The early 1980s saw a new generation of sex bombs that included Sri Gudhi Sintara, Enny Beatrice, Wieke Widowati and Meriam Bellina. Of these Bellina attracted significant attention for her scenes of undress in historical drama *Roro Mendut* (Ami Priyono, 1982) when she was just seventeen (Figure 7.4). A scheduled screening of the film at the Indonesian Film Festival at the Tropenmuseum, Amsterdam was cancelled because the film was reportedly too 'hot'. Bellina's role in the prostitution film *Sorga Dunia di Pintu Neraka* (Heaven on Earth at the Gates of Hell, Henky Solaiman, 1983) and then the Indonesian remake of *The Blue Lagoon* (Randal Kleiser, 1980), called *Pengantin Pantai Biru* (Blue Beach Wedding, Wim Umboh, 1983), further cemented her reputation as a talented young actress able to embody the sex bomb role and its on-screen demands.

Throughout the 1980s, an important platform for emerging sex bombs was the popular comedies of the all-male Warkop DKI trio who appeared in over thirty titles between 1979 and 1994 (Figure 7.5). Double entendre titles such as *Depan Bisa Belakang Bisa* (In Front Can, Behind Can, H. Tjut Djalil, 1987) and *Mana Bisa Tahan* (Cannot Hold On, Arizal, 1990) hinted at the sexual innuendo of the Warkop style of comedy. Women in these films acted as foils and eye-candy and presented themselves on-screen seductively and flirtatiously. Many young actresses earned their first or establishing roles in Warkop films, initially as *figuran* (extras/supporting roles) and later in speaking roles or named billing. Sex bombs of the 1980s including Sally Marcellina, Diah Permatasari, Gitty Srinita, Kiki Fatmala, all took roles in Warkop films propelling them into the mainstream by highlighting their sexiness and sexuality.

As the film industry entered a period of decline in the 1990s due to a number of factors that included competition from private television and a creative slump, its output shifted to erotica with much more explicit sex themes. Some sex bombs from the 1980s successfully made the

Figure 7.4 Original poster for *Roro Mendut* starring Meriam Bellina.

Figure 7.5 Original poster for the Warkop DKI film *Depan Bisa Belakang Bisa* featuring the three comedians and Eva Arnaz. Image courtesy of Soraya Intercine Films.

transition out of film and into television, especially the new format of *sinetron* akin to soap opera. At the same time, a new set of actresses came to be featured in the films of the 1990s. These films and the roles within them were much more focused on sexual themes, and the actresses much more confined to these roles. Prominent names from this period include Febby Lawrence, Inneke Koesherawaty, Ayu Yohana, Rika Herliana, Megi Megawati, Malvin Shayna and Windy Chindyana. Their legacies are not as pronounced as the sex bombs from the 1970s and 1980s who lived much more public lives in gossip columns and tabloid newspapers and had longer careers.

Sex bomb as star image

Following Richard Dyer, Hollinger says that star image is the 'combination of the ordinary and the extraordinary' or the 'integration of the everyday and the exceptional' (Hollinger 2006: 229). Most Indonesian sex bombs have ordinary or unremarkable backgrounds giving them a proximity to the people. Although not following the usual light-skinned Eurasian or 'Indo' look, most sex bombs do have mixed ethnic origins including Chinese-Filipino (Yurike Prastica), Sunda-Pakistan (Kiki Fatmala), Afgani-Palembang (Ayu Azhari) and Indian (Sri Gudhi Sintara). They often begin their careers as models or by winning beauty pageants before making a transition into film in their late teenage years. Often the young star juggles secondary school (SMA) with a budding acting career. Few seem to see film as their career choice, and when asked, identify other careers such as air steward or policewoman as their preferred choice. While these humble or unremarkable origins speak of their ordinariness, it is by becoming a sex bomb that these women become extraordinary.

For the Indonesian sex bomb, her extraordinariness comes not just from her physical attractiveness but from her willingness (*berani*) to take on sexually charged roles. This sets the sex bomb apart from other actresses and from the general public and puts her into conflict with prevailing gender norms and moral codes. Yet when asked, they tend to downplay their *berani*-ness by offering such explanations as 'If from the outset I agree, why should I refuse?' ('Meriam Bellina' 1984: 27)[1] and 'It's just normal, it's nothing special. It's up to the public to make their judgement' ('Yenny Farida' 1985: 140).[2] They say there are limits to what they will do and argue that they are not fully naked when acting, that there are many camera tricks, with some admitting to using body doubles for some scenes.

One way in which both producers and sex bombs justify their roles and scenes of sex and seduction is by insisting that the films are morality tales discussing the follies of infidelity, the dangers of excessive desire, and the risks of 'free sex'. Sally Marcellina justified one of her roles arguing that her films were vehicles for important moral messages:

> My films in circulation have already passed the censorship board. So, there's no problem, right? [...] Just so you are satisfied, let me make it clear: If I make a film, if you look carefully, there's a moral message, don't just see the images. So, try and see from other perspectives.
> ('Sally Marcellina Sering' 1996: 48)³

Posing as moral education created a loophole for producers: as long as there was moral retribution or a moral message certain leeway could be made for sexual content.

According to Richard Dyer (1986), star image is created in extra-filmic media material including publicity and press coverage. In magazine coverage the sex bomb's body is displayed in photographs while accompanying articles discuss her private life, often speculating whether her on-screen persona carries over into her private life. Other topics of interest include her relationship status, especially who she is dating, her thoughts on premarital sex, and plans for marriage. Yenny Farida was asked in a 1985 interview about *kumpul kebo* (couple living together unmarried) – she disagreed with the practice, and as a widow with a child preferred to find a man who was loyal, responsible and handsome. Kiki Fatmala by contrast thought *kumpul kebo* was good for 'exploration and getting to know each other better' ('Kiki Fatmala' 1989: 3). As actresses entered their mid-twenties they were pressed on their desire to get married, like Lela Anggraeni, who was asked in a 1990 interview about her plans to marry when she was aged twenty-five ('Lela Anggraeni Takut' 1990: 16). Whilst pushing a normative line, these questions also allowed the actresses to express a variety of viewpoints on marriage, relationships and sex thereby contributing to public discourse on these topics.

Sex bombs earned more notoriety and status as rumours suggested their involvement in prostitution, extra-marital affairs, 'free sex' and 'sugar daddy' relationships. In many articles, doing sex for reward is insinuated by describing the car that the actress drives, property she owns or other material possessions she flaunts. In a 1989 interview, actor Adam Jawaqni, who was in a relationship with Yenny Farida, asked: 'It should be these things [possessions] we question. Where did they get the money from if not from . . .', implying money-for-sex relationships ('Yenny Farida Cerai' 1989: 17).⁴ In a 2012 interview with *Detik*, Eva Arnaz recalls being made offers 'starting from officials, businessmen, and directors. But how much were they willing to pay? In a year, I could act in ten films, not that I want to be arrogant' ('Diajak Tidur Pejabat' 2012).[5] Here sex bombs become salacious tabloid fodder and a star type through which issues of sexuality are investigated, exposed and discussed.

Discussions of morality and broader social issues began to disappear in the 1990s with the declining popularity of local cinema and the turn by local producers to much more explicit sexual content. Mainstream outlets were less willing to indulge in gossip and speculation about these women because their films were now well outside the norm. As one reader's letter to *Majalah Film* noted in 1995: 'evidently this is a symptom, producers prefer to pay a lot for hot actresses rather than pay for quality stories available in the market' ('Komentar Film Berhadiah' 1995: 39).[6] When asked in a 1992 interview, Yatti Octavia noted the generational difference: 'Now the young ones are sexy in the film and sexy outside. We weren't like this before. When we are shooting we do it, but when the shooting is done, we return to normal. I became myself again, I didn't take my roles into my daily life' ('Kata Yati Octavia' 1992: 9).[7]

Here we see a difference between the actresses of the 1970s–80s and those of the 1990s. On reflection, an earlier generation of sex bombs see their entry into acting and especially in taking up *berani* roles as a result of their naiveté or forced choice. Debbie Cynthia Dewi, for example, says that: 'I started from not understanding anything at all. [If I was] told to shower, I showered. Told to take my clothes off, I took them off' ('Debbie Cynthia Dewi' 1986: 27).[8] Lina Budiarty recounted her first role:

> Well I felt like I was trapped at that time. To refuse was not possible since I had already been paid. But to do this kind of scene also felt impossible. It's bad for me as a mother of my children. What will people say later? ('Lina Budiarty' 1989: 3)[9]

Budiarti likened her first film role to prostitution: 'I was really like a hostess or prostitute. First time I acted I was given 60 thousand [rupiah] and told to get naked.'[10]

This experience differs from the sex bombs of the 1990s who use sex and their bodies to get into acting and onto the screen. Ayu Yohana, who found most of her roles in the 1990s, says that 'At that time people said that only rich people can become film stars', whereas she became an actress by wanting 'sexy' roles (Pudyastuti et al. 1994).[11] Kiki Fatmala, for example, proudly claimed: 'Beauty, allure, daring and youth are the way to achieve opportunities' ('Kiki Fatmala Setuju' 1989: 3).[12] But it also means that they were mostly cast not because of their acting ability, but because of their look and their willingness to act in the new kinds of sex content prevalent in the 1990s. This was indicative of the changing fortunes of the local film industry, as more mainstream audiences moved to television, and feature film producers turned almost exclusively to *filem esek-esek* (soft porn) to attract audiences. These differences impact the career trajectories of these actresses, their star images, and their declining significance to Indonesian sexual politics.

Career trajectories

It can be argued the sex bomb's star image continues to be meaningful even as she is no longer willing or able to do the kinds of roles that defined her as a sex bomb. Often though there comes a time when the sex bomb role no longer fits whether due to age, personal choice, or changing audience tastes. Invariably all sex bombs age and are replaced by younger actresses who rise to fame or notoriety in their place. Generational replacement is common to the acting profession, with female stars carrying the extra burden of being subject to much greater scrutiny over their appearance and youthfulness (Hollinger 2006: 55). How the star navigates and shapes her career and the kind of agency she has also adds meaning to the sex bomb phenomenon. Indonesia's sex bombs typically follow one of three general career trajectories: disappear, adapt or repent. The post-sex bomb career also provides insight into norms of sexuality and gender, and about women's careers in media more generally.

Whilst at the peak of their stardom, many sex bombs find themselves typecast and work to the will of producers who bank on their continued willingness to act in sexy roles. Two years into her decade long film career, Yenny Farida noted that: 'Producers have not given me opportunities (for other types of roles). Or maybe they think that I am not yet able to act in films without scenes of undress. So, until now I haven't got those scenes' ('Yenny Farida' 1985: 12).[13] Over time though, a desire to escape being typecast becomes an important aspect of their career narrative. Enny Beatrice in 1985 began to question her image saying: 'I don't want to be known as an artist whose only selling point is her audacity' ('Enny Beatrice' 1985: 38).[14] For Debbie Cynthia Dewi, after a decade in film, she decided it was time to change her trajectory: 'Hot scenes? No, I don't like them anymore. I am now avoiding those kinds of scenes. Basically, if it's titillating, I'm not interested anymore' ('Debbie Cynthia Dewi' 1982: 17).[15]

A number of sex bombs move beyond their sex bomb image by proving their acting skills and transitioning into more serious roles. Meriam Bellina, for example, won Best Actress at the 1984 Indonesian Film Festival for her role in *Cinta di Balik Noda* (Love Behind the Stain, Bobby Sandy, 1984), prompting her to claim that 'Obviously the Piala Citra [Acting Award] will push me in a better direction' ('Meriam Bellina Tak Pernah' 1984: 26).[16] She received praise from senior actor Zaenal Abidin who said 'She has the potential to be an actress' ('Meriam Bellina Tak Pernah' 1984: 26)[17] and she would later be dubbed the '*magma perfilman Indonesia*' (lava of Indonesian cinema) by director Arifin C. Noer. In an article from 1990 she was referred to as a 'first class sensual actress' ('Tetap Tampil Sensual' 1990: 18),[18] quite a different connotation to being described as 'young and willing' as she was in 1984 ('Meriam Bellina Tak Pernah' 1984: 27).[19] Proving their acting skills enables some sex bombs to gain more serious roles through which they are able to move beyond their sex bomb image.

The expansion of private television in the 1990s provided many actresses with opportunities to move into *sinetron* (soap opera). Yurike Prastica, for example, had become famous for her role in *Pembalasan Ratu Pantai Selatan* (Revenge of the South Sea Queen, H. Tjut Djalil, 1988) which had been released in the cinemas but then withdrawn for its nudity and sex scenes.[20] Looking back in a 1997 interview, she says that: 'As I was getting older and becoming more aware it was time to leave behind those kinds of films' ('Mereka (sebagian)' 1997: 19).[21] Yet she acknowledges that she cannot escape her previous reputation and roles: 'I became the South Sea Queen and it won't be forgotten by the public, [...] for me it is not bad [sex bomb image], but it's an experience. It doesn't matter that people remember me like that. What matters is that I follow the process and change' (Kurniawan 2015).[22] Prastica, along with Debbie Cynthia Dewi, Sally Marcellina and Meriam Bellina became television actresses and are examples of 'successful aging' (Rowe and Kahn 1997). Inneke Koesherawaty even juggled both during the 1990s: acting in sex films and *sinetron* at the same time.

A second set of sex bombs stop acting and disappear from public life altogether. Usually this follows a marriage in which their duties to husband and household take priority. Others leave a significant gap between their 'sex bomb' period and their return to acting. Sally Marcellina took a seven-year hiatus to raise her children and manage her restaurant in Bintaro, South Jakarta, before returning to acting in 2005. In the case of Enny Beatrice, who began acting at age sixteen in 1982, she retired from acting in 1989 age twenty-three after meeting future husband and Malaysian politician Tengku Adnan Tengku Mansor. As a result, she gave up her celebrity and acting life to become a mother and wife. Yati Octavia also retired from acting and moved to Purwokerto with her actor husband Pangky Suwito. When asked in a 1992 interview about her former acting career she replied: 'I have never regretted what I did before. Maybe it was necessary for me to follow that path in life. A kind of process' ('Kata Yati Octavia' 1992: 9).[23]

Often family duties and instruction from a husband end a woman's acting career. Sri Gudhi Sintara, active from 1981 to 1984, received praise for her role in *Kawin Kontrak* (Contract Marriage, Maman Firmansjah, 1983) and was 'crowned the Malay sex bomb' (Iwan 1983: 7).[24] After her marriage in 1983, she reassured readers in interviews that she would continue acting:

> My husband understands my profession. Just that now I have to divide my time between my career and household. Like it or not I am now a wife who must privilege her husband. But trust me, despite my status there will be no change to the fundamentals of my career. Maybe now I have to consult with my husband about the roles I want to take. If he agrees, then I take it. If he doesn't, then I have to listen to him. (Iwan 1983: 49)[25]

> I will continue acting in films. The film world is the world I am familiar with. But of course, I prioritise the needs of my family over film. If my family demands that I no longer act, what can I do? ('Gudhi Sintara Menikah' 1983: 33)[26]

In the same edition her husband is also interviewed, and he is quoted as saying: 'Before marrying her, I know that her hobby is to act in film, so I don't want to limit her or stop her career in film. What's important is that she takes care of herself' (ibid.: 121).[27] Yet in an interview a year later (in November 1984) her husband says he wants her to stay home and to no longer act in films ('Gudhi Sintara Setelah' 1984). Sri Gudhi Sintara disappeared from the public eye and has never acted in film or television again.

A third route that some former sex bombs take involves a process of transformation through repentance which involves not only disavowing their former roles and image but crafting an image antithetical to a sex bomb. The new image often involves appropriating symbols of piety and a religious transformation called *hijrah* (turn to Islam). In 1983, as sex films became more prominent, actress Jenny Rachman felt she needed to 'limit herself' as she had just completed the hajj (pilgrimage to Mecca), letting other actresses such as Meriam Bellina take on more risqué roles ('Meriam Bellina' 1983: 9). Karim Tartoussieh (2007) documents the phenomenon of actresses repenting in Egypt where they often undergo a spiritual and/or religious reform to shed their former image and 'sins' of the past. However, as Tartoussieh (2007: 32) notes, repenting is gendered as it is actresses not actors who typically undergo this morality shift in their image.

Of the 'repenters', Eva Arnaz underwent one of the most profound transformations. Eva Arnaz was one of the most prominent sex bombs of the 1980s but by 1991 she had decided to repent and had begun wearing the *kerudung* (headscarf) and announced that she wanted to *hijrah*. In 1991 she went on the hajj to Mecca. This aligned her with an emerging piety movement in Indonesia in which a religious identity is prioritised. She then distanced herself from her previous roles and image as a sex bomb. In an interview from 2015 she says:

> I scream when my films are screened, because the sins repeat, [but] if I have truly repented then god willing I can. I destroyed all of my film collection in my house, I burned them. I asked producers not to screen my films anymore. Although that may not be acceptable to the producers, but I strive to ensure my films are no longer shown. (Merdekawan 2015)[28]

She is now known by her Muslim name – Siti Syarifah – rather than her stage name Eva Arnaz. In recent interviews she is photographed dressed in full *hijab*, standing in her humble shop where she sells Muslim fashion and food (Merdekawan 2015).

It is also possible to repent and maintain a star image through a self-refashioning as is the case with Inneke Koesherawaty (Figure 7.6). Prominent as a sex bomb in the 1990s, Koesherawaty decided on a different route in 1997: 'I've had enough of acting in films. As long as the film industry continues to sell breasts and thighs I won't return' ('Inneke Koesherawaty' 1997: 19).[29] Noting that her parents had gone on the hajj, she herself turned to Islam and began wearing the *hijab* in 2001. This led her to take roles in religious programmes, including the Islamic *sinetron* serial *Padamu Aku Bersimpuh* (To You I Kneel, 2001) and a year later she won the Best Ramadhan Show Host (Pembawa Acara Ramadhan Terbaik) award from the Indonesian Council of Ulamas (MUI, Majelis

Figure 7.6 Original poster for *Pergaulan Metropolis 2* (Metropolitan Relationships 2, Acok Rachman, 1995) starring Inneke Koesherawaty. Image courtesy of Soraya Intercine Films.

Ulama Indonesia). In 2003 she was the cover model for the inaugural edition of *Alia*, a new Muslim women's magazine (Figure 7.7). She has become an important figure in the Islamic entertainment mainstream, having severed all ties with her past as an actress in sex roles.[30]

Figure 7.7 Front cover of issue 1 of *Alia* magazine (July 2003) featuring Inneke Koesherawaty in headscarf. The text says she is 'Ready to give up her career' (Siap Melepas Karir).

All sex bombs age and are forced by circumstances to adapt or disappear. This is common around the world for women who have built their stardom on their sexual attractiveness (Feasey 2012). For Indonesia's sex bombs, the maturing process is inflected through local mores and gender expectations, especially the expectation that actresses will get married and have children or return to proper morality through religion. Nevertheless, the sex bombs remain important personalities in the ongoing debates over gender roles and sexuality in Indonesia. Likewise, the post 2000 revival of the film industry also features several prominent actresses (notably Dewi Perssik and Julia Perez) who have taken the mantle of the sex bomb from early generations. But the nature of celebrity and stardom has changed, especially with the arrival and widespread use of social media. New types of celebrity have emerged – not tied to traditional media and the press – but rather made and often self-made in social media. It may be the case that the sex bombs considered here were a phenomenon particular to the New Order period.

Conclusion

As the first substantive study of the Indonesian sex bomb, this chapter can only offer a limited account that opens the way for further study of the star phenomena in Indonesia. Sex bombs are a significant part of Indonesian cinematic history and their stories and biographies are important to ongoing studies of Indonesian cinema and society. Sex bombs are a star type whose careers and images tell us not only about the nature of the film industry but also changing ideas of sexual morality and gender roles. The sex bomb also provides a counterpoint to the revival of modesty and morality underway in modern day Indonesia. This has been evident in the emergence of new Islamisation and the visibility of the *hijab*, a return to values of family, marital duty and domesticity for women, and the legislation of an Anti-Pornography Law in 2009, ensuring films with the same imagery as in the past would be almost impossible to make now. As a result, there is increased caution around topics related to sex and sexuality. This can also explain some of the nostalgia for the film and the sex bombs of the past as many come to terms with the changed cultural and moral landscape of Indonesia after 1998.

References

Barker, Thomas (2014), 'Sex on Indonesia's screens', in Linda Rae Bennett and Sharyn Graham Davies (eds), *Sex and Sexualities in Indonesia: Sexual Politics, Diversity and Representations in the Reformasi Era*, London: Routledge, pp. 253–72.

Bonnie, Lala (1977), *Doris Callebaut*, Jakarta: Karya Baru.

'Debbie Cynthia Dewi Kadang Kadang Rindu' (1986), *Ria Film* 622, 2–8 April, p. 27.
'Debbie Cynthia Dewi Mulai Tinggalkan Adegan Merangsang' (1982), *Ria Film* 403, 20–6 January, p. 17.
'Diajak Tidur Pejabat, Eva Arnaz Tantang Berani Bayar Berapa' (2012), *detikHOT*, 17 April, <http://hot.detik.com/celeb/1894569/diajak-tidur-pejabat-eva-arnaz-tantang-berani-bayar-berapa> (last accessed 13 November 2018).
Dyer, Richard (1986), *Heavenly Bodies: Films Stars and Society*, London and New York: Routledge.
'Enny Beatrice' (1985), *Hai* IV-IX, 29 October–4 November, p. 38.
Feasey, Rebecca (2012), 'The ageing femme fatale: sex, stardom and Sharon Stone', in Aagje Swinnen and John A. Stotesbury (eds), *Aging, Performance, and Stardom: Doing Age on the Stage of Consumerist Culture*, Zurich and Münster: LIT Verlag, pp. 109–30.
Grossman, Julie (2007), 'Film noir's 'femme fatales' hard-boiled women: moving beyond gender fantasies', *Quarterly Review of Film and Video* 24, pp. 19–30.
'Gudhi Sintara Menikah Secara Diam-Diam' (1983), *Ria Film* 483, 10–16 August, p. 121.
'Gudhi Sintara Setelah Mempunyai Anak Berhenti Main Film' (1984), *Ria Film* 549, 7–13 November, pp. 26, 27, 145.
Hangguman, Willy A. (1990), *Johny Indo: Tobat dan Harapan*, Jakarta: Pustaka Sinar Harapan.
Hollinger, Karen (2006), *The Actress: Hollywood Acting and the Female Star*, New York: Routledge.
'Inneke Koesherawaty: Ingin Bertobat' (1997), *Majalah Film* 2999-265-XIV, 29 November–12 December, p. 19.
Iwan Ch. (1983), 'Sri Gudhi: Bom Seks Baru Film Nasional', *Variasi Putra Indonesia* 18:X, pp. 7, 49.
Jordan, Jessica Hope (2010), *The Sex Goddess in American Film, 1930–1965: Jean Harlow, Mae West, Lana Turner and Jayne Mansfield*, New York: Cambria Press.
Junaidi, Ahmad (2012), *Porno! Feminisme, Seksualitas, dan Pornografi di Media*, Jakarta: Gramedia Widiasarana Indonesia.
'Kata Yati Octavia, Jadi Ibu Rumah Tangga juga tak Kalah Membahagiakan Dibanding dengan jadi Bintang Ternama' (1992), *Bintang* 50, February, p. 9.
'Kiki Fatmala: Setuju Kumpul Kebo' (1989), *Majalah Film* 085-53-VI, 30 September–13 October, p. 3.
'Komentar Film Berhadiah' (1995), *Majalah Film* 226-192-XI, 11–24 February, p. 39.
Kurniawan, Ari (2015), 'Imej Bom Seks Masih Melekat, Yurike Prastika Anggap Sebagai Perjalanan Hidup', *Tabloid Bintang*, 5 March, <https://www.tabloidbintang.com/berita/gosip/read/18977/imej-bom-seks-masih-melekat-yurike-prastika-anggap-sebagai-perjalanan-hidup> (last accessed 13 November 2018).
'Lela Anggraeni Takut Kawin' (1990), *Majalah Film* 095-63-VI, 17 February–2 March, p. 16.
'Lina Budiarty: Saya ini Memang Pantas Jadi Hostes atau Pelacur. Pertama Main Film Honornya 60 Ribu Disuruh Telanjang' (1989), *Majalah Film* 073-41-V, 15–28 April, p. 3.
Merdekawan, Guntur (2015), 'Tobat, Eva Arnaz Bakar dan Hancurkan Semua Film Panasnya di Rumah', *Kapanlagi*, 22 November, <http://www.kapanlagi.com/showbiz/

film/indonesia/tobat-eva-arnaz-bakar-dan-hancurkan-semua-film-panasnya-di-rumah-a7339c.html> (last accessed 13 November 2018).

'Mereka (sebagian) yang Berpeluang Wajah Baru, Berenerji Besar' (1997), *Majalah Film* 298-264 XIV, 18–31 October, p. 19.

'Meriam Bellina: Akan Mengorbit Perkawinan 83' (1983), *Ria Film* 452, January, p. 9.

'Meriam Bellina: Kenapa Sangat Berani?' (1984), *Ria Film* 543, 26 September–2 October, pp. 27, 144.

'Meriam Bellina Tak Pernah Mencurigai Produser' (1984), *Ria Film* 543, 26 September–2 October, p. 26.

Paramaditha, Intan (2017), 'Film studies in Indonesia: an experiment of a new generation', *Bijdragen tot de Taal-, Land- en Volkenkunde* 173:2–3, pp. 357–75.

Pudyastuti, R. Sri, Muryadi, Wahyu and Indrawan (1994) 'Suara dari balik seluloid yang panas itu', *Tempo* 17/XXIV, 25 June.

Rowe, John W. and Robert L. Kahn (1997), 'Successful aging', *The Gerontologist* 37:4, pp. 433–40.

Said, Salim (1991), *Shadows on the Silver Screen: A Social History of Indonesian Film*, Jakarta: Lontar.

'Sally Marcellina Sering Orang Keliru Menilai Saya' (1996), *Majalah Film* 256-22-XII, 6–19 April, p. 48.

Sen, Krishna (1994), *Indonesian Cinema: Framing the New Order*, London: Zed Books.

Suryakusuma, Julia (1996), 'The State and sexuality in New Order Indonesia', in Laurie J. Sears (ed.), *Fantasizing the Feminine in Indonesia*, Durham, NC: Duke University Press, pp. 92–119.

Tartoussieh, Karim (2007), 'Pious stardom: cinema and the Islamic revival in Egypt', *Arab Studies Journal* 15:1, pp. 30–43.

'Tetap Tampil Sensual' (1990), *Majalah Film*, 095-63-VI, 17 February–2 March, p. 18.

Weintraub, Andrew (2010), *Dangdut Stories: A Social and Musical History of Indonesia's Most Popular Music*, New York: Oxford University Press.

Welly K, 'Eva Arnaz: Mendampingi Liem Swie King' (1980), *Ria Film* 307, 5–11 March, p. 5.

'Yenny Farida: Anti Hidup Bersama Tanpa Pernikahan' (1985), *Ria Film* 576, 15–21 May, pp. 12, 13, 140.

'Yenny Farida Cerai Setelah Kumpul Bareng' (1989), *Majalah Film* 073-41-V, 15–28 April, p. 17.

Yngvesson, Dag (2014), 'The earth is getting hotter: urban inferno and outsider women's collectives in Bumi Makin Panas', *Plaridel* 11:2, pp. 54–94.

Notes

1. 'Kalau semula saya sudah setuju, kenapa harus menolak?'
2. 'Hanya biasa-biasa saja, tidak ada yang istimewa. Entah kalau masyarakat yang menilainya.'
3. 'Film-filmku yang sudah beredar itu, sudah melewati saringan jalur badan sensor film. Jadi, tidak ada masalah kan? [...] Biar lebih puas lagi, saya jabarkan: Saya itu kalau

membuat film, jika anda perhatikan dengan teliti, selaku ada pesan moral dan tolong jangan dilihat hanya gambarnya saja. Tapi, coba dilihat dari sudut-sudut lainnya.'
4. 'Seharusnya yang begini yang perlu kita pertanyakan. Mereka dapat duit darimana kalau nggak . . .'
5. 'Mulai dari pejabat, pengusaha, sampai sutradara. Tapi, berani bayar berapa mereka? Setahun saja, tante bisa main sampai 10 film, bukan mau sombong.'
6. 'Nampaknya ada gejala, produser lebih suka membayar mahal artis panas daripada membayar cerita novel bermutu yang ada di pasaran.'
7. 'Kalau anak-anak sekarang [artis panas], ya seksi di film, seksi di luar. Kalau kita dulu nggak. Kalau pas main film, ya main, tapi begitu syuting selesai, semua kembali seperti semula. Saya ya menjadi diri saya lagi, tidak membawa-bawa sosok peran dalam kehidupan sehari-hari.'
8. 'Saya mulai dari tidak ngerti sama sekali. Disuruh mandi, ya mandi. Disuruh buka baju, ya buka.'
9. 'Wah saya merasa terperangkap waktu itu. Untuk menolak tidak mungkin karena honornya sudah saya terima. Tapi kalau harus melakukan adegan seperti itu rasanya juga mustahil. Jelek-jelek saya ini kan ibu dari anak-anak saya. Apa kata orang nanti?'
10. 'Saya ini memang pantas jadi hostess atau pelacur. Pertama main film honornya 60 ribu disuruh telanjang'
11. 'Waktu itu ada yang bilang bisa jadi bintang film hanyalah orang-orang kaya.'
12. 'Kecantikan, kemolekan, keberanian dan usia muda adalah bagian dari jalan meraih kesempatan yang menjanjikan.'
13. 'Namun produser belum memberikan kesempatan pada saya. Atau mungkin mereka beranggapan, saya masih belum mampu berakting untuk film tanpa adegan buka-bukaan. Dan tentu saja hingga kini adegan semacam itu belum pernah saya peroleh.'
14. 'Saya tak mau dikatakan artis yang punya modal keberanian saja.'
15. 'Adegan hot? Tidak, saya tidak suka lagi. Saya mulai jauhi adegan-adegan seperti itu. Pokoknya yang rada merangsang tidak kepingin lagi.'
16. 'Yang jelas Piala Citra harus menjadi dorongan saya kearah yang lebih baik.'
17. 'Dia bakal jadi aktris nantinya.'
18. 'aktris sensual kelas satu.'
19. 'muda dan berani.'
20. Released internationally as *Lady Terminator*.
21. 'Seiring dengan kedewasaannya dan juga kesadaran sudah saatnya meninggalkan film-film jenis begituan.'
22. 'Saya pernah jadi Ratu Pantai Selatan, dan itu enggak akan pernah hilang dari ingatan masyarakat. [. . .] Jadi buat saya itu (imej bom seks) bukan enggak baik, tapi jadikan pengalaman. Enggak apa-apa, orang mengingat saya begitu. Yang penting gimana saya jalani proses itu sampai berubah.'
23. 'Saya tidak pernah menyesali yang telah saya lakukan dulu-dulu. Mungkin memang harus begitu jalan hidup yang saya lalui. Jadi semacam proses, gitu.'
24. 'digelari bom seks Melayu.'
25. 'Suami saya sudah mengerti profesi saya itu. Cuma sekarang ini saya harus bisa membagi waktu antara karir dan rumah tangga. Sebab biar bagaimanapun, saya kini telah menjadi seorang istri yang harus memperhatikan suami. Tapi percayalah,

dengan status ini tidak ada perubahan yang mendasar dalam karir saya. Tapi mungkin saya kini harus berkonsultasi dengan suami saya mengenai peran yang bakal saya mainkan. Kalau memang disetujui, baru saya lakukan. Kalau tidak, saya pun harus menurutinya.'

26. 'Saya tetap akan main film. Dunia film sudah menjadi dunia saya yang akrab. Tetapi tentu saja saya lebih mementingkan keperluan keluarga daripada film. Bila keluarga saya menuntut agar saya tidak boleh main film lagi, ya apa boleh buat.'
27. 'Sebelum menikah dengannya, saya sudah tahu kalau Gudhi itu hobiya main film, maka itu saya tidak akan membatasi atau menghentikan karirnya di dunia film. Yang penting, dia bisa menjaga diri.'
28. 'Film (panas) diputar saya ngejerit, karena dosa berjalan terus, kalau bener tobat, Insya Allah bisa. Semua koleksi film saya yang di rumah saya hancurin semua, saya bakar. Saya sempat minta tolong ke produser untuk tidak lagi memutar film-film saya. Tapi itukan nggak mungkin begitu saja bisa diterima produser, tapi saya tetap berusaha agar film itu tidak diputar lagi.'
29. 'Saya sudah jenuh main film! Selama perfilman nasional masih menjual paha dan dada saya tidak akan kembali.'
30. In 2018, Inneke Koesherawaty and her husband Fahmi Darmawansyah were arrested by the Corruption Eradication Commission.

Chapter 8

Nora Aunor and Sharon Cuneta as migrant workers: stars and labour export in Filipino commercial films

Katrina Ross Tan

This chapter examines the star images of Philippine cinema's two biggest stars, Nora Aunor and Sharon Cuneta, and the ideological functions they serve in films about Filipino migrant workers. Nora, who rose to fame in the 1970s, is known as the 'Superstar', while Sharon, who first became popular in the 1980s, is known as the 'Megastar'. Both stars achieved enormous success in their music, film and television careers and attracted legions of devoted fans – the Noranians and Sharonians, respectively. Although their star images differ in many ways, there are some significant similarities. Both started out in the music industry before venturing into making movies, and early in their careers they starred in youth-oriented romantic films before later tackling more serious roles. Nora and Sharon are also known for their roles as *babaeng martir* (the long-suffering female) and recently their roles as Filipino migrant workers, or Overseas Filipino Workers (OFWs).

This chapter analyses the star images of Nora in *The Flor Contemplacion Story* (Joel C. Lamangan, 1995) and Sharon in *Caregiver* (Chito S. Roño, 2008) and the roles they play in shaping the meanings of these films in relation to discourses on migrant labour. I argue that the star images of Nora and Sharon as *babaeng martir* are mobilised for different ideological purposes in the OFW films according to the larger social context which shapes the evolving discourses on migrant work. While star images can be used to personalise the collective suffering of OFWs, they can also amplify its dangers and cultivate collective action to respond to abuses and injustices. As the analysis below shows, Sharon's star image arouses individualised aspirations that are fulfilled through migrant work, while

Nora's evokes collective empathy and solidarity with the OFW. In what follows, I discuss stars as primary ideological vehicles in films, drawing from the works of Richard Dyer (1998) and Janet Thumin (1986). Then, I briefly sketch the emergence of OFW films in Filipino commercial cinema in the context of the country's increasingly naturalised labour export policy, demonstrating how OFW films have become part of the machinery of stardom in Philippine film and media. I then analyse the representation of migrant work in *The Flor Contemplacion Story* and *Caregiver* and identify how the star images of Nora and Sharon frame possible readings of these representations.

Stardom and the OFW

In his pioneering work in *Stars*, Richard Dyer (1998: 3) analyses stars as 'texts' that are capable of shaping the ideological meanings of the films they appear in. He explains (20) that the 'ideological effect' of stars rests in part on the conflation of the star as character and the star as person. As he points out, the star personality revealed through the character is 'a construction known and expressed only through films, stories, publicity ...' (20). This web of discourses builds an image for the star and embeds within this image a particular set of ideas. Moreover, as images, stars produce a 'finite multitude of readings' and restrict the 'meanings and affects [that] can legitimately be read in them' (3). When these images intersect with films, limited ways of reading these films are produced. Thumin (1986: 75) believes that 'star texts act on the film text to privilege a particular reading while not, of course, making other readings impossible'. In the context of OFW films, then, stars imbue their characters with their personas and, in doing so, can lead audiences to particular ideological viewpoints, while masking this process through the glamour of stardom.

OFW films are characterised by a narrative that focuses on an OFW character, usually female and usually played by a major star (Tan 2017: 153). Patrick Campos (2016: 528) argues that the OFW film is a 'uniquely Filipino (i.e. national) genre' which corresponds with the prevalence of labour export in the country. These films narrate OFW experiences, highlighting the sacrifices the migrant worker makes for her/his family. They are usually set in whole or in part in other countries outside the Philippines, which means that they require larger production budgets. Campos (2016: 528) notes that companies gamble with making large investments in these films, but that they often prove to be profitable by attracting large diasporic as well as domestic audiences. Aside from theatrical screenings, Filipinos overseas can view OFW films through cable channels like The Filipino Channel and, lately, through streaming sites like Netflix. This extended distribution chain generates further profit for OFW films.

Emerging against the backdrop of decades of labour export policy (LEP) in the Philippines, OFW films serve as a cultural site in which the 'heroic' image attached to the OFW figure is redeployed. Former President Corazon Aquino proclaimed the OFWs as *bagong bayani* (modern-day heroes) to recognise their economic contributions. Bach and Solomon (2006: 3) suggest that such a proclamation is necessary in order for the Philippine state to justify its 'unusual approach toward the state-led export of labor'. That 'unusual approach' is characterised by the nation state's aggressive 'brokering' of the Filipino labour force within the global economy (Rodriguez 2010: 4). With thousands of Filipino workers departing daily, the Philippines is among the top labour exporters in the world (Rodriguez 2010: xii). The latest figure from the Philippine Statistics Authority (Mapa 2020: n.p.) records approximately 2.2 million Filipino workers deployed overseas in 2019 alone. With the total number of overseas Filipinos exceeding 10 million, the Philippines receives billions of dollars in remittance each year. The Bangko Sentral ng Pilipinas ('Overseas Filipinos' Cash Remittances' 2020) reports that Filipino migrants sent a total of $30 billion to their families in 2019. Rolando Tolentino (2009: 432) notes that OFW remittance serves as a reliable source of government income, which is then used for debt servicing, military spending and even corruption. From being a temporary solution to unemployment problems, LEP has morphed into an integral development strategy of the Philippine government (Asis 2017), which has in turn led to overseas work being characterised by the nation state as a 'heroic' act. Robyn Rodriguez (2010: 84) argues that overseas work frames 'international migration as a voluntary act of self-sacrificing individuals ... akin to those made by anticolonial nationalists'. Given the government's reliance on the economic role played by migrant workers, it is understandable that it perpetuates the narrative of the OFW as 'modern-day hero'.

OFW films have evolved to become a key aspect of the machinery of stardom in the Philippines. As the discussion on Nora and Sharon below shows, these films have served as star vehicles to revive their careers from hibernation, and as vehicles their roles were made to fit their star images (Dyer 1998: 89). More importantly, their roles bring them closer to the mass audience who know or are related to OFWs. In some instances, actors play OFWs in order to accelerate an up-and-coming career, widen their fan base or attempt to make a comeback, as is the case with the two examples discussed in this chapter. Taking an OFW role has, therefore, become a useful strategy for stars to advance their careers: it reinforces their popularity among domestic fans and expands it among Filipino audiences overseas.

Stars as OFWs, however, also serve ideological purposes as they invite certain readings of migrant work in the films in which they appear. In the sections that follow, I analyse the ideological meanings the star images of Nora and Sharon created as they performed their OFW roles in *The Flor Contemplacion Story* and *Caregiver*, respectively.

The superstar in *The Flor Contemplacion Story*

Considered 'Philippine cinema's grand dame' (Tsui 2015), Nora Aunor is known in the entertainment industry as 'the Superstar' (Figure 8.1). She began her career in the 1960s by winning a national singing contest in a television show called *Tawag ng Tanghalan* (Call of the Stage). Her golden voice captured the public's imagination and launched her career as a recording artist and, later, a movie star. This petite, short and brown-skinned *probinsyana* (from the province) was from Iriga, Camarines Sur, hundreds of kilometres away from the world of showbiz in Manila. Before she became famous, Nora sold water at a train station and joined singing contests in her hometown to help with her family's finances. Her rise to fame exemplifies a rags-to-riches story which attracted the adoration of Noranians. Scholars have noted that Nora's phenomenal rise as a star ushered in a new dynamic of stardom in the Philippines (Lim 2009; Tadiar 2002). Bliss Cua Lim (2009: 323), for example, argues that Nora signalled a 'profound' change 'in the racialized, classed terms of Philippine stardom'. She deposed the dominance of the lighter skinned *mestiza/o* actors and gave ordinary movie goers a star they could identify with (for more on the significance of the *mestiza/o* star in Philippine cinema see Sebastiampillai's discussion of John Lloyd Cruz and Bea Alonso in Chapter 9). Lim (2012: 181) states that Nora's exceptional success in this regard has been read 'as a collective embodiment' of her fans who were 'widely perceived

Figure 8.1 The young Nora Aunor in the 1970s. Photo courtesy of Oliver Inocentes.

as lower-class, feminized and dark-skinned' like her. Nora's star image is thus made up of her individualised characteristics as 'the dark-skinned superstar' and the collectivity of her fans (Lim 2012: 180–1).

As an actor, Nora was first known for her youth-oriented films in the late 1960s, particularly those she made opposite Tirso Cruz III. Guy and Pip, as they were known in these films, reigned at the box office for many years. In 1972, Nora established her own production company, NV Productions, which produced almost thirty films including *Bona* (Lino Brocka, 1980), in which she played one of her memorable roles as a devoted fan. NV Productions also produced *Banaue: Stairway to the Sky* (Gerardo de Leon, 1975) and *Tatlong Taong Walang Diyos* (Three Years without God, Mario O'Hara, 1976), which are among the early films in which Nora took on more serious roles. Notably, her company also produced her directorial debut, *Niño Valiente* (Brave Boy, Nora Aunor, 1975). As an actor, she ventured into more serious roles in the late 1970s, a period known as Philippine cinema's 'second golden age', owing to the critically acclaimed work of several new directors, including Lino Brocka, Ishmael Bernal and Mike de Leon, among others, produced despite (or because of) the repressive military rule. These films altered Nora's image from that of a youth in love to one of a long-suffering female. Lim (2009: 321) points out that this image is characterised by her enduring mistreatment and putting the needs of others before her own, as in her role as a domestic servant in *Atsay* (Maid, Eddie Garcia, 1978).

Her OFW role in *The Flor Contemplacion Story* exemplifies Nora's long-suffering female image. In it she gives life to the convicted domestic helper's tragic story of suffering and death in Singapore. Contemplacion was accused of killing Delia Maga, a Filipino domestic helper, and her ward. The film was Nora's comeback film after a year of not working in the cinema. Patrick Flores (2000: 91) notes that this film became an opportunity for the 'has-been' Nora to revive her wavering career by resurrecting her portrayal of the *babaeng martir* from her previous work. Nora went on to win awards for her performance, including the first award given to a Filipino actor at the Cairo International Film Festival. These recognitions, however, did not translate into more film projects in the following years. By the end of the 1990s, Nora had only made ten films in total. In 2003, she went to the USA and stayed there for almost a decade. During her absence from the industry, controversies hounded her, with her allegedly suffering from gambling and drug problems. Even though she was not convicted of any drug-related crime, former President Benigno Aquino III used her alleged offences as a reason for blocking her confirmation as a National Artist for Film in 2014. Having been denied the country's highest honour for an artist, Nora received recognition from various groups and institutions. For instance, the women's group Gabriela declared her 'Artista ng Bayan' (Artist of the People) in 2014.

In addition, the Cultural Center of the Philippines and the Manunuri ng Pelikulang Pilipino (Critics of Filipino Films) honoured her work with lifetime achievement awards.

As a biopic, *The Flor Contemplacion Story* highlighted aspects of Contemplacion's life that fitted Nora's established star image. Nora was also made to look like the character she portrayed by sporting short curly hair and wearing the printed dresses Contemplacion was seen wearing in photographs. Like Contemplacion, Nora came from a poor family in the provinces. Consistent with Nora's *babaeng martir* persona, the film underscored the mother's sacrifice with Contemplacion working abroad and away from her children in order to support them. In addition, *The Flor Contemplacion Story* explored marital problems experienced between Contemplacion and her husband, which also paralleled events in Nora's real life. Even the casting of Nora's son, Ian de Leon, and Contemplacion's real life twins can be considered as an attempt to highlight similarities between the two women.

A central part of Nora's star image is her skilful talent as a performer (Lim 2012: 190), which is evident in *The Flor Contemplacion Story*. Alice Guillermo (2000: 108) declares Nora's performance in the film as 'exceptional' and closest to the actual Contemplacion as compared with the performance given by Helen Gamboa, who also played Flor in *Bagong Bayani* (A New Hero, Tikoy Aguiluz, 1995). One scene that demonstrates Nora's exceptional acting skill occurs when the Singaporean guard announces her execution day. Hysterical, Nora/Flor curses the guards before suddenly falling silent. From here, Nora's bodily gestures express her deep sadness and resignation with her fate. Nora/Flor slowly walks towards the rear of her cell and sits with her arms crossed over her legs, burying her head between her legs and crying silently. The camera, positioned outside her cell, lets the audience see her behind bars. Nora/Flor is at the back of the frame and a ray of dim light shines on her in this darkly lit scene, enough for the audience to discern the restrained expression of her emotions. Foreign film critics, such as Emmanuel Levy (1995) of *Variety*, also note Nora's powerful performance in the film, with him commenting on the 'powerful emotions and utmost conviction' that she invested in her role. For Levy, Nora provides an effective portrayal of a 'humble, self-sacrificing mother [who] became a victim of corruption and abuse – and later, a national symbol adored by her countrymen'. In this regard, she embodies the transformation of a personal tragedy into a national one.

As a *babaeng martir* Nora fosters identification with her audience. Lim (2012: 184) calls this the 'Noranian embodiment', explaining that Nora 'closes the gap' between her and her fans not only through the physical attributes she shares with them, but also by providing Noranians with someone they can champion 'against the neo-colonial conflation of beauty and whiteness' (Lim 2012: 184). This racial logic has denigrated people with dark skin and the lower-class origins associated with it. Lim views Noranian embodiment as a form of 'solidarity mapped on the axes of racial, classed and gendered alliances' (184). This Noranian embodiment thus makes it possible for Nora to 'coordinate collective sentiment' in *The Flor Contemplacion Story* and transform it into something productive (197). Flores (in Lim 2012: 197) argues that Nora coordinates mourning for the executed domestic helper in the film, pointing out that it is a mourning that transforms *awa* (pity) into a more productive form, such as *pakikidalamhati* (sharing of grief) and *pakikiisa* (solidarity). The film supports this view through its emphasis on people's actions. For instance, Philippine NGO Migrante International provided a lawyer to reopen Contemplacion's case, while her fellow domestic helpers testified to her innocence. People joining mass demonstrations declared, 'Flor, hindi ka nagiisa!' (Flor, you are not alone!) in their chants. In real life, Nora has elicited offers of help from Noranians every time she has experienced financial troubles, although she always refused to accept such offers (Lim 2012: 190). In this respect, Noranians, like the people who helped Contemplacion, demonstrate that 'suffering is not only borne by an individual' (190). This illustrates Nora's capacity to embody suffering in a manner which helps to bring about forms of collective power (Flores in Lim 2012: 190).

The film did not stop at depicting such collectivity, however, as it also clearly held the Philippine government accountable for Contemplacion's death. *The Flor Contemplacion Story* suggests Contemplacion is innocent and a victim of foul play and government neglect, a position similarly argued by the organisations that helped her. Many scenes show the lack of appropriate response from relevant government offices. For instance, a scene shows a staff member of the Philippine Embassy in Singapore telling reporters they did not provide a lawyer to Contemplacion because they did not want to pay for it. Another scene reveals how the Foreign Affairs Secretary disparaged Contemplacion as he did not think she deserved the government's attention. In this regard, the film politicised Contemplacion's case by underlining the government's failure to save her from execution. This detail suggests the cruel irony of the government abandoning its 'modern-day heroes', while also bringing to light the disastrous risks involved in labour export. The film, then, engages with the larger discourse of LEP by linking it with Contemplacion's case.

In this regard, Nora's star image was similarly politicised, which is consistent with her persona and previous roles. For instance, in *Minsa'y Isang Gamu-Gamo* (Once a Moth, Lupita Aquino-Kashiwahara, 1976), she transforms from being a nurse eager to work in the USA to someone who loathes the country after a US soldier kills her brother. As Bona, she ends her obsession as a fan of a stuntman when he fails to reciprocate her devotion. Nora's star image, thus, incites action against the injustices her characters face. Moreover, the context of the film's release conditioned the politicised use of Nora's star image, particularly as *The Flor Contemplacion Story* premiered at a time when Contemplacion's execution was still fresh in the public's minds. Protests against the Ramos administration's failure still resonated, and the public continued to express their outrage. The film's release in 1995 came at a time when the government was scrambling to legislate the Migrant Workers Act of 1995 as a response to these protests. Thus, this particular historical juncture in LEP's history shaped Nora's politicised star image.

The Flor Contemplacion Story exposed the dangers brought about by LEP and the government's inability to protect OFWs. It shows the strength of collective action to stop Contemplacion's execution though it came too late to save her from death. Like Nora, whose star image can cultivate a collective response to individual suffering, Contemplacion ignited collective action to pressure the government to pass legislation to ensure protection for OFWs. Her case roused the people to act against government negligence and their lack of compassion for a domestic helper on death row. In this respect, Nora's star image serves as an ideological force, which helps to articulate the collective dimensions of the migrant experience and, as such, demonstrates the power that collective actions can have in responding to the abuses and suffering that migrants face.

The megastar in *Caregiver*

Sharon's stardom shares some parallels with that of Nora (Lim 2009: 329), particularly her entry into show business as a singer before becoming a movie star (Figure 8.2). After an unsuccessful first single, she managed, at

Figure 8.2 Sharon Cuneta, a new star in the 1980s. Photo courtesy of Jerrick David and Angelo de Guzman.

the age of twelve, to break into the music industry with the song 'Mr. DJ'. A few years later, she starred in her first film despite her father's opposition. Lim (2009: 328) recounts that movie producers paid her P200,000 for her first film, making her 'the highest paid neophyte in Philippine cinema'.

Like Nora, Sharon began by making youth-oriented films, with her first being the highly successful *Dear Heart* (Danny Zialcita, 1981), in which she starred alongside Gabby Concepcion, with whom she also starred in her follow-up film, *P.S. I Love You* (Eddie Garcia, 1981), as well as in several other romance films. In 1984 the two got married and had a daughter, but they ended their marriage after just three years. Sharon got married again in 1996 to Francisco Pangilinan, who has served as a senator since his first election in 2001.

Unlike Nora, Sharon comes from a well-off family. She studied in a private school for girls at St Paul's College and later on at an international school in Manila (Lim 2009: 327–8). Jerrick Josue David (2015: 333) notes that although she is from a wealthy family, Sharon is not like an ordinary *mestiza* who has strong Spanish features. He believes this worked to her advantage since Nora's popularity had ended the reign of the *mestizo/a* actors at that time. While Sharon may not have a *mestiza*'s physical features, Lim (2009: 329) argues that she 'introduced a new brand of *mestiza* stardom', which partly rested on her use of *Taglish* – a combination of English and a few Tagalog words – in her early roles as *kolehiyala* or college student (330). Lim explains *Taglish* acts as 'a form of cultural capital, an index of belonging to the latter-day Spanish mestizo elite' (330). She adds that Sharon's signature *Taglish* performance differentiated her as a star. In this regard, Sharon expands *mestizo/a* stardom through her adoption of a distinct use of language.

Entering the film industry in the wake of Nora's reign, Sharon had to refashion her *mestiza* image to appeal to the audience that had made Nora a star. Lim (2009: 331) argues that to secure her rise to stardom Sharon's image in the 1980s had to undergo a shift, described by Lim as a 'Noranian Turn', which involved taking roles in films with rags-to-riches plotlines, reminiscent of Nora's own personal story. Films such as *Bukas Luluhod ang mga Tala* (Tomorrow the Stars will Kneel, Emmanuel H. Borlaza, 1984) and *Bituing Walang Ningning* (Star without Sparkle, Emmanuel H. Borlaza, 1985) uncannily resemble Nora's beginnings when she joined an amateur singing contest and rose to fame. In *Pasan ko ang Daigdig* (World on my Shoulders, Lino Brocka, 1987), Sharon plays Lupe, who lives and scavenges in a landfill before she and her mother rise from poverty through her talent at singing. These films installed Sharon as the new star of the 1980s.

Sharon is generally recognised for her wholesome image, but she is also well-known for trying out new roles. The most recent example of this was in *Crying Ladies* (Mark Meily, 2003) in which she played an ex-convict hired by a wealthy Chinese man to cry at his father's wake. This willingness to try new roles gives Sharon's image an adventurous quality, which has proven beneficial in her role as a brand endorser. Cecile Gabutina-Velez (in de Quiros 2010), an advertising executive, notes her 'universal appeal' and her possession of 'the credibility to embrace change and espouse new or revolutionary ideas'. In doing so, her star image places emphasis on her adventurousness and a desire to seek positive change.

Sharon's role in *Caregiver* exemplifies these themes. The film focuses on Sarah (Sharon) and her attempts to regain control of her life. At the beginning of the film, she follows the plans made by her husband Teddy, who wants her to join him in the UK where he has been looking for work as a nurse, and eventually migrate there with their son. She leaves her teaching career and her son in the Philippines to work in the UK as a caregiver, but she discovers that Teddy has been unable to find a job as a nurse and has taken a position as a hospital janitor instead. Owing to the difficulties he has faced, he decides that they should return to the Philippines. She agrees to his plan yet again, but when they arrive at the airport, she changes her mind and decides to stay in the UK, telling him that there is nothing for her in the Philippines (even though her son and family are there). The two separate and the final scene shows Sarah reunited with her son in the UK years later.

Caregiver associates migrant work with Sarah's empowerment by framing it as something she has chosen rather than something that has been forced upon her. Although working in the UK was initially Teddy's idea, Sarah's migrant labour gives her the opportunity to free herself from her husband's control. This choice, however, is restricted to middle-class professionals like Sarah, Teddy and another Filipino character called Joseph, who is a doctor in the Philippines but becomes a nurse in the UK. While their choices involve moving to a career that is perceived as a downgrade from their previous occupations, they can achieve greater financial stability than they would have had in the Philippines.

The film represents not only migrant labour, but also the struggle to overcome the difficulties that migrant workers face. Sarah keeps her problems to herself, confiding occasionally in Karen, a fellow caregiver, while Teddy suffers from his failure to find a position as a nurse. Aside from Karen and Joseph, the couple do not have other OFW friends to share their problems with. One reason for this is because Teddy forbids Sarah to mingle with other women who work as 'DH' or domestic helpers – in his mind, his and Sarah's professional degrees and middle-class backgrounds distinguish them from the low-skilled domestic workers who usually come from a lower social class. Ironically, his job as a janitor and Sarah's caregiving job are not too dissimilar to the domestic work he looks down on. By invoking their class distinction, he removes them from the collective migrant experience and compels them to personalise their struggles.

As a female-centred film, *Caregiver* puts the spotlight on its main star, Sharon, whose star persona shapes the representation of Sarah's life. For example, Sarah's characterisation as a supportive wife is enhanced by Sharon's star image. Sarah decides to leave her job and sacrifice her promotion in order to follow her husband's plan, which is similar to Sharon's experience when she moved to the USA when her second husband was studying there (David 2015: 316). Another parallel stems from the emphasis on Sarah as self-sacrificial and long-suffering. Even though Teddy lies to Sarah about his job, she forgives him and also turns a blind eye to his drunkenness and consumerist behaviour. The film also shows her enduring the difficulties of her job, like working long hours and doing 'dirty' tasks, such as wiping a resident's bottom. The long-suffering character is a component of Sharon's *'perpetwal na birhen'* (perpetual virgin) image, which Rolando Tolentino has discussed (in David 2015: 316). David (2015: 316) cites Tolentino, describing this image as being meek, obedient, patient, kind and virtuous, characteristics which corroborate Sharon's wholesome image discussed above.

Caregiver showcases, however, another side of Sharon's star persona – her feistiness. In rereading Sharon's image, David (2015: 326) argues that she is a *dulsita*, a combination of her 'perpetual virgin' image with feistiness (326). The term is a portmanteau of the Spanish terms *dulce*, which means sweet, and *maldita*, which means feisty (326). David describes the *dulsita* image as involving a transformation from being weak and subservient into becoming a fighter who stands up against her enemies (327). Two scenes from *Caregiver* demonstrate this *dulsita* persona. In one of these, Teddy comes home enraged because Sarah was unable to prepare dinner for him since she was working longer hours. She offers to cook, but Teddy harshly replies that he will just go to bed. She retorts that she will cook anyway even if he does not eat, which begins to show her shift away from her earlier servile attitude towards her husband. The other scene is more climactic and involves Sarah calling out the abuse she experiences from Mr Morgan, a grumpy wealthy resident she is assigned to look after, who gives her a difficult time and talks to her as though she is a lowly servant.

While she has previously endured this treatment, this time she fights back, confronting Mr Morgan with a litany of sacrifices she has made for her 'thankless job'. She tells him, 'I care about my job, Sir! I care about you.' This instance transforms her character from being a meek caregiver to one who stands up for herself.

Sharon's stardom also contributes to the meaning of the film through her bringing glamour to the difficult and sometimes dirty work of care giving. Marketed as Sharon's comeback film after several years away from the cinema, *Caregiver* includes numerous close-up shots of the star, not all of which are motivated by the narrative. The star's glamour, which is enhanced by the shots of London, shown through the touristy treatment of the city in the film's *mise-en-scène*, helps mask the nature of care giving: dirty, dangerous and difficult. Additionally, London's representation as a cosmopolitan city lends overseas work a sense of modernity that could attract Filipino workers. Outside the film text, *Caregiver*'s promotion and marketing events reinforced the spectacularisation of overseas work. For instance, the film's premiere was a glitzy showbusiness affair. One entertainment reporter wrote about the Hollywood-style premiere of the film in SM Megamall, which was attended by Sharon, the director Chito Roño, and a number of other stars (Dimaculangan 2008), while another described the long lines of fans waiting outside Alex Theater in Glendale, California, hours before the screening started (Llanes 2008).

This use of Sharon's stardom plays a role in diminishing the political dimensions of migrant labour. Although the film represents some of the difficulties that Sarah faces as part of the migrant workforce, Sharon's stardom brings forward notions of individual agency. From this perspective Sharon helps audiences accept that Sarah's decision to remain in the UK to work as a caregiver is her own 'choice', rather than something she had to do, and in doing so the film and the star disengage migrant work from the larger discussions surrounding labour export. As King (in Dyer 1998: 27) has argued, the star can 'promote depoliticised modes of attachment (i.e. acceptance of the status quo) in its audience. The stars promote a privatisation or personalisation of structural determinants, they promote a mass consciousness in the audience'. In *Caregiver*, Sharon personalises the migrant work experience, shifting attention towards her glamorous stardom and notions of individual agency and away from the collective struggles and strength of the Filipino migrant workers.

Conclusion

As the above discussion shows, stars have served different ideological purposes in OFW films, in line with the larger evolving discourses on migrant work. Nora's performance as Contemplacion stresses the potential of the star image to generate collective action in responding to a migrant's suffering, which *The Flor Contemplacion Story* frames as caused by the nation state's LEP. The film politicised Contemplacion's death, and Nora's star text aided in raising political awareness among audiences. As noted, Nora's star text has the capacity to evoke collective sympathy and translate it into more productive energy that generates solidarity and action. Conversely, Sharon's OFW role established migrant work as a personal choice, which can empower and emancipate an individual. *Caregiver* uses her star image to articulate the character of Sarah, who takes risks and works to achieve her dream for her son. While *The Flor Contemplacion Story* presents migrant suffering in collective terms, in *Caregiver* it has been shown in a more glamorous and attractive light, while also being reduced to a personal, rather than a collective, experience. Here Sharon's star image has been used to disconnect migrant work from the politics of labour export and instead frame it as an individual choice. Tolentino (2009: 425) has observed that the use of stars in OFW films is part of a strategy to sell 'aspiration for [transnational] identity and regulate the flow and circulation of prospective and ongoing OCWs'. In other words, the star aids in naturalising migrant work. The star image, however, holds the potential to challenge this naturalised state. As Nora's case demonstrates, star images can serve to expose the dangers of labour export. What this chapter offers is a nuanced look at the ways star images engage with migrant work discourse. Stars, as ideological texts, can be employed to shape a film's discourses that either invite the audience to aspire for personal gain or evoke solidarity and collective action to respond to the everyday violence that OFWs experience in a foreign land.

References

Asis, Maruja M. B. (2017), 'The Philippines: beyond labor migration, toward development and (possibly) return', *Migration Policy Institute*, 11 July, <https://www.migrationpolicy.org/article/philippines-beyond-labor-migration-toward-development-and-possibly-return> (last accessed 19 June 2020).

Bach, Jonathan and M. Scott Solomon (2006), 'Labors of globalization: emergent state responses', *New Global Studies* 2:2, <https://doi.org/10.2202/1940-0004.1025>.

Campos, Patrick (2016), *The End of National Cinema: Filipino Film at the Turn of the Century*, Quezon City: University of the Philippines Press.

David, Jerick Josue (2015), 'Dulsita, ang Kabuuan ng Kontradiksyon ng Imahen ni Sharon Cuneta sa Pelikulang Pilipino', *Kritika Kultura* 25, pp. 314–43.

de Quiros, Melissa Andrea (2010), 'Top 10 most in-demand celebrity endorsers', *Spot. Ph*, 26 January, <https://www.spot.ph/entertainment/36607/top-10-local-celebrity-endorsers> (last accessed 18 June 2020).

Dimaculangan, Jocelyn (2008), 'Caregiver' international screenings', *PEP.ph*, <http://www.pep.ph/guide/movies/1992/updated-caregiver-international-screenings> (last accessed 23 September 2018).

Dyer, Richard (1998), *Stars*, new edition with supplementary chapter by Paul McDonald, London: BFI Publishing.

Flores, Patrick (2000), 'The dissemination of Nora Aunor', in Rolando B. Tolentino (ed.), *Geopolitics of the Visible: Essays on Philippine Film Cultures*, Quezon City: Ateneo de Manila University Press, pp. 77–95.

Guillermo, Alice (2000), 'The Filipino OCW in extremis', in Rolando B. Tolentino (ed.), *Geopolitics of the Visible: Essays on Philippine Film Cultures*, Quezon City: Ateneo de Manila University Press, pp. 107–24.

Levy, Emanuel (1995), 'The Flor Contemplacion Story', *Variety*, 10 December, <https://variety.com/1995/film/reviews/the-flor-contemplacion-story-1200444108/> (last accessed 20 June 2020).

Lim, Bliss Cua (2009), 'Sharon's Noranian turn: stardom, embodiment, and language in Philippine cinema', *Discourse: Journal for Theoretical Studies in Media and Culture* 31:3, 318–58.

Lim, Bliss Cua (2012), 'Fandom, consumption, and collectivity in the Philippine New Cinema: Nora and the Noranians', in Youna Kim (ed.), *The Precarious Self: Women and the Media in Asia*, London: Palgrave Macmillan, pp. 179–203.

Llanes, Rommel R. (2008), 'It's a sold-out "Caregiver" premiere in Glendale, California', *PEP.ph*, 6 June, <https://www.pep.ph/guide/movies/2066/it39s-a-sold-out-caregiver-premiere-in-glendale-california> (last accessed 1 June 2020).

Mapa, Claire Dennis (2020), 'Total number of OFWs estimated at 2.2 million', *Philippine Statistics Authority*, <https://psa.gov.ph/content/total-number-ofws-estimated-22-million> (last accessed 20 February 2021).

'Overseas Filipinos' cash remittances' (2020), *Bangko Sentral ng Pilipinas*, March, <http://www.bsp.gov.ph/statistics/keystat/ofw2.htm> (last accessed 20 June 2020).

Rodriguez, Robyn Magalit (2010), *Migrants for Export: How the Philippine State Brokers Labor to the World*, Minneapolis: University of Minnesota Press.

Tadiar, Neferti X. M. (2002), 'Himala (miracle): the heretical potential of Nora Aunor's star power', *Signs: Journal of Women in Culture and Society* 27:3, pp. 703–41.

Tan, Katrina (2017), 'Spectacularization of overseas work in commercial films', *UPLB Journal* 15:1, pp. 151–61.

Thumin, Janet (1986), '"Miss Hepburn is humanized": the star persona of Katharine Hepburn', *Feminist Review* 24, 71–102.

Tolentino, Rolando B. (2009), 'Globalizing national domesticity: female work and representation in contemporary women's films', *Philippine Studies* 57:3, 419–42.

Tsui, Clarence (2015), 'Taklub': Cannes review, *The Hollywood Reporter*, <https://www.hollywoodreporter.com/review/taklub-cannes-review-796465> (last accessed 23 September 2018).

Chapter 9

One more second chance: love team longevity and utility in the era of the television studio

Chrishandra Sebastiampillai

On 25 November 2015, *A Second Chance* (Cathy Garcia Molina) was released by Philippine production company Star Cinema. The film broke Filipino box office records, earning figures that redefined previously accepted ideas of success in contemporary popular Philippine cinema. In 2019, it was the sixth highest grossing Filipino film of all time at PHP556 million (US$11.7 million) and one of only seven local films to gross more than half a billion pesos. The love team films of John Lloyd Cruz and Bea Alonzo have been perennial tent poles for ABS-CBN since 2002, working together in seven *teleserye* (television series) and eight films. The pair are a product of the modern television studio and yet they also hark back to the love teams of the past in Philippine cinema in their construction.

Mainstream filmmaking in the Philippines was dominated by the television studio ABS-CBN,[1] a sprawling multimedia conglomerate owned by the Lopez family. It has multiple arms within the entertainment industry including television channels such as ABS-CBN 2, mainstream and 'maindie' filmmaking companies in Star Cinema and Skylight Films respectively, the Star Studio magazine, DZMM-AM, a radio station, and even the means to transmit internationally via their global subscription television network, The Filipino Channel. ABS-CBN took over the creation of stars and films from the more traditional film studios of the past, dominating the industry from the 1990s onwards. This chapter will examine the studio's chief export of love teams and romance films, particularly the marketing and management of the popular long-term Cruz–Alonzo love team. With a shared history of nineteen years together, their love team is particularly successful with a unique nostalgia and evolution shared with the audience. It explores how the television studio utilises love teams, and how this compares historically to prior Philippine studios. It considers how the love team is marketed through social media, particularly Instagram, and examines how *A Second Chance* and its publicity is informed by the history and longevity of the Cruz–Alonzo love team.

The role of the studio and its employees in shaping and marketing the love team image, and how that role has evolved to embrace the new possibilities offered by social media, illustrate an evolving empire that employs both the traditional tactics of 1950s Philippine studios as well as contemporary marketing strategies. These traditional strategies extend to creating a family atmosphere at the studio that demands accountability and upright moral character from its stars, plots that promote good Christian values, and a vigorous studio that develops, trains and governs stars. The entrance of social media into the marketing practices of the studio devolves the traditionally held power of publicity from the studio elite and distributes it into the hands of its many employees and consumers. *A Second Chance* marks the eighth film collaboration of the love team and was built entirely on nostalgia, shared history and more informally perceived methods of marketing via the social media accounts of key personnel working closely with the stars.

The television studio as film and star maker

The rise of the television network studio as the dominant force in star and film production began in the early 1990s with ABS-CBN. Tired of paying exorbitant talent fees for freelancing stars or negotiating with established film studios to hire their talent, ABS-CBN built its own stable of exclusive stars to be paid fees that they could control (Paredes 2012). Subsequently, ABS-CBN Talent Development and Management Centre (now known as Star Magic) was set up in 1992, grooming aspiring teenagers to become stars for ABS-CBN, first on television and then in cinema (Paredes 2012).

This decision yielded several benefits – reasonably priced home-grown talent, a more manageable talent fee for big stars who now had competition, and the ability to make their own films, possessing both the infrastructure and talent rather than paying to redistribute films made by film studios. This led to the establishment of Star Cinema, the filmmaking arm of ABS-CBN, which dominates contemporary film production. GMA (the main rival of ABS-CBN at the time) soon followed suit and thus, television studios took control of the production and deployment of stars, once the sole domain of film studios. In making films and stars, the studio employed a strategy that has been effective in Philippine cinema from the very outset – love teams in romance films.

A love team is a film couple, two stars whose personas combine to create a joint image of coupledom in Philippine cinema. Sometimes love teams are one-off pairings, while other love teams are recurring couples that run for years of onscreen partnership. Through their multiple performances together they are able to convey more nuanced and complicated notions of love, gender, class and many other ideologies (Nochimson 2002: 6). Love teams and romance films are an ideal form of risk management for studios as they are a tried and tested formula used since the very beginning of Philippine cinema in its early adaptations of the *sarsuwela*, or musicals with romance plots originating in the theatre (Tiongson 1983: 87). The fact that both stars are owned by ABS-CBN and paid controlled fees means that it is financially viable and a guarantee of profit for studios to cast them repeatedly in love team projects. In return, the tandem also represents a promise to the audience of the same quality and unique brand of entertainment and romance that their tandem provides.

Cruz and Alonzo are veteran talents of ABS-CBN and thus hold privileged positions in the studio. Their joint image combines Cruz's friendly and approachable boy-next-door persona with Alonzo's more reserved, elegant and professional one. Where Cruz has a specific talent for relating with the public, Alonzo has the poise to make them look good while they do it. Both are endorsers of several fashion and beauty products and share a passion for fine clothes, which ensures that their combined image is mature and fashionable. This marks a contrast from their early partnership when sneakers, t-shirts and trendy teenage hairstyles were the norm. As they have grown older, their image has become a throwback to the stars of the past with glamour emphasised but without alienating the public because of their much more accessible personas and modest backgrounds, which they emphasise in their interviews. They both share *mestizo* ('mixed ethnicity') good looks, another long-standing tradition of Philippine cinema still as relevant today as a condition for stardom as it was in the 1940s (Figure 9.1).

At the height of their work together, both stars worked to maintain family-friendly personas. Alonzo is especially scandal-free, with only the standard speculation about her love life sometimes in the press. With Cruz the matter is less simple, and rumours of alcoholism circulated in the late

Figure 9.1 Cruz and Alonzo star in *A Second Chance*. Star Cinema and ABS-CBN Film Productions Inc.

2000s. These were mostly suppressed in everything but tabloids, which demonstrates the ability of ABS-CBN to regulate press about their stars through their impressive cross platform media ownership. His charm in interviews and air of 'niceness' helps dispel any doubts that remain, and often other stars come off worse in any mudslinging against him.[2] Talent managers also work hard to ensure the good behaviour of their charges with a fining system implemented for misdemeanours. This echoes the strict code of behaviour and conduct that studios of the past insisted on for their stars, who were rigorously trained in aspects that included acting, etiquette, posture, dress and elocution (Almajose and Ramos 2013: 16). Scandals were carefully covered up, but recurring misbehaviour would earn the displeasure of the head of the studio, something that stars were careful to avoid then, and remain wary of today.

The professional teams that surround the couple keep them in peak condition. Talent managers, handlers, road managers, stylists, hair and makeup artists, acting coaches, directors and producers keep their stars current, appropriately exposed and scandal-free. This is aided by the sense of family that the studios cultivate. Early Philippine studios were family owned and run, usually with the patriarch or matriarch of the family in daily contact and administration of the studio, such as Doña Sisang of LVN Pictures and Doc Perez of Sampaguita Pictures. ABS-CBN is owned by the Lopez family who have members working in various positions in the conglomerate. Supervising Star Cinema and ABS-CBN at the peak of the Cruz–Alonzo love team were the Santos sisters who were executive producers of all the films that came out of the studio. The stable of talent is respectful of the women and defers to them in all matters. In this manner, the family-oriented running of the studios of the past lives on. This is reinforced by the name that ABS-CBN has for its employees and viewers – *kapamilya*, which means 'family member'. As in the past, loyalty to the mother studio is paramount, and stars openly declare their gratitude and affection for the studio. Cruz and Alonzo's success is due in no small part to team members who have worked with them long term, such as noted romance film director Cathy Garcia Molina, screenwriters Carmi Raymundo and Vanessa Valdez, their talent managers who have been with them for their entire careers and their relationship with the Santos sisters at the top of the studio hierarchy. Charo Santos-Concio (President of ABS-CBN Corporation 2008-16) recognised their worth early on, cast them together originally and has taken an interest in their tandem, personally championing their projects.

Another throwback to the first studios is the plots of the films that are made. LVN Pictures was always meticulous in ensuring that their films taught good values and that right would prevail (Almajose and Ramos 2013: 8). This is echoed in modern Star Cinema releases, though of course some latitude exists for modern times. Perhaps modern stars may show a little more skin, but at heart, the values they embody are as relevant today as they were in the 1950s – loyalty, filial piety, sacrifice, truthfulness, faithfulness and commitment. Clear distinctions are usually made between right and wrong, and prize talents are carefully cast in appropriate roles. Cruz and Alonzo are always cast as *bida* or protagonists and care is taken to ensure that they do not portray unlikeable characters or *kontrabida* (antagonists) onscreen.

These values echo the majority Catholic values of the Philippines. Christianity is often portrayed in films, sometimes with a church scene such as a wedding, or at other times in the plot with prayer and blessings bestowed upon loved ones. Elements of Catholicism follow in other aspects of the studio, such as the ABS-CBN chaplain (known as the Showbiz Priest) who holds thanksgiving masses during successful releases and other occasions at the studio. Prayers and thanksgiving are a central element to the operation of the studio, with most shoots beginning with a prayer led by the director and some television programmes ending with 'To God Be The Glory' in the credits. The end goal of many romance films tends to be a wedding or a committed relationship leading to one. As the plot comes to closure, traditional values of marriage and heteronormativity are reinforced.

But the main form of divergence in the way the studios and love teams of old and present operate lies in technological differences and opportunities for fan engagement that modern social media presents. The Cruz–Alonzo love team has recently become a cross-platform digital and social media presence while younger tandems are native to social media (Bolisay (2019) examines a popular young love team's fandom on Twitter). Where once there were social events, press releases, newspaper interviews and profiles, there are now also concerts, albums, world tours, television appearances, engagement with online fan communities and the smooth publicity machine that characterises ABS-CBN, extending even into the social media accounts of its employees. Managers, handlers, road managers, writers, directors, authors, music executives, crew members and cast members all work to casually promote stars and films. With a single picture upload or status update by the right individual, fans speculate and in turn provide publicity through their social media sharing and discussion of the text. Because their work together pre-exists social media, the Cruz–Alonzo love team are an ideal site to examine the ways ABS-CBN adhere to traditional methods of star production and dissemination and how they transitioned to include social media as a key tool in their publicity machinery. Publicity on *A Second Chance* was from the very outset almost entirely a social media production supplemented by the official branch of ABS-CBN's marketing division.

Love team nostalgia and Instagram

Because Cruz and Alonzo have worked together so long, their films have had to innovate to remain relevant. They can no longer rely on simple boy-meets-girl or love triangle formulas, resulting in more sophisticated projects which they excel in because of the trust and relationship they have with each other and their audience. They began to innovate in their fourth film, *One More Chance* (Cathy Garcia Molina) in 2007. At the time, the plot was reasonably unique: a couple, Popoy and Basha, have been together for some time in a committed relationship that everyone assumes will end in marriage. They are middle-class early career professionals, with a close-knit group of friends, who go through a rough patch and break up. The film was very popular upon release, in part because of its many melodramatic quotable lines that immediately entered popular culture ('She loved me at my worst. You had me at my best . . . And you chose to break my heart'); in part because of the relatable nature of a break-up narrative and the characters featured in it; in part because of the director who is well-known for her work in the popular romance genre, particularly with Cruz and Alonzo; and in part because the love team a generation of Filipinos had grown up with, whom they had watched fall in easy, perfect love so many times before on film and television was facing the same real struggles that everyone else in real life did. In short, this was not a perfect happily-ever-after romance film but rather the anatomy of a break-up accompanied by a soaring and oft-played theme song, 'I'll Never Go' by Erik Santos, itself a cover of a nostalgic Philippine song released in the mid-1990s. Of course, in the end, the two are seen patching up their relationship, hence the title *One More Chance*. This film definitively marked a shift in their careers to more complex narratives and cemented their image as the love team of their generation. It remained their most popular film and the one that generated the most interest among fans.

A Second Chance was marketed in a radically different way from the love team's previous films – a testament to the power of social media and the comprehensive team structure built around the stars. Their previous film, *The Mistress* (Olivia Lamasan, 2012), came out at a time when the studio was still learning how to use social media in their favour. Instagram would prove to be a useful tool in the Philippines, a nation that has held the record globally for the most social media use for three years in a row (Kemp 2018). Nostalgia plays a big role with the sharing of images on social media, a phenomenon aptly documented by the popular hashtags #ThrowbackThursday, #TBT, #FlashbackFriday and #FBF. The marketing for the tandem and film embodies this nostalgia and features a series of cues that reference the past to fans. *A Second Chance* provides a good case study of the strategies used by the studio to market their love team while also allowing the love team's longevity and resultant audience nostalgia to drive the narrative of that promotion.

The marketing of *A Second Chance* began before a sequel was even announced, with initial publicity built around the nostalgia and love for *One More Chance*. It began on 13 December 2014, when key members of the cast and crew assembled at Bellini's, the location of a particularly emotional scene in the first film. The restaurant had since become a place of pilgrimage for fans of the film seeking the chance to sit at the same table as Cruz/Popoy and Alonzo/Basha. The restaurant played on this attraction, marking the chairs that the stars had sat on with their names, the title of the film, and the director's name. The meeting consisted of several people significant to the film – the love team, its two writers, and the director. Several pictures appeared on Instagram of the occasion, evoking the nostalgia of the place and the people reunited after seven years. The presence of a camera at the meeting raised questions of what might be going on after all this time – would there be a sequel? The date of the meeting was no coincidence – 12.13.14, echoing a favourite moment from the conclusion of *One More Chance* when Popoy promises to love Basha for '12, 13, 14 [years] . . . Forever and ever!' (Figure 9.2).

The photos include the five of them at the infamous table, another with the famous neon sign bearing the restaurant's name, and crucially, a throwback image to seven years ago when they gathered during the production of the original film, pre-dating the existence of Instagram (Raymundo 2014). These images were shared on the Instagram account of Carmi Raymundo, one of the two writers of the original film. Star Cinema, the filmmaking arm of ABS-CBN posted images of the event on their official website ('#SNAPSHOTS: Team "One More Chance" Reunites' 2014). They rapidly became the source of gossip, appearing on the ABS-CBN news website featuring an official comment from Star Cinema that remained ambiguous about a sequel but stated that a project

Figure 9.2 The iconic quote from the Cruz and Alonzo film, *One More Chance*. Star Cinema and ABS-CBN Film Productions Inc.

related to the film would be announced in January 2015. Speculation on a sequel was raised in the opening sentence of the same article, demonstrating ABS-CBN's powerful ability to present a mystery, pose a question and supply answers through three different channels. Raymundo's Instagram post was particularly effective because it seemed like a glimpse into a personal moment with the cast and crew rather than the crafted formality of an official press release, a tone reinforced by Raymundo's personal reflection of gratitude that accompanied the pictures in captions.

Instagram allowed ABS-CBN to exploit the film's visuals to market the love team – a key aspect of their success. Pictures released on the Star Cinema site included a close-up of the detail of the backs of the love team's chairs, with their names stencilled in white fading paint on the backs and supplemented with new plastic name tags. The chairs are symbols laden with meaning, representing the history of the tandem with the fading white paint a testament to their longevity. Seven years had passed since they had sat there and created an iconic cinematic moment, with a drunken and distraught Popoy breaking down and confronting Basha, spawning the oft-memed and repeated quote listed in any collection of quotes from the film:

> 'Bash, don't you know about the three month rule? Everyone who has been in love and broken up knows it. Bash, you wait for three months. Three months, and only then you have another boyfriend. Don't you know that? Bash, I still have two weeks left.'

Within the film, the restaurant functioned comparably to Central Perk in *Friends*, with the young group of friends meeting there regularly to catch up with each other and celebrate all their important milestones. Bellini's and its chairs thus represented the highest and lowest points of the relationship between Basha and Popoy in *One More Chance*, forming the emotional centre of the film. And the new name tags on the chairs invited speculation of what would happen to the pair now.

The next step on the publicity for *A Second Chance* was the announcement of the novelisation of *One More Chance* in June 2015, released on Star Cinema's website. The book was promoted heavily on official Instagram accounts related to ABS-CBN and more subtly by the handler of Alonzo, Monch Novales, on her personal account. Novales posted two collages of the pair consisting of four images each, featuring the pair in an intimate setting lounging on a hotel room bed, Alonzo in a bathrobe and Cruz reading the novel (Novales 2015). The pair are relaxed and playful, demonstrating the chemistry and close relationship that fans had come to expect from them. Later during the same trip, an ensemble concert by Star Magic talent in Spain, Raymundo posted another image to her personal account of the pair sharing a bowl of ice-cream along with a quote from the novel. The image was credited to Cruz's handler Nenette Demillo-Rustia. Road managers and handlers of the stars use their personal Instagram accounts to document their charges during publicity engagements and other candid off-camera moments, and in this case to help drive interest in the publishing of a novel that contributed to the formal announcement of an upcoming sequel in August 2015. This announcement was made during another event built on the nostalgia for *One More Chance* – this time the release of a re-mastered DVD of the film. Subsequently, a short documentary on the film was released, finally revealing the purpose of the meeting in Bellini's in December 2014.

Throughout filming, cast and crew uploaded images to personal social media accounts, including a cast party for Halloween featuring Cruz and Alonzo in matching pirate outfits and other intimate behind-the-scenes images. The work of promotion had moved from being solely the responsibility of a department and was now in the hands of cast, crew and even casual bystanders. The employees of ABS-CBN, particularly the unit built around the talent are key in framing their offscreen images without revealing the heavy machinery that the formal marketing team possesses. Fans in turn share the images on their personal social media accounts, spreading the publicity in a much more informal way than Star Cinema's publicity department can. The use of nostalgia as a selling point of the film was also vital, allowing the team to sell memories of a beloved film often described as the film that defined an era in the lives of young working adults who had grown up alongside the love team, while also making the promise of new memories to come. This meant that the promotion of *A Second Chance* hinged far less on its own merits but rather on the films that preceded it and the long and skilled careers of its beloved stars. The marketing of the film celebrated the longevity and durability of the pair's careers, a strategy continued in the immediate aftermath of the film's release in November 2015.

Once playing in cinemas, the marketing team released videos on social media and their television channel of other popular stars of ABS-CBN endorsing the film. Some of the stars were featured alone, with box office favourites Vice Ganda, Coco Martin and veteran star Dawn Zulueta encouraging viewers to watch the film, while other videos featured younger love teams – tandems who grew up directly influenced by the popularity and impact of the Cruz–Alonzo love team, popular with a much younger demographic than the contemporary fans of the love team. These young stars directly referenced the nostalgia for the first film and the veteran talent of Cruz and Alonzo, with several love teams including KathNiel (Kathryn Bernardo and Daniel Padilla) (mis)quoting the popular line 'You had me at my best, she had me at my worst' of *One More Chance*. These reaction videos work on several levels – firstly, they promote the film to television and social media audiences. Secondly, they reinforce the importance of the Cruz–Alonzo love team, both as popular stars as well as being an influence and inspiration to the careers of the new stars following in their footsteps. Finally, they also serve as a chance to promote themselves, directing viewers towards their own current projects while encouraging their fans to enjoy a favourite film of their favourite stars. Younger stars possess a formidable reach on social media with followers numbering in the millions and all willing to do the informal work of promoting their stars, and by extension, promoting *A Second Chance* and Cruz and Alonzo. Teen stars also appeared in person at the premiere of the film, a star-studded event that attracted significant media coverage and fan attendance, generating more content on social media.

Continuing with the theme of engaging fans for publicity, the marketing team also featured reaction videos by 'real-life couples' for their opinion on the love team and the film, filmed casually outside theatres after viewing *A Second Chance* (Star Cinema YouTube 2015). The official Star Cinema Instagram account updated the box office figures every time it broke a new record, which happened on its first, third and fifth days of running. Star Cinema executive Roxy Liquigan made the final announcement on his Instagram account at the end of its four-week run that it had created a new box office record – PHP556 million (US$11.7 million) ('"A Second Chance" Hits P566M in Box Office' 2015). The longevity and resulting nostalgia for the Cruz–Alonzo love team fuelled this success, but a key element was in the film itself, particularly in how the stars were used and its narrative, both reflecting on the history of the tandem and the first film while setting up new challenges to overcome.

Longevity and *A Second Chance*

A sequel is unusual in the Philippine romance genre where recurring screen couples rarely make direct sequels but more often a series of unrelated films together during the course of their careers. In Cruz and Alonzo and *One More Chance*, the studio had a guarantee that they were about to capitalise on. Both *One More Chance* and *A Second Chance* deal with themes of troubled committed relationships in crisis, with the plot working to bring the couple back together. The two films feature the love team in their ugliest moments: shouting, throwing breakables, crying, drunken self-hatred and bitter accusations. The Cruz–Alonzo love team excels in drama, evident from their *teleserye* and history of tearful parting scenes over the course of their partnership. Popoy and Basha are not perfect but flawed individuals who struggle to come to terms with the challenges of life and relationships.

Jovenal Velasco theorised in 2008 that the new Philippine screen man and woman are '"Feminized" Heroes and "Masculinized" Heroines', arguing that men were becoming softer and more in tune with their emotions while women abandoned traditional roles to instead provide for their families, or to embrace a modern liberated identity. Cruz certainly conforms to these broad strokes, projecting a softer and emotional masculinity – he cries frequently in his films. But Alonzo has in the past closely resembled the traditional *'babaeng martir'* (female martyr) (Tadiar 2002) instead of the modern masculinised heroine (for more on the *babaeng martir* see Tan's discussion of Nora Aunor and Sharon Cuneta in Chapter 8 of this book). In *A Second Chance*, Basha and Popoy appear disenchanted in their marriage of seven years. The marriage is on the rocks along with their business, verging on bankruptcy due to misfortune and mismanagement. After suffering a miscarriage, Basha (an architect), chooses to stay at home to aid the conception and safe pregnancy for a future baby. In her absence, Popoy (an engineer), faces many obstacles before crumbling under the weight of having sole responsibility for their construction company. The cause of the conflict is simple – he is a dreamer bent on building only the best, which in the case of the Philippines is calamity-proof housing. She is the realist, able to look at things with a clear head and eliminate the unnecessary to prioritise the vital. In the absence of her anchoring hand, Popoy's idealism invites calamity.

Popoy uses the word 'dream' often for houses, marriage and other hopes and aspirations. Conversely, Basha tends towards negating things or questioning the wisdom of them. 'Calamity-proof' has a dual meaning – firstly, the natural disasters that plague the Philippines and regularly destroy houses, which he wishes to remedy, and secondly, their marriage, which he hopes to keep intact by not speaking of the danger the company is in until Basha discovers it herself. Basha subsequently takes control of the situation herself, returning to work, speaking with clients, running site meetings and fixing the finances. Relegated to menial work, Popoy sinks into depression as his self-worth crumbles and is chipped at further by her negative comments daily. The first part of the film places Basha in the traditional female role of housewife while the second part sees her forcing Popoy into the same role against his wishes. Emasculated and heartbroken, Popoy considers working abroad to gain some measure of self-esteem while helping to pay off the debt of the company.

Thus, Alonzo is thrust into her first role that requires her not to just play at being a career woman, but to fight to keep a business afloat – where her job is central to the plot, not a minor detail mentioned in passing. And Cruz is a broken man trapped by his dreams and criticism from an overwhelmed wife trying her best to keep them solvent. His legendary charm ensures that the audience is sympathetic and his tearful speech to Basha that refers to the iconic line about being at his best in the first film also becomes memorable: 'I lost him. I lost the man you married, and I'm so sorry. This is me at my worst. Can you still love me? Can you honestly love a failure?' Alonzo for the first time not only suffers for her family – she rises above the suffering, claims a modern and independent identity for herself and saves not just her company but her marriage.

The film does not focus on a new romance or even a romantic plot. Instead, it depicts the difficulties of being married; the struggle of middle-class Filipinos in a difficult economy; and the importance of marrying idealism to pragmatism. Pursuing either one in isolation makes for disaster, but together, they do their best work. Popoy learns to allow Basha to be her own person and that that person is vital to their success, while Basha learns that being coldly capable can be isolating if effective. The film makes a persuasive argument for equal partnership between husband and wife and is unafraid to hack away at the traditionally sacred masculinity of its leading man. Cruz is particularly effective for this purpose because his masculinity is not a traditional one, but a gentler and more emotive one, with his charm able to sustain audience sympathy even as he sinks into a drunken, depressed mess. And Alonzo puts away the *martir* persona to fully and proactively take control rather than meekly accepting oppression as her fate.

Conclusion

One More Chance had Basha seeking more beyond what her boring and stifling relationship with Popoy gave her, while *A Second Chance* features masculinity in crisis with Basha stepping in to fix Popoy's missteps in handling their fledgling business. These are complex and unlikeable character beats that Cruz and Alonzo play, entire films about discord and angst made possible because the rest of their careers have shown them to be destined for one another as they navigate the different stages of a relationship, from puppy love to a rocky marriage. The subject matter is risky for a love team in its ambition to tackle the very real but ordinary problems of a middle-class married couple, and not something that a one-off love team would be able to carry off as successfully without the shared history of the love team to ground the ugly, unvarnished breakdown of a marriage. There is little glamour in the plot – instead there are the realities of debt, disillusionment, crumbling self-esteem and insecurity.

This is in contravention to one of the practices the studio has with its prize talents that is outlined above – taking care to avoid portraying negative or unsympathetic characters. It is a testament to their trust in these stars and their relationship with their audience that they can make a film that has their prize love team do everything that you should not do in a romance film but still have the audience satisfied with fewer than thirty minutes of screen time in a two hours and ten minutes long film in which the couple get along. This is made up for by including not just one, but two church weddings for the couple – a flashback to the original lavish and dreamy ceremony as well as a more grounded rededication at the end of the film. The memorable quotable lines make a reappearance and new lines are added to the collection. The work of the love team lies in making the old new again, an act of recreation they excel in with the trust of their audience.

A Second Chance and the love team of Cruz and Alonzo demonstrates many of the studio practices shared across decades and different iterations of studios in the Philippines. The strategy of love teams and romance films remains a sound investment for studios as proven in the record-breaking run of the film. This is aided by the specific joint image of Cruz and Alonzo which lends a distinct flavour to their partnership and projects together. For their part, the studio exerts care in their stewardship of this image through several strategies that include keeping star images clean by imposing sanctions and controlling the narrative through their impressive cross-media ownership and influence. The studio also takes care to assemble skilled professional teams that encourage a family environment at the studio, building on relationships between the team and the audience over the course of their work and the love team's career. The studio also chose a relatable plot that imparts good values and explores the identity of a contemporary middle-class Filipino couple in crisis while representing in their film the nation's majority religion and values of marriage and fidelity. The work of promoting stars has evolved to include modern means of social and cross platform media, democratically empowering the studio's entire staff as well as the public to perform the work of informal promotion through sharing, an ethos reflected in their shared history with the stars they have loved since 2002.

References

'"A Second Chance" Hits P566M in Box Office; Makes History as New Highest Grossing Filipino Film' (2015), *ABS-CBN*, 23 December, <http://ABSCBNpr.com/a-second-chance-hits-p566m-in-box-office-makes-history-as-new-highest-grossing-filipino-film/> (last accessed 2 July 2018).

Almajose, Kathy and J. V. Ramos (2013), *Kakaibang Tingin, Kakaibang Titig: An Appreciation of the Golden Period in Philippine Cinema*, Santo Tomas: La Abuela Publishing House.

Bolisay, Richard (2019), '"Yes, you belong to me!": reflections on the JaDine love team fandom in the age of Twitter and in the context of Filipino fan culture', *Plaridel* 16: 2, pp. 41–62.

'Drunk Anne Curtis slaps John Lloyd Cruz' (2013), *ABS-CBN News*, 3 December, <https://news.abs-cbn.com/entertainment/12/02/13/drunk-anne-curtis-slaps-john-lloyd-cruz> (last accessed 18 March 2021).

Kemp, Simon (2018), 'Digital in 2018: world's Internet users pass the 4 billion mark', *We Are Social*, 30 January, <https://wearesocial.com/blog/2018/01/global-digital-report-2018> (last accessed 2 July 2018).

Nochimson, Martha P. (2002), *Screen Couple Chemistry: The Power of 2*, Austin: University of Texas Press.

Novales, Monch (2015), '"Popoy and Basha Discussing the #onemorechance Book."' Instagram, 14 June, <https://www.instagram.com/p/35zBxRQ0Vc/> (last accessed 2 July 2018).

Paredes, Andrew (2012), 'Behind the magic, 20 years of star magic', *YES! Magazine*, July.

Raymundo, Carmi (2014), 'Carmi Raymundo on Instagram: "Photos Taken 7 Years Apart...."' Instagram, 14 December, <https://www.instagram.com/p/wkXAKtwgXt/> (last accessed 2 July 2018).

'#SNAPSHOTS: team "One More Chance" reunites' (2014), *Star Cinema*, 15 December, <https://starcinema.abs-cbn.com/2014/12/15/news/snapshots-team-one-more-chance-reunites-6775> (last accessed 2 July 2018).

Star Cinema, YouTube (2015), '"A Second Chance" Reactions Real Life Couples', YouTube, 1 December, <https://www.youtube.com/channel/UCgKeTXD5Jl9Eyk6hny4En4Q> (last accessed 2 July 2018).

Tadiar, Neferti X. M. (2002), 'Himala (miracle): the heretical potential of Nora Aunor's star power', *Signs: Journal of Women in Culture and Society* 27:3, pp. 703–41.

Tiongson, Nicanor G. (1983), 'From stage to screen: Philippine dramatic traditions and the Filipino film', in Rafael Ma Guerrero (ed.), *Readings in Philippine Cinema*, Manila: Experimental Cinema of the Philippines, pp. 83–94.

Velasco, Jovenal D. (2008), '"Feminized" heroes and "masculinized" heroines: changing gender roles in contemporary Philippine cinema?', *Philippine Studies: Have We Gone Beyond St. Louis?*, Diliman, Quezon City: University of the Philippines Press, pp. 444–54.

Notes

1. Since this chapter was originally written, several major changes have occurred. Cruz went on a showbiz hiatus in 2017 and became a father. ABS-CBN was shut down under the Duterte administration in May 2020, and subsequently the head of its Star Magic talent management arm, Johnny Manahan, left in September 2020, alleging the existence of a 'shadow talent centre' undermining the official management's work. Manahan moved to rival station TV5, where he works with several veteran talents of ABS-CBN. Alonzo is now managed independently and is currently in pre-production for a reunion film with Cruz, who is staging his comeback to showbusiness through the strength of their love team.
2. When another popular star, Anne Curtis, reportedly drunkenly slapped him and called him an addict in an upscale club, ABS-CBN and most mainstream coverage downplayed the label 'addict' and reported widely on Curtis's drunkenness and bad behaviour ('Drunk Anne Curtis slaps John Lloyd Cruz', 2013). Curtis does not belong to the ABS-CBN stable of stars.

Chapter 10

The changing status of the Thai *luk khrueng* (Eurasian) performer: a case study of Ananda Everingham

Mary J. Ainslie

Literally translated as a 'half-child', the *luk khrueng*[1] (Thai Eurasian) is a ubiquitous figure in Thai entertainment. Famous male and female *luk khrueng* performers such as Mario Maurer, Willy McIntosh, Nadech Kugimiya, Mick Tongraya, Krissada Sukosol Clapp, Eve Pancharoen and many more occupy a prime place in Thai music, advertisements, film and television, attracting both criticism and admiration for their talents and beauty. Possibly the most famous and successful of all *luk khrueng* performers in Thailand, however, is the actor and model Ananda Everingham, whose film career spans the birth of the New Thai industry from the late 1990s up to the present day. Publicity material, websites and blogs hail Ananda as the foremost Thai movie star, with the *Bangkok Post* describing the performer as a 'legend', who 'has been everything to everyone' (Panya 2016), while a co-star states 'I think of him as a superstar' (Bunnag 2016). Such accolades continue and demonstrate the longevity of Ananda's career, with one Bangkok blogger referring to the performer as '2010's man of the moment' (Ilbonito 2010b) and still 'one of the country's top box office draws' (Ilbonito 2010a). Indeed, Ananda's IMDb page lists over thirty-six films since the late 1990s, including significant box office hits such as the internationally renowned *Shutter* (*Shutter Kòt tìt Winyaan*, Banjong Pisanthanakun, 2004), *Shambala* (Panjapong Kongkanoy, 2012), *Ploy* (Pen-Ek Ratanaruang, 2007) and *Eternity* (*Chua faa din sa-laai*, M. L. Pundhevanop Dhewakul, 2010). The performer has also been an effective 'brand ambassador' for international companies and products in Thailand such as Seiko watches and Magnum ice cream and is credited with significantly increasing these product sales in Thailand. Despite such success, however, as the son of an Australian father and a Laotian mother (whose famous love story during the Cold War was portrayed in the Hollywood film *Love Is Forever* (Hall Bartlett, 1982)) Ananda only officially received full Thai citizenship in 2010, and has at times expressed ambiguity as to his overall relationship to Thailand and Thai-ness.

This chapter examines the position of the *luk khrueng* in contemporary Thailand, deploying Ananda and his film career as a case study through which to highlight some of the recent changes enacting upon representations of this figure. The chapter approaches the *luk khrueng* performer as a recognised signifier of 'cosmopolitanism and global mobility' that grew following the 1980s economic boom, and bespeaks the continuing rigid racial hierarchies that have shaped Thailand and Thai nationalism. It argues that such a construction has resulted in an advantageous yet still nevertheless restrictive social construction, in which the otherwise desirable *luk khrueng* is still 'othered' and not considered to be fully Thai. Exploring representations of the *luk khrueng* in Thai media and through attention to Ananda in particular, it highlights the construction of this figure as both a tragic misfit and highly feminised. Then, through examining Ananda's more recent roles which actually move away from dominant *luk khrueng* constructions, the chapter addresses how Thai constructions of race, gender and national belonging are becoming increasingly fluid in the globalised context. Finally, it ultimately questions whether such changes should be seen as entirely progressive, with the increased opportunities offered to performers such as Ananda unlikely to filter down to the provincial and marginalised minorities who were also subject to racial stereotyping, albeit at the bottom of the Thai social hierarchy.

The emergence of the *Luk Khrueng* performer

The popularity of the Eurasian figure in the late twentieth and early twenty-first centuries is a phenomenon often associated with non-Western countries and societies that were strongly affected by both European colonialism and later American imperialism. The lauding of Eurasian features can be typically interpreted as a lasting preference for white Western European-originating signifiers that reflects the previous global dominance of the European powers up to the early twentieth century and later the advent of American consumer capitalist culture since the end of the Cold War.

In Thailand specifically, such appeal can certainly be traced back to the colonial era and the endorsing of European models of dress and behaviour that were promoted by Thai elites as part of a quest to 'civilise' the nation, a discourse transliterated into Thai as *siwilai* (Thongchai 2000: 528-49). This was a delicate balancing act, as Thai elites were anxious to maintain their own control over this land and people in the face of a strong colonial presence in the region, so promoting a vehement (and at times contradictory) strain of nationalism at the same time they presented Western-ness as sophisticated and desirable.[2]

Despite the promotion of Western-orientated notions of 'civilisation' and the social elevation of this aesthetic, unlike in some other Southeast Asian nations the now-ubiquitous Caucasian-associated features of the Eurasian *luk khrueng* did not become desirable and prominent in Thai media until much later in the twentieth century. Instead, the *luk khrueng* as a figure was particularly derided in a position similar to that of the 'tragic mulatto' character of Classical Hollywood, and was not yet positioned as particularly desirable. This is reflected in Thai literature. In the famous Thai novel *Letters from Thailand*, first published in 1969, the main character, a Chinese immigrant to Thailand in the 1940s, speaks of how physically strange he finds a Caucasian Western woman who has married a local man. Yet this reaction is much more negative and pronounced when referring to the racial make-up of the supposed offspring:[3] 'if she bears her husband children, I expect they will look even more peculiar. Would they have pink skin, blue eyes, and black hair, I wonder? Or brown skin and red hair?' (Botan 1977: 127).

This very negative construction has specific origins. The number of *luk khrueng* people in Thailand increased dramatically after the Vietnam War and the stationing of over 50,000 troops in Thailand. At first, such people carried a strong social stigma, being constructed as 'outcasts' and 'leftovers' (Jiraporn 1996). Many, including those who were eventually to become media stars later in the century, such as actress Jarunee Suksawat, also either did not grow up with or did not know their Western fathers, while their mothers could be stereotyped as sex workers.

In Thai cinema, the post-Second World War 'golden age' of Thai cinema did not easily accommodate *luk khrueng* performers. With urban audiences fed by a steady stream of high-quality imported American films, the unfunded, unsupported and financially unstable indigenous industry targeted upcountry provincial viewers, urban lower-classes and those who were generally 'left behind' by the new modern and Americanised culture that was sweeping Thailand (see Boonrak 1992 and Ainslie 2017 for articles discussing this period). The films in this highly successful mass-produced low-budget era tended to depict situations pertinent to provincial Thai village life (most notably the effects of rural to urban migration, changes in gender roles and the encroachment of modernity) and incorporated a *mise-en-scène* of 'traditional' rural Thailand, including songs, clothing, and, notably, performers. Performers from this 'golden age' of Thai film were physically very recognisably Thai, the most famous of which, the dark-skinned Mitr Chaibancha, came from Phetchaburi province, south of Bangkok. After 1970 and the reorientation of Thai film towards more urban (though still largely lower-class) audiences, many films still tended to focus upon issues pertinent to the Thai experience at this time, including the developing social inequality connected to rapid urban growth and questions of what now constituted authentic *Thainess* (Sasinee 2020: 273).

It was in the 'teen industry' of the mid-1980s, a very much overlooked and often derided historical period in Thai film history, that the *luk khrueng* performer began to become a fixture of Thai entertainment. This period began due to the recognition of a new urban, modern teen audience and sparked an industrial reorganisation of the exhibition industry to cater for this viewer (Ingawanij 2006: 152–3). The Eurasian performer is therefore associated with Thailand's 1980s economic boom and entry into a global system of modernity, when urban centres swelled with rural migrants and the country became increasingly affluent. The increased ubiquity of *luk khrueng* performers in the late twentieth century then reflects the general worldwide increase in the number of mixed marital and cohabiting unions resulting from global migration, with mixed-race people becoming reflective of this social change (Aspinall 2018: 1991).

Macha Watthanaphanit (known as Marsha) was one of the first famous and successful *luk khrueng* performers in Thailand. Marsha began modelling and acting in the late 1980s, and is still an active performer today. Encouraged by her Thai aunt she went to a casting call and was noticed by agents, who decided they could use what they saw as her 'international' image, with much success. Originally, it appears that *luk khrueng* characters were somewhat masculinised. Marsha was originally cast in quite aggressive roles in films such as *Tamruat Lek* (Kom Akadej,

1986) and *Phetchakhat Si Chomphu* (Supharuek, 1988) and another well-known 1980s *luk khrueng* actress Jarunee Suksawat is described as being a 'tomboy' in her early roles (Wise Kwai 2013). In the early 1990s talent scouts then started targeting international schools, with performers identified when they were still in their early teens; Marsha was 'spotted' at age fifteen, while Ananda himself began acting in his mid-teens.

The increasing presence of *luk khrueng* performers on television soap operas (known as *Lakorn*) then followed in the 1990s, with the first (openly) *luk khrueng* 'Miss Thailand' in 1996. The first wave of *luk khrueng* stars then emerged, including Tata Young, Champagne X, Cindy Bishop and Willy McIntosh, most of whom combine acting, modelling and singing, and many of whom are still active today. *Luk khrueng* performers are now so ubiquitous in Thailand and so strongly associated with the entertainment industries that such individuals are even pushed into these careers regardless of personal desires or ability. *Luk khrueng* singer Lana Cummings laments this pressure, suggesting that her own aspirations and individuality are overlooked:

> If you're *luk khrueng*, you're almost expected to be in the entertainment business. I used to get really bored with that kind of expectation – people always seem to expect me to be a certain way – but really that's not what I'm about. (Kemasingki and Atkins 2008)

This frustration is echoed in this online forum posting from a father with a *luk khrueng* daughter, who felt that such pressures caused his daughter's own personal achievements to be ignored:

> I do get very irritated that 'Luk Kreung' ... are somehow automatically consigned to the 'Entertainment' field in their career prospects ... My own daughter – British father, Thai mother – graduated from ISB here in Bangkok, went on to attend the London School of Economics and is currently working at a very Senior level with a Multi-national Corporation in London. ('What do Thai people think about *luk kreung*' 2014)

Cosmopolitanism and Thai nationalism

In the contemporary Thai media industries, *luk khrueng* performers now appear frequently, and their construction adheres to the recognised complex signifiers of the mixed-race figure. Race and ethnicity must be recognised as an ongoing construction, with previous research tending to construct a binaristic 'black' and 'white' position while studies addressing the mixed-race position specifically are a relatively recent phenomenon. Dominant identity politics and postcolonial theory from the 1990s is generally inappropriate to exploring the mixed-race figure as the position is ultimately too varied and depends too heavily upon the speaker and their context (Matthews 2007: 42).

Recent scholarship highlights how increased interest in the representation and social position of Eurasian figures in countries such as Thailand is very different to both the previous colonial-era lauding of the 'civilising' Western world and the post-Second World War 'tragic' construction of the mixed-race person. Instead in the contemporary context, mixed-race attributes have become a sign of being internationally savvy, something that is increasingly a part of defining oneself as successful in the current globalised context. The term that encapsulates this 'success' and globalism is 'cosmopolitan,' defined as 'a commodity whose value lies in its diffuse associations with worldliness, refinement, enlightened sophistication, and intercultural aptitude' (Matthews 2007: 49); in the contemporary context 'Cosmopolitanism has become global merchandise and Eurasians are its principal conduit' (Matthews 2007: 49). Eurasian-ness has therefore become an embodiment and commodification of cosmopolitanism, globality, success and mobility, with scholars highlighting class, future prosperity and modernity as important variables associated with this figure (Aizura 2009: 304).

The increased visibility of the *luk khrueng* performer in wider Thai media since the 1980s reflects how this figure has become a desirable representation of cosmopolitan 'high culture', and an embodiment of the modernity and success associated with contemporary Thailand's entry into global consumer culture. The European whiteness the *luk khrueng* embodies functions as a 'classed physical feature', rather than a 'surface level' attempt at physical emulation (Aizura 2009: 304). Those in the Thai entertainment industry recognise and are very explicit about this appeal, with one 'talent scout' remarking 'My clients prefer them to present their products as they look more international' (Jiraporn 1996). Eurasian people themselves also acknowledge this appeal, with the *luk khrueng* Thai film and television performer Willy McIntosh similarly remarking upon these signifiers of globality, education and wealth, stating 'Eurasians look more international and many have a high degree of education ... Thais are attracted to that high quality of life' (Pruzin 1997).

Yet this positive construction of the *luk khrueng* is questioned and strongly critiqued by scholars of Thai studies (see, for example, Van Esterik 2000; Reynolds 2002; Persaud 2005). Rather than an emancipatory action, scholars see the lauding of the *luk khrueng* as part of an overall self-orientalising sexist and racist regime based upon older colonial hierarchies that strongly informed the post-1980s Thai adoption of global modernity (Persaud 2005: 214). The Caucasian whiteness of the *luk khrueng* is still central to the modernity and sophistication associated with this figure, who is then placed at the top of an internal racial hierarchy reminiscent of older European-originating colonial discourses. Darker and poorer provincial Thais are at the bottom and Bangkokian light-skinned elites at the top (see, for example, Streckfuss 2012; Keyes 2002); the cosmopolitan *luk khrueng* then reinforces such racism by operating as an aspirational pinnacle exemplifying the rewards of whiteness.

While this racist system may result in significant social advantages and economic opportunities for individuals, the general power relations which still govern notions of race, parentage and national belonging even into the twenty-first century, mean that the Thainess of the *luk khrueng* is also constantly under question. The mixed-race person is still subject to an intrusive gaze that stems from a general construction of the mixed-race body as 'abnormal' (Jin 2009: 73). This reflects the general struggle of mixed-race individuals to reconcile their own (often deeply personal and very complex) racialised experiences with society and the state's increasingly narrow racial categories (Yeoh et al. 2018: 4).

In Thailand, heightening these narrow racial categories and the 'abnormality' of the *luk khrueng* is the strong historical association between Thai nationalism and race. This constructed discourse was historically designed to subsume the many ethnically diverse citizens into a nation state by describing everyone as Thai. This created a mono-cultural mono-ethnic nation of authentic Thainess largely through 'forced inclusion'; to be a Thai citizen was to be of the Thai race, an ideal that is represented most completely by central Bangkokian Thainess (Streckfuss 2012: 307). While such a construction is deeply problematic in terms of its racist implications to the aspirations of darker-skinned provincial Thais, this ethnic homogenisation does not easily accommodate Western-associated features either. Along with the ethnic 'Other within', the West also functioned as an 'Other without' against which to construct authentic Thainess. Such 'Otherness' is still very apparent: while the adoption and use of the term 'Eurasian' can be seen as a 'category of resistance' against both avoiding the potential hazards of being 'uncategorised' and the previous lexicon of derogatory terms such as 'mongrel' 'half-caste' and the question 'where are you from' (Matthews 2007: 47), the term *luk khrueng* still remains the primary Thai axiom to describe the mixed-race body. This operates as a linguistic signifier of this abnormality and lack of belonging, often translated into the English-language description of 'she/he's a half'.

This lack of belonging is also played out through assumptions made about *luk khrueng* peoples' national belonging. For instance, one Western parent of a *luk khrueng* child describes the Thai attitude towards *luk khruengs* as 'schizophrenic', further stating 'On the one hand they are not Thai, on the other they are handsome, beautiful, talented stars!' ('What do Thai people think about *luk kreung*' 2014). Such a statement highlights the continuing lack of acceptance of Eurasian people as 'truly' Thai and the extent to which Thai discourses of national belonging are still integrated with race. Another parent describes their Eurasian child's difficulty at a Thai school: '[the] Teacher [is] more interested in my daughter's hair and fingernails because she is a *luk khrueng* rather than her learning anything' ('What do Thai people think about *luk kreung*' 2014), indicating how the child's 'othered' Eurasian body invites scrutiny at the expense of educational interactions. Even as the top film star in Thailand, Ananda himself also expresses his own sense of disconnection within Thailand, highlighting his inability to 'fit' into both Thai and Australian society due to his mixed-race status: 'I definitely have an identity crisis. I'm not Australian; I'm not Thai at all ... When I went to school in Australia, I didn't feel Australian. I had issues of fitting in. And Thais [also] treat different people differently' ('Q&A: Ananda Everingham' 2008).

The *luk khrueng* in post-97 Thai film

While *luk khrueng* figures may be somewhat ubiquitous in Thai media, their depiction in the big budget internationally savvy post-97 New Thai film industry reflects this reductive and problematic status. Further highlighting the connection between race and national belonging, films in the New Thai industry that purport to represent nationalist topics and discourses seemed to avoid casting *luk khrueng* performers. Certainly, highly nationalistic films such as the historical epic *Bang Rajan* (Bang Rajan: The Legend of the Village Warriors, Tanit Jitnukul, 2000) and *Suriyothai* (The Legend of Suriyothai, Chatrichalerm Yukol, 2001), do not contain recognisably *luk khrueng* performers. Likewise, *muay thai* boxing films, a very successful film genre in the New Thai industry and a topic heavily attached to Thai nationalism and tradition (see Pattana 2007 and Vail 2014 for in-depth discussions of this link), also tend to shy away from *luk khrueng* performers. This is evident in successful high grossing films such as *Ong-Bak* (*Ong-Bak: Muay Thai Warrior*, Prachya Pinkaew, 2003), *Tom Yum Kung* (*The Protector*, Prachya Pinkaew, 2005) and *Koet Ma Lui* (*Born to Fight*, Panna Rittikrai, 2004) (see Ancuta's discussion of *muay thai* cinema in Chapter 11 of this book for more about this genre).

Instead, films which directly address the mixed-race *luk khrueng* often place these characters within an overly negative narrative of violence and/or tragedy. Such a construction speaks of both Jin Haritaworn's (2009) 'intrusive' gaze upon the mixed-race body and position as well as the overall assumed 'lack' of identity and belonging associated with this figure as a misfit who is not truly Thai. For instance, *Thirteen Beloved* (*13 Game Sayong*, Chukiat Sakveerakul, 2006) depicts the *luk khrueng* Chit as the victim of an unstable childhood and a violent white Western father. *Killer Tattoo* (*Mue Puen Lok Phra Chan*, Yuthlert Sippapak, 2001) involves a character expressing their dislike of foreigners to a violent *luk khrueng* character, who is then shot by the protagonist. The historical drama *The Siam Renaissance* (*Tavipob*, Surapong Pinijkhar, 2004) depicts its time-travelling French-educated *luk khrueng* protagonist learning how to 'be' traditionally Thai and warning of the threat of Western influence in modern Thailand.

Ananda's long career reflects this dominant construction of the *luk khrueng*, with media products directly engaging with the 'internationalised' and cosmopolitan connotations of the performer's ethnicity, as well as raising questions around issues of identity and national belonging. The narratives of many of Ananda's films directly engage with the *luk khrueng* experience, depicting this as a difficult negotiation of two separate worlds, a familiar construction of the mixed-race experience. Films such as *Hi-So* (Aditya Assarat, 2010), *Sway* (Rooth Tang, 2014) and *Concrete Clouds* (Lee Chatametikool, 2013) follow a troubled character returning to Thailand from the West or considering emigrating from Thailand to the West. *Hi-So* in particular explicitly represents (and highlights) the contradictory position of the *luk khrueng*, with the film set over two separate parts which both see the character negotiating Thai and Western relationships. Similarly, *Concrete Clouds* involves Ananda's character choosing between Thai and Western partners and locations, again with a bittersweet and melancholic unfinished resolution.

The internationalised cosmopolitanism associated with the *luk khrueng* figure is also represented in the significant number of Ananda's films set in or taking place outside of Thailand and also made in the wider Asia region, including *Shambhala, Pleasure Factory* (Ekachai Uekrongtham, 2007), *Sabaidee Luang Prabang* (Sakchai Deenan and Anousone Sirisackda, 2008), *Love H20* (*Kon Ook Hak*, Suttasit Dechintaranarak, 2015) and *Sway. Fatherland* (*Pitupoom*, Yuthlert Sippapak, 2012) is also set in the south of Thailand and *Happy Birthday* (Pongpat Wachirabunjong, 2008) also involves travelling to other parts of Thailand. Promotional material for Ananda's brand ambassador role for Seiko watches also builds upon this internationalised image, with the performer positioned as an 'adventurer', in one image dressed in scuba gear and another standing next to a Land Rover. Seiko even uses the slogan 'Fusion of Perfection' next to an image of Ananda and the product, so directly referencing the performer's mixed-race status and highlighting the desirability of this particular biological 'fusion'.

Gender stereotyping: the feminisation of the *luk khrueng*

Alongside such narrow constructions, the *luk khrueng* is also strongly feminised within Thailand, becoming a literal 'gendered embodiment of racialisation' (Aizura 2009: 309). This is reflected in wider research, in which the mixed-race and Eurasian figure is often represented or analysed purely as female: in Matthews's very influential paper, for instance, references to Eurasianness almost completely construct this body as feminine (Matthews 2007). The *luk khrueng* attributes of white flawless skin, a high bridged narrow nose and double-fold eyelids are associated with an idealised version of femininity, and one which contrasts with the Orientalised construction of Thai women as imagined within the West (Aizura 2009: 307), with female performers embodying a hypersexual hyperfemininity (Jin 2009: 66).[4] The advantages associated with the aforementioned celebratory and desirable discourses of internationalism and cosmopolitanism are therefore profoundly different for Eurasian men and women, with Eurasian femininity becoming particular marketable (Jin 2009: 60).

In the contemporary Thai film industry, this gendered construction is reflected in the seemingly narrow range of roles open to male *luk khrueng* performers. Such performers most often appear as romantic leads, particularly in Thai *Lakorn* and also in successful Thai urban-based romantic metrosexual-esque comedy films. The latter association recalls the metrosexual 'Soft Masculinity' embodied in East Asian cultural products, particularly those of the Korean Wave, popular across East and Southeast Asia since the mid-2000s (see Jung 2009; Song 2016; Louie 2012 for discussions of this phenomenon). 'Soft Masculinity' is a progressive form of hybrid masculinity involving both increased recognition of female agency and a more flexible and inclusive model of masculinity in East Asia (Louie 2012). Yet in contrast to the much more mono-racial societies of Japan and South Korea where Soft Masculinity challenges traditional notions of masculinity, in Thailand this phenomenon instead affirms the feminised racial stereotype of the *luk khrueng*, so losing its progressive connotations from the East Asian context.

The male *luk khrueng* Thai figure seems to embody this Soft Masculinity in films such as *Heart Attack* (*Freelance: Ham puay . . . Ham phak . . . Ham rak* mor, Nawapol Thamrongrattanarit, 2015), *I Fine . . . Thank You . . . Love You* (Mez Tharatorn, 2014), *30+ Single on Sale* (*30+ Soht On Sale*, Puttipong Pormsaka Na-Sakonnakorn, 2011), *Bangkok Traffic (Love) Story* (*Rot Fai Fa Ma Ha Na Thoe*, Adisorn Tresirikasem, 2009) and *ATM: Er Rak Error* (Mez Tharatorn, 2012) which all embrace such a model and are popular with urban female viewers. Similar to the original Korean films and television shows, the narratives of these Thai films often focus upon professional urban unmarried women in their thirties who are looking for love, and take place within a *mise-en-scène* of coffee shops, offices, bars and shopping malls.

Ananda's career certainly reflects this racial feminisation. Romance features strongly in the performer's repertoire, with films such as *The Leap Years* (Jean Yeo, 2008), *Sabaidee Luang Prabang*, *Sway*, *Love H20*, *Happy Birthday* and *Eternity* placing the performer as a romantic lead. For some this is part of a melancholic and tragic sacrificial narrative while others bleed into metrosexual romantic comedy, with Ananda taking on the role of a seemingly arrogant *luk khrueng* superstar who eventually falls for the heroine in *Love H20*. Tragic romance also informs Ananda's horror roles, with *Shutter*, *Memory* (Torpong Tunkamhang, 2008) and *The Coffin* (*Long To Tai*, Ekachai Uekrongtham, 2008) entwining horror with romance, and depicting a deeply regretful and tormented character who is trying to make up for past transgressions. His breakthrough role (for which he is probably still most internationally famous) in *Shutter* depicts

Ananda's *luk khrueng* character, Thun, as more thoughtful and kinder towards women than the gang of Thai boys who eventually abuse Thun's former girlfriend and lead their friend to participate in sexual assault.

Other roles engage strongly with topics around sexuality and sensuality and several are deeply homoerotic, demonstrating the extent to which the feminisation of the male *luk khrueng* allows sexuality to be somewhat flexible. *Ploy* and *Pleasure Factory* involve nudity and sex scenes and also include much emphasis upon the physicality of the performer. Such depictions echo the intrusive gaze invited by the mixed-race body in a similar way to Mulvey's famous male gaze, which scrutinises and objectifies the abnormal body from an ideologically hegemonic perspective, albeit through racialised connotations of femininity in the Thai context. In *Bangkok Time* (Santi Taepanich, 2007) the performer is a male sex worker, and in *Me … Myself* (*Khaw Hai Rak Jong Jaroen*, Pongpat Wachirabunjong, 2007) plays a former transvestite who, after amnesia from an accident, has begun a relationship with a woman. Such homoeroticism is also reflected in many of his publicity photos, which are heavily objectified and sexualised for a male performer. Images of him shirtless were used on the front cover of the September 2011 Thai edition of the gay lifestyle magazine *Attitude*. Likewise, Ananda's promotional material as a brand ambassador for Magnum ice cream in particular is highly sexualised; high angle shots depict him surrounded by women and positioned with an open mouth about to eat an ice cream.

Contemporary changes to the *luk khrueng* construction

Yet in the contemporary context, the hierarchical and reductive Thai constructions of race and nationalism are beginning to change. Access to a 'cosmopolitan identity' is no longer purely associated with the Caucasian Western-ness embodied in the *luk khrueng*. 'Alternative forms' of cosmopolitan transnationalism in this region are now forming, attributable to the diverse non-white global migrants, professional workers and consumers attracted to Thailand's international travel, tourism and 'cosmopolitan' image, and whose desires are comparable to migrants from (white) European descent (Hickey 2018: 739–40).

These alternative forms are also exacerbated by other internal challenges to hegemonic discourses around race. Scholars note that the nationalist model based upon cultural and ethnic homogeneity is beginning to collapse (Streckfuss 2012: 307). The rise of the rural middle-class, increased challenges to government control, diversity in religion and challenges to official bias are all evident, with increased lese-majesty laws and persecution making up the authoritarian backlash against such changes.[5]

Such a reorientation of discourses around race and belonging is reflected in wider media; 2014 saw dark-skinned Nonthawan Thongleng crowned 'Miss Thailand', who then made very explicit her rejection of skin whitening products and insecurity around darker skin in well-received publicity interviews (Fredrickson 2014). In Thai film, the rejection and critique of previous hegemonic rigid racial hierarchies and corresponding unfair class privilege can be seen in films from contemporary director Kongkiat Khomsiri (known as Kom) such as *Muay Thai Chaiya/ Muay Thai Fighter* (*Chaiya*, Kongkiat Khomsiri, 2007), *Slice* (Kongkiat Khomsiri, 2009) and *The Gangster* (*Anthaphan*, Kongkiat Khomsiri, 2012), which explore the Thai lower-classes, provincial Thais of darker ethnicities and Thai masculinity. Characters are strongly masculinised Thai men such as boxers, cops and gangsters, who are placed within very violent, dark and tragic narratives that are 'worlds apart from the more mainstream media representations of "ideal" Thai males that privilege light-skinned, "soft," metrosexual, sensitive urbanites' (Ancuta 2013), an ideal embodied by the feminised *luk khrueng*.

As a major star with significant box office clout, longevity and considerable freedom of choice within his industry, the increased diversification of Ananda's roles becomes indicative of these wider changes to the construction of race in Thailand. Recent years see attempts by the performer to move beyond the confines of *luk khrueng* connotations, coupled with an expressed desire not to be stereotyped (Suebsaeng 2010). This increased flexibility in the last decade has been recognised, with one 2015 commenter referring to Ananda as 'a chameleon when acting and choosing roles' (Sirinya 2015).

The late 2000s and into the 2010s saw Ananda begin to move beyond overly romantic, sexualised and feminised *luk khrueng* roles into characters that embody notions of Thai national identity and Thai masculinity. This included a foray into action cinema, which arguably began with *Queens of Langkasuka* (Nonzee Nimibutr, 2008), followed with *Insi Daeng* (*The Red Eagle*, Wisit Sasanatieng, 2010) and finally the *Khun Pan* (Kongkiat Khomsiri, 2016) series. All of these films are significant and high-budget action films from prominent Thai directors, demonstrating Ananda's reputation as a performer. In contrast to the typical feminised and 'misfit' mixed-race position, Ananda's roles in these films now embody and are attached to traditional notions and symbols of Thainess and are embedded within stories and characters that, in various ways, are closely connected to both Thai national identity and masculinity.

Queens of Langkasuka is an adaptation of a historical fantasy which tells the story of three female rulers from the Southern Thai/Malay kingdom of Langkasuka who are tasked with defending their territory from pirates. Ananda plays the role of Pari, a young sea gypsy who can magically communicate with sea creatures and assists the queens in their battle. The performer was very aware of Pari's difference to his previous roles, specifically highlighting his movement to the action genre in publicity interviews: 'Pari is different from my previous roles. Playing an action role is exciting and I enjoyed every moment' (Kamal 2009). Following on from Queens of Langkasuka, Insi Daeng is a high concept stylised superhero film from notable Thai auteur Wisit Sasanatieng set in the near future of 2013 Bangkok. The film contains extensive action and fight scenes and was a remake of the Red Eagle superhero figure from an older post-war film series, the most famous of which, the film *Insi Thong* (*Golden* Eagle, Mitr Chaibancha, 1970), resulted in the on-screen death of Thailand's superstar at the time, Mitr Chaibancha.

Featuring characters connected to hegemonic notions of masculinity and Thai national identity, these two films are highly significant in moving a *luk khrueng* performer outside of *luk khrueng* connotations. Yet while these productions are indicative of potential changes to constructions of race, close attention also highlights the continuing limitations of the *luk khrueng* construction. For instance, the character of Pari in *Queens of Langkasuka* is still a naïve, confused and romantic figure, connotations coded as feminine. *Insi Daeng* was also problematic, being widely considered unsuccessful and promptly putting an end to the intended rebooted franchise of this superhero. While this can be attributed to its convoluted plot and overlong action sequences, animosity was also directed towards casting Ananda as the central character, perhaps signalling a continued residual disjunction between the feminised Soft Masculinity of the performer's *luk khrueng* image and a masked crime-fighting superhero. Casting Ananda in a role previously associated with the dark-skinned provincially Thai and strongly masculinised 1960s performer Mitr Chaibancha was regarded within critical and popular opinion as a strong example of miscasting for this previously romantic lead. It appears that Ananda's crime fighting *Insi Daeng* figure could not yet embody these masculine connotations, despite the 2010 character's association with martial arts (rather than *muay thai* specifically) and his location within the metropolis (rather than ethnic provincial Thailand).

However, it is in Kom's late 2010s *Khun Pan* series that Ananda seems to have overcome the limits of the *luk khrueng* connotations and finally moved beyond the tragic misfit narrative, the feminisation and the cosmopolitanism that so heavily informed his previous roles. Set around the Second World War, the series tells the story of the famous Thai policeman Khun Pan, who fought against a notorious group of bandits in southern Thailand (while *Khun Pan 2* (Kongkiat Khomsiri, 2018) moves the action to central Thailand). A real figure in Thai history, the ethnically southern Thai Khun Phantharakratchadet (known as Khun Pan) is much celebrated in Thailand and has become a strong signifier of both Thainess and masculinity, with his death in 2006 receiving much publicity. With a *mise-en-scène* of cowboys, horses, saloons and gunfights, the film can be considered a Western, yet it also contains fantasy elements such as magical weapons, spells and amulets, in a nod to the prevalence of such an aesthetic in the previous post-Second World War golden age of Thai film. In contrast to the Soft Masculinity of the *luk khrueng*, the Khun Pan character is unemotional and extremely violent, with the character willing to break rules, shoot bad guys without hesitation and team up with gangsters when necessary in a bid to maintain a moral order. Echoing the corruption associated with Thai politics, police and politicians, the film also constructs an environment in which few individuals or systems can be trusted, and the Khun Pan character must work largely in isolation (a feature seen in many characters and situations in Kom's films, indeed the character even goes 'rogue' in *Khun Pan 2* after being suspended due to corruption in the police system).

Ananda's portrayal in the film has been particularly lauded, and represents possibly his most successful crossover into the historical and action genres. Ananda himself expressed significant awareness around the potential difficulties in taking on a role that was so different to both his previous star image and his own ethnicity, stating 'I'm not Southern, nor biologically Thai' and 'I look nothing like the real-life Khun Phan' (Duangkamol 2016). Yet despite his own misgivings, there appears to have been very little backlash against Ananda's casting in such a recognisable and nationalistic Thai role, with his appearance in the film, in which he sports an impressive handlebar moustache, rides horses and has a whip, now somewhat iconic. Such a transformation was even surprising to the performer himself, who confessed 'When I look at the poster, I'm like, "Man, that's not me"', before further indicating the satisfaction he evidently experienced in being able to move beyond hegemonic racial stereotypes: 'It's strange but it's nice' (Duangkamol 2016).

Publicity material also seeks to attribute masculine prowess to the performer, with reports celebrating the film's excessive violence and stressing how stunts are performed by Ananda himself, also claiming that the second film toned down CGI (due to budget constraints) and relied more upon the performer's own stunts and skills. Likewise, Ananda performs alongside *muay thai* boxing stars such as Dan Chupong, illustrating his ability to now 'blend in' with performers who have been associated with the nationalistic genres that previously did not cast *luk khrueng* performers. It seems that in the late 2010s, the parameters governing racial connotations and constructions are now less rigid, and a performer whose star image was deeply embedded within his *luk khrueng* ethnicity can now begin to embody very different connotations. Such increased opportunities are also seen across Thai media, with younger *luk khrueng* performer Mario Maurer now taking the lead role in Kom's latest historical action fantasy *Khun Phaen Begins* (Kongkiat Khomsiri, 2019).

Furthering *luk khrueng* privilege

However, such changes should not be seen as equivalent to increased opportunities for darker-skinned Thais. While racial hierarchies are certainly breaking down, the position of the 'other within' (provincial ethnic minorities) and the 'other without' (the 'West' and the globalised *luk khrueng*) are not comparable and do not break down equivalently; increased opportunities come to those at the top of this hierarchy first, namely the privileged *luk khrueng*.

Likewise, while the *luk khrueng* is undoubtedly a victim of racial stereotyping, there is also a worrying lack of awareness and concern from performers about the social and economic privileges the racial hierarchy has awarded. For instance, Ananda's publicity interviews around the *Khun Pan* series fail to acknowledge any potential problem with a privileged *luk khrueng* performer taking on a provincial ethnic character of marginalised (and in some cases state-persecuted) southern Thai ethnicity: 'I'm not acting to prove that I'm a different ethnicity. That's not the point. I'm acting to convey the spirit of the character. The spirit of the character does not essentially have something to do with ethnicity or where you are from' (Duangkamol 2016). In seeking to remove race as a criterion for the performer, Ananda then curiously references the Caucasian performer Jake Gyllenhaal playing an Iranian character in the Hollywood film *Prince of Persia: The Sands of Time* (Mike Newell, 2010) as a justification as to why he should be able to play Khun Pan, stating 'Jake Gyllenhaal can be the Prince of Persia, and I can be a southern guy' (Duangkamol 2016).

Such equivalence fails to note that Gyllenhaal's performance was not well received by critics or audiences, is regarded as one of the worst examples of contemporary whitewashing, and that the actor himself later expressed regret for taking on the role. This also questions whether Ananda's actions in taking on the role of Khun Pan can be viewed as equivalent to whitewashing and, furthermore, whether the increased opportunities awarded to *luk khrueng* performers could remove opportunities for performers from marginalised provincial and subaltern groups to represent their own traditions and communities onscreen. If so, then Eurasian-ness has been able to break out of racial stereotypes merely to fully realise its privileges, ones which may not then filter down to those at the other end of the Thai racial hierarchy. While there has been no backlash towards Ananda for taking on the southern Thai role of Khun Pan equivalent to that against Gyllenhaal, such silence may merely highlight how marginalised provincial voices and perspectives remain within dominant discourse in Thailand, a subaltern status that cannot be recognised by the privileged *luk khrueng*.

Conclusion

This chapter has examined the contradictory and complex construction of the Eurasian *luk khrueng* in Thai society, individuals who are 'othered' and heavily stereotyped. It outlined how Eurasian-ness has shifted dramatically from a socially undesirable to a socially desirable position in the contemporary context, embodying connotations of globality, internationalisation and cosmopolitanism. Through close analysis of the top Thai *luk khrueng* performer Ananda Everingham, the chapter outlined how Ananda's career demonstrates the popularity and complex position of the *luk khrueng* performer in contemporary Thailand, highlighting media that addresses the performer's 'otherness' and stereotypes his Eurasian-ness as romantic, sexual and feminised.

However, the chapter then argued that Ananda's more recent roles have moved beyond the romantic feminised 'Soft Masculinity' of the *luk khrueng* figure, becoming symptomatic of an increasing flexibility around race in the new globalised Thai context. Such developments suggest a general positive trend towards breaking down restrictive racial barriers and stereotypes, all of which can potentially offer some very welcome new opportunities and freedoms for those previously subject to narrow racialised constructions. However, the dismantling of such hierarchies and stereotypes manifest differently across the Thai social spectrum, and the degree of increased opportunity depends upon an individual's previous position within such constructions. While *luk khrueng* performers such as Ananda may welcome the increased opportunities these changes present, the inherent privilege that still underlies their general position should strike a note of caution against overly social progressive interpretations.

References

Ainslie, Mary J. (2017), 'Post-war Thai cinema: audiences and film style in a divided nation', *Film International* 15:2, pp. 6–19.

Aizura, Aren Z. (2009), 'Where health and beauty meet: femininity and racialisation in Thai cosmetic surgery clinics', *Asian Studies Review* 33:3, pp. 303–17.

Ancuta, Katarzyna (2013), 'Sons, husbands, brothers: the Gothic worlds of Thai men in the films of Kongkiat Khomsiri', Paper presented at the 11th Biennial IGA Conference: Gothic Technologies – Gothic Techniques. University of Surrey, UK, 5–8 August.

Aspinall, Peter J. (2018), 'What kind of mixed race/ethnicity data is needed for the 2020/21 global population census round: the cases of the UK, USA, and Canada', *Ethnic and Racial Studies* 41:11, pp. 1990–2008.

Boonrak Boonyaketmala (1992), 'The rise and fall of the film industry in Thailand 1897–1992', *East West Film Journal* 6:2, pp. 62–98.

Botan, Susan Fulop Kepner (1977), *Letters from Thailand*, Bangkok: D. K. Book House.

Bunnag, Tatat (2016), 'Police and thieves', *Bangkok Post*, 30 July, <http://www.bangkokpost.com/learning/learning-entertainment/1047593/police-and-thieves> (last accessed 3 March 2018).

Esterik, Penny Van (2000), *Materializing Thailand*, Oxford and New York: Berg.

Fredrickson, Terry (2014), 'Maeya: dark beauty', *Bangkok Post*, 27 June, <https://www.bangkokpost.com/learning/advanced/417680/maeya-dark-beauty> (last accessed 3 April 2018).

Hickey, Maureen (2018), 'Thailand's 'English fever', migrant teachers and cosmopolitan aspirations in an interconnected Asia', *Discourse: Studies in the Cultural Politics of Education* 39:5, pp. 738–51.

Ilbonito (2010a), 'Eternity (Chua Fah Din Salai)', *Ilbonito*, 28 September, <https://ilbonito.wordpress.com/2010/09/28/eternity-chua-fah-din-salai/> (last accessed 9 April 2018).

Ilbonito (2010b), 'More, more, more: 2010's man of the moment, Ananda Everingham', *Ilbonito*, 7 October, <https://ilbonito.wordpress.com/2010/10/07/more-more-more-2010s-man-of-the-moment-ananda-everingham/> (last accessed 9 April 2018).

Ingawanij, May Adadol (2006), 'Un-Thai sakon: the scandal of teen cinema', *Southeast Asia Research* 14:2, pp. 147–77.

Jackson, Peter A. (2003), 'Performative genders, perverse desires: a bio-history of Thailand's same-sex and transgender cultures', *Intersections: Gender, History and Culture in the Asian Context* 9, pp. 1–52.

Jin Haritaworn (2009), 'Hybrid border-crossers? Towards a radical socialisation of "mixed race"', *Journal of Ethnic and Migration Studies* 35:1, pp. 115–32.

Jiraporn Wongpaithoon (1996), 'Once outcasts, mixed-blood Thais ascend to pop stardom as hip icons', *Los Angeles Times*, 23 June, <https://www.latimes.com/archives/la-xpm-1996-06-23-mn-17748-story.html> (last accessed 3 April 2017).

Jung, Sun (2006), 'Bae Yong-Joon, hybrid masculinity and the counter-coeval desire of Japanese female fans', *Participations* 3:2, <https://www.participations.org/volume%203/issue%202%20-%20special/3_02_jung.htm>.

Kamal, Hizreen (2009), 'Ananda thrives on challenges', *New Straits Times*, 6 April, <http://pages.citebite.com/c1c3n8f4k3nsa> (last accessed 3 April 2017).

Kemasingki, Pim and Mike Atkins (2008), 'Half Thai and half foreign', *Citylife Chiang Mai*, 25 November 2008, <http://www.chiangmainews.com/ecmn/viewfa.php?id=894> (last accessed 3 April 2017).

Keyes, Charles (2002), 'Presidential Address: "The Peoples of Asia" – Science and politics in the classification of ethnic groups in Thailand, China, and Vietnam', *Journal of Asian Studies* 61:4, pp. 1163–203.

Kitiarsa, Pattana (2007), 'Muai Thai cinema and the burdens of Thai men', *South East Asia Research* 15:3, pp. 407–24.

Louie, Kam (2012), 'Popular culture and masculinity ideals in East Asia, with special reference to China', *Journal of Asian Studies* 71:4, pp. 929–43.

Matthews, Julie (2007), 'Eurasian persuasions: mixed race, performativity and cosmopolitanism', *Journal of Intercultural Studies* 28:1, pp. 41–54.

Panya, Duangkamol (2016), 'A legend becomes bulletproof', *Bangkok Post*, 10 July, <https://www.bangkokpost.com/life/social-and-lifestyle/1032217/a-legend-becomesbulletproof> (last accessed 3 April 2018).

Persaud, Walter H. (2005), 'Gender, race and global modernity: a perspective from Thailand', *Globalizations* 2:2, pp. 210–27.

Pruzin, Daniel (1997), 'In mother's land, Tiger Woods finds he's on par', *Christian Science Monitor*, 7 February, <http://www.csmonitor.com/1997/0207/020797.intl.intl.1.html> (last accessed 3 April 2007).

'Q&A: Ananda Everingham' (2008), *The Hollywood Reporter*, 5 June, <https://www.hollywoodreporter.com/news/qampa-ananda-everingham-113260> (last accessed 3 April 2007).

Reynolds, Craig J. (2002), *National Identity and Its Defenders: Thailand Today*, Chiang Mai: Silkworm Books.

Sasinee Khuankaew (2020), 'The Boonchu comedy series: pre-1990s Thai localism and modernity', in Gaik Cheng Khoo, Thomas Barker and Mary J. Ainslie (eds), *Southeast Asia on Screen: From Independence to Financial Crisis (1945–1998)*, Amsterdam: Amsterdam University Press, pp. 271–90.

Sirinya (2015), 'Ananda Everingham on personality and hi-so (high society)', *Sirinya's Thailand*, 15 May, <http://www.sirinyas-thailand.de/2015/05/14/ananda-everingham-on-personality-and-hi-so-high-society/> (last accessed 3 April 2017).

Song, Geng (2016), 'Changing masculinities in East Asian pop culture', *East Asian Forum Quarterly* 8:2, pp. 3–5.

Streckfuss, David (2012), 'An 'ethnic' reading of 'Thai' history in the twilight of the century-old official 'Thai' National Model', *Southeast Asia Research* 20:3, pp. 305–27.

Suebsaeng, Asawin (2010), 'Ananda Everingham on movies, politics and becoming a Thai', *Bangkok Post*, 22 August, <http://pages.citebite.com/k1l4e2q7dfuq> (last accessed 3 April 2017).

Thongchai Winichakul (2000), 'The quest for "*Siwilai*": a geographical discourse of civilizational thinking in the late nineteenth and early twentieth-century Siam', *Journal of Asian Studies* 59:3, pp. 528–49.

Vail, Peter (2014), 'Muay Thai: inventing tradition for a national symbol', *SOJOURN: Journal of Social Issues in Southeast Asia* 29:3, pp. 509–53.

'What do Thai people think about *luk kreung*' (2014), *Thaivisa*, 28 July, <https://forum.thaivisa.com/topic/746771-what-do-thai-people-think-about-luk-kreung/> (last accessed 3 April 2017).

Wise Kwai (2013), 'Queen of action, queen of drama', *The Nation*, 15 November, <http://www.nationmultimedia.com/life/Queen-of-action-queen-of-drama-30219603.html> (last accessed 3 April 2007).

Yeoh, Brenda S. A., Kristel Acedera and Esther Rootham (2018), 'Negotiating postcolonial Eurasian identities and national belonging in global-city Singapore', *Social Identities* 25:3, pp. 294–309.

Notes

1. Terms in the Thai language (including film titles) have been transliterated in accordance with the Royal Thai General System of Transcription (RTGS) in order to standardise the spelling.
2. Thai state nationalism, with the country's name changed from Siam to Thailand in 1939 in part to increase inclusiveness to non-Siamese identified citizens, was designed to consolidate a nation that was ethnically, culturally and geographically diverse, so giving all citizens a form of national identity to adhere to. This discourse was consolidated into a strict ideology made up of the trilogy nation, religion and monarchy.
3. The Thai-Western partnering is typically constructed as a Western male/Asian female pairing, and one that reflects the heightened sexualisation of the Orientalised Asian female body, a construction that was heightened during and after the Vietnam

War. From a Thai perspective, theorists understand and interpret this phenomenon largely as a means by which lower-class women (often from Thailand's darker skinned ethnic minorities) can seek social advancement and financial security, as well as a status symbol for wealthier (and in some cases older) women. Such a pairing is a recent phenomenon. Intermarriages earlier in the twentieth century tended to be between the outer rings of Thai elites and Caucasian women, many of whom were Russian aristocratic emigres, in the late nineteenth century and early twentieth century.

4. Such 'ultra-femininity' is particularly recognisable in the figure of the Thai *kathoey*, the transgender individual or 'ladyboy', for which Thailand is particular famous and who is understood to be the product of gendered forms of dress and behaviour solidified during the early twentieth century, when Thai culture and society was re-ordered to adhere to global, namely Western, cultural norms (Jackson 2003). *Kathoey* individuals often take aesthetic procedures to extremes due to the importance of cultivating femininity within the adoption of this form of identity (Aizura 2009).

5. Notably, one way in which progressive scholars are also attacked, some of whom are *luk khrueng* themselves, is through highlighting their supposed connection to the 'West' and so othering their way of thinking as unThai.

Chapter 11

Fight like a girl: Jeeja Yanin as a female martial arts star

Katarzyna Ancuta

Thai martial artists have dreamt of outshining Bruce Lee, Jet Li and Jackie Chan ever since Hong Kong martial arts films became popular in Thailand in the 1970s. The influence of Hong Kong was felt in Thai cinema of the period and, mixed with American-style action, inspired the production of local action films, known as *nang bu* or *nang tosu*. Popular with many 16-mm era directors and launching the cinema careers of stars like Mitr Chaibancha and Sombat Metanee, these films told stories of cops and gangsters, set masked heroes and undercover agents against organised crime rings, or followed mercenaries into the jungle in search of missing treasure. But while their heroes often took to throwing punches amidst copious explosions and gratuitous gun violence, none of the actors showcased their martial arts skills as none were trained for that purpose. Martial arts films are a recent addition to Thai cinema, owing much to the vision of the director/producer Prachya Pinkaew, whose work with the late stunt choreographer Panna Rittikrai defined the genre through films like *Ong-Bak: The Thai Warrior* (*Ong-Bak*, 2003), *The Protector* (*Tom Yum Kung*, 2005), and *Chocolate* (2008).

Pinkaew's idea to create a specifically Thai brand of *muay thai* cinema that could compete with Hong Kong *kung fu* and *wuxia* films, appealed both to local audiences, culturally conditioned to view *muay thai* as an expression of 'Thainess', and foreign ones familiarised with this martial art through Jean-Claude Van Damme's *Kickboxer* (Mark DiSalle and David Worth, 1989). Pinkaew's plan relied on his ability to create iconic martial arts stars that would become the instantly recognisable faces of the genre. The three martial artists originally selected for this purpose were Tony Jaa, Jeeja Yanin (Figure. 11.1),[1] and Dan Chupong. Tony Jaa's career skyrocketed after his appearance in *Ong-Bak*, which, arguably, remains the best known Thai film outside of Thailand. His cooperation

Figure 11.1 Spin-kicking into fame – Jeeja in her impressive screen debut in *Chocolate*.

with foreign stars like Dolph Lundgren or Van Damme and recent cameo roles in Hollywood action films certainly make him the biggest star of the three. Dan Chupong's solid performances in films like *Born to Fight* (*Koet Ma Lui*, Panna Rittikrai, 2004) or *Dynamite Warrior* (*Khon Fai Bin*, Chalerm Wongpim, 2006) have won him a steady following in Thailand and abroad. Jeeja Yanin's rise to stardom, however, is all the more intriguing as female martial artists who specialise in full contact sports are still relatively rare in martial arts cinema. Best known for her roles in *Chocolate* and *Raging Phoenix* (Rashane Limtrakul, 2009), today Jeeja is frequently mentioned alongside such stars as Cynthia Rothrock, Michelle Yeoh (formerly Michelle Khan) or Yukari Oshima.

Although Jeeja has mostly trained in *taekwondo*,[2] she is often promoted as a *muay thai* star. This is highly significant for the production of her star image, since in the ritualised Thai world of *muay thai* boxing, where arduous physical training goes hand in hand with reliance on magical amulets and sacred tattoos, women are generally positioned as inferior to men. While today many Thai camps accept women for training and the number of female *muay thai* fighters is on the rise, women are often segregated from men and expected to adhere to different rules. They are also excluded from the national myth that utilises the figure of the male boxer as the vehicle to portray the 'ideal Thai'. *Muay thai*, the creation of which is often attributed to the legendary boxer Nai Khanom Tom, said to have singlehandedly defeated a procession of Burmese fighters during the Siamese-Burmese war in 1774 (although historical records suggest it was likely practised much earlier than that), is an important part of Thai cultural heritage. The figure of a *muay thai* boxer is highly symbolic in Thai national ideology. Jakkrit Sangkhamanee explains: 'For the Thais, the boxing has often been viewed as embodying their great courage, nationalism, historical achievements, performing arts and literatures, rituals and spiritual expressions, and representing their social norms, hierarchy, ethics and ideology' (2012: 162). Pattana Kitiarsa notices that 'boxing as a type of fighting skill and a social ideology constitutes a key part of the Thai concept of masculinity' (2011: 200), which in its traditional format defined a 'manly' man as one who possesses knowledge, politeness, morality, spirituality (religious and magical), and physical skills, such as boxing (201). Thai *muay thai* films are thus generally vehicles of masculine nationalistic propaganda.

This chapter examines the specific positioning of martial arts stars within cinema and investigates the gendered construction of the female martial artist. It discusses the development of the *muay thai* film as a specifically Thai contribution to martial arts cinema and the genre's vindication of the ideological construction of *muay thai* as an expression of heroic masculinity and patriotism. The chapter focuses on Jeeja Yanin to examine how the introduction of a female *muay thai* star affects the heroic/nationalistic narrative of Thai *muay thai* cinema and how this, in turn, affects the construction of Jeeja's star image.

The martial artist as a film star

Richard Dyer (1998) claims that stars are images created by the film industry, circulated by the media and consumed by the audiences. He views stars as a phenomenon of production – discussing film production in terms of a capitalist venture and evaluating stars according to the function they play within this specific economy, and a phenomenon of consumption – exploring the relationship between stars and audiences. The creation of stars is thus said to depend on both the filmmakers (and film economies) that make them and the audiences that consume them (1998: 11). Paul McDonald observes that stars operate within a *star system*, a component of film business that allocates a specific place to stars within the film industry organisation and sets the conditions for the production and use of star images (2000: 3). McDonald examines the evolution of the Hollywood star system – from the earliest days when film business, driven by film technologies rather than actors, was not conducive to the production of stars; through the age of studio dominance, when '[s]tars became a vital asset in maintaining the hegemony of the major studios over the whole domestic film industry' (40); to the rise of film agents who negotiate deals for stars, now seen as 'freelance labour, hired for short periods on separate film projects' (74) as part of package-unit production. Not all film stars, however, are made in Hollywood. The production of stars depends on the star system operating within the industry they are a part of.

Star images are 'always extensive, multimedia, intertextual' (Dyer 2004: 3). They are constructed, adjusted and reinforced in films, posters, stills and promotional materials, public appearances, press coverage and interviews, but also in critical commentary, advertising and various incarnations of popular culture (2–3). Star images are based on real people – part of the film labour force employed for their individual looks, talents and skills that are profitable for the industry – but these people cannot be seen as stars without a specific media discourse evaluating performances and examining the work of actors (McDonald 2000: 29) that conflates their public appearances with a glimpse of their private lives. Star images are perpetuated by the media, which simultaneously makes the stars familiar and keeps them at a distance, contributing to the creation of *celebrity culture*, where stars/celebrities 'circulate as images in everyday life and public space [and] thrive on the response these images invoke and circulate even more as a result' (Nayar 2009: 2).

Many scholars feel the need to distinguish stars from celebrities. For Kelly McWilliam, a star is 'a person who plays a prominent leading role, eclipsing others with their excellence in some widely recognised way' (2009: 249). Stars are given an *achieved* celebrity status, which Chris Rojek describes as the attention capital derived from the perceived artistic or sporting accomplishments of individuals said to 'possess rare talents or skills' (2001: 18). Martial artists possess unique skills that identify them as both athletes and performers. They are capable of accomplishing physical feats that put regular humans in awe. Yet relatively few martial artists achieve stardom while the rest continue to be seen as supporting/second-rate actors, body doubles or stunt persons. How different then is the image of a martial arts star and does it matter if the martial artist is a woman?

The use of martial arts is a genre-defining characteristic. Films that involve performances of martial artists are likely to be seen as martial arts films regardless of their plots, settings, or iconography. Martial arts films are, generally speaking, action films that feature actors trained in combat sports, whose skills are showcased in highly choreographed fight sequences during the movie. In contrast to regular action films they do not involve gunplay but rather hand-to-hand combat, swordplay and fights with all kinds of bladed weapons and staffs, the use of which requires rigorous training. The films feature performative combat oriented towards others, where practitioners 'demonstrate techniques or engage in more-or-less scripted mock-fight for the purpose of communicating with and/or entertaining an audience' (Channon and Matthews 2015: 13). Martial arts films originated in Hong Kong cinema with *wuxia pian*, derived from Peking Opera performances, telling tales of sword-wielding heroes, magic and chivalry set in ancient China, and *kung fu* films reinvented by Bruce Lee. Exported to Hollywood in the 1970s, they blended with American productions and contributed to the rise of the 1980s action films focused on the muscular hero whose body becomes a deadly weapon thanks to competitive combat sports and Eastern martial arts.

The martial artist is first and foremost an action actor, associated with the genre that foregrounds the physicality of the body. Unsurprisingly then, the martial artist's star image is inextricably tied to their bodies, perceived and promoted as functional and aesthetic objects. These bodies are inevitably gendered and racialised, and so is the action film as such. While martial arts cinema allows certain privilege to Asian bodies, action films tend to be overwhelmingly masculine, promoting hegemonic versions of masculinity. Yvonne Tasker argues that action cinema 'often operates as an almost exclusively male space, in which issues to do with sexuality and gendered identity can be worked out over the male body' (2002: 17). Such a distinction derives from the perception of gender in terms of the 'presentation of more-or-less masculine and feminine selves within a culturally accepted, gendered system of signification' (Channon and Matthews 2015: 4), where masculinity and femininity are polarised and associated with complementary qualities: strength/weakness, rationality/emotionality, autonomy/dependence, etc. This gender hierarchy presupposes a different orientation towards the body, where men are encouraged to develop strength and muscular physique, and women are trained to engage in 'softer,' more artistic pursuits and restrict their bodies by fashion (5).

Seen from this angle, the muscular gun-wielding heroines who can 'express their rage, defend their bodies, and usurp some of manhood's most vital turf' (King and McCaughey 2001: 5) are judged to be more masculine and 'unladylike' to the point of becoming 'symbolically male' (Brown 2011: 21), although their recurring appearance can contribute to changing gender expectations, redefining traditional notions of femininity and empowering women. Yet, long before the 'hardbody, hardware, hard-as-nails heroine who can take it – and give it – with the biggest and the baddest men' (Brown 2011: 20–1) took centre stage in Hollywood, Hong Kong martial arts film had already featured female leads. In the 1960s/early 1970s, the Shaw Brothers' Cheng Pei Pei and Golden Harvest's Angela Mao Ying were among the most admired fighting ladies, and the genre saw the rise of many female martial artists including Wei Yin Hung, Michelle Yeoh, Moon Lee, Cynthia Rothrock or Yukari Oshima, and encouraged the turn of mainstream stars like Anita Mui or Maggie Cheung to action.

One reason for that, as Catherine Jean Gomes observes, may be the fact that since martial arts focus on channelling one's inner strength and transforming it into physical action, the discipline is 'blind to gender distinctions' (2004: 16). Gomes and Tasker also argue that the performative nature of martial arts cinema with its dance-like choreography that showcases the body in motion makes the genre more feminised, as it allows for an expression of feminine sensuality with the moving body becoming the object of our gaze (Gomes 2004: 16). This means that, unlike in the case of action heroines, the star image of female martial artists does not necessarily revolve around their lethal and muscular bodies but also highlights the more traditionally feminine aspects of their physique, preferring graceful movement over brutal strength, precision over blind force, elegance and poise over rough un-coordinated attacks. What happens then when the female martial artist takes the lead in the genre that serves a masculine national ideology?

Jeeja Yanin and *muay thai* cinema

The late 1990s mark the beginning of the New Thai Cinema, not a coherent movement but rather a reflection on 'the process by which contemporary Thai cinema and its film industry morphed into a much more internationally savvy industry catering for a new bourgeois urban spectator' (Ainslie 2018: 76). As Lauren Steimer observes, Thai action films have also benefited from this cinematic revival. Steimer argues that the New Thai action cinema successfully combined the Hong Kong action model with what May Adadol Ingawanij calls the Thai 'heritage' film (2013: 143). Ingawanij describes the 'heritage' genre as geared towards nostalgically oriented high-quality productions that glamourise selected parts of Thai history and promote the concept of 'Thainess' (2007: 180) adjusted to the national ideology of the three pillars – Nation, Religion (i.e. Buddhism) and Monarchy – that entered Thai socio-political discourse in the 1950s. She links the popularity of such films, made at the time when Thailand was recovering from the 1997 Asian Financial Crisis, with their ability to match the tastes of the urban middle-class audience simultaneously yearning for the 'old' Thailand as the imaginary site of 'Thainess' and the 'new' Thailand marked by economic prosperity and globalisation (181). *Muay thai*, portrayed as the 'ancient' uniquely Thai martial art and Thai contribution to the modern world of sports, meets both these requirements.

To Prachya Pinkaew *Ong-Bak* was the answer to what Thai action cinema was missing: a specifically Thai version of the martial arts film. Pinkaew explains:

> Before we made *Ong Bak* we thought of martial arts movies in terms of Chinese Kung-Fu movies. Thai boxing has been accepted as a unique form of martial arts but not in the movies. You could find a lot of Muay Thai boxing schools all over the world but not so many Muay Thai martial arts films. So perhaps that's yet another chance for Thai films to find their niche in the film world. We could create a new category – a Muay Thai movie. I had this idea before I started making *Ong Bak* and I felt it was going to be a hit. (2007: 91)

Pinkaew understood that although *muay thai* represents different things to national and international audiences it can be appealing to both, and the rapid rise of Tony Jaa to fame confirms it. Steimer argues that Tony Jaa's body spectacle draws on and improves the formula used by Hong Kong martial artists by making the fights more authentic, which she sees as a trademark of Thai action filmmaking, and incorporating elements of Thai culture – from the promotion of the 'original' art of *muay boran* (ritualised Thai 'ancient boxing', the records of which go back to at least the sixteenth century) rather than the modern version of *muay thai* (the internationally regulated modern combat sport) to Buddhism and elephants (2013: 144). Such a model, however, visibly favours male over female performers.

Muay thai holds a special position in the Thai cultural worldview. Kitiarsa argues that *muay thai* is a prominent site for the production and consumption of Thai hegemonic masculinity that is 'highly situated in the country's discourse of race and nationalism' (2011: 202). *Muay thai* is masculine because it foregrounds the concept of the 'real man' (*luk puchai*) who acts with dignity (*saksi*) and shows pride (*kiattiyot*) in being a man (Kitiarsa 2005: 82). *Muay thai* also conveys the poetics of Thai manhood and nationhood (82) and is consequently constructed in Thai scholarship as the evidence of Thai superiority over other races. Thai critics have argued that '[t]he sport of *muai Thai* arose with the nation of Thailand, and is a sport for true Thais' (Posawat Sangsawan 1979, in Vail 1998: 91) and that '*muai Thai* is truly our national [martial] art, which is difficult for other nations to imitate' (Rangsarit Bunchalor 2000, in Kitiarsa 2005: 62). They have claimed that *muai thai* is 'in the blood' of Thai men (Thanaboon Wutharasathien 1996, in Kitiarsa 2005: 62) and that indeed '[a]ll Thai men have an instinctive talent for Muay Thai … and it happens almost automatically' (Suthon Sukphisit 1997, in Vail 1998: 91).

Kitiarsa highlights the discrepancy between representation and reality where 'poverty produces muai Thai fighters. Boxing is a tough career sought almost exclusively by poor young boys from working-class backgrounds; boxing serves as an escape from poverty and a venue for geographical and socioeconomic mobility' (Kitiarsa 2011: 197). Boxers live the lives of 'hunting dogs': 'They train, they sweat, they fight, they get injured, but they have no control over their destiny' (2005: 65). Thai *muay thai* film narratives contribute to the creation of the myth that portrays Thai boxers as patriotic, courageous defenders of Thai cultural heritage. In *Ong-Bak*, Tony Jaa plays a naïve simpleton whose journey from the idyllic northeastern village to the sin city of Bangkok to recover the stolen head of a Buddha statue – a symbol of Thai religious identity and culture – turns him into the champion of the faith and the nation. *The Protector* and *The Protector 2* (*Tom Yum Kung 2*, Prachya Pinkaew, 2013) are larger-scale realisations of practically the same plot, sending Tony Jaa in pursuit of a stolen elephant for a change. Dan Chupong's films also reinforce the myth of the heroic warrior: in *Born to Fight* he leads a team of Thai athletes to liberate a village from armed intruders and foil a terrorist plot to launch a nuclear missile into Bangkok, while in *Dynamite Warrior* he appears as a Robin Hood-esque protector of the weak, saving poor farmers from their corrupt overlord. Things change, however, when a female martial artist enters the scene.

Ten years after her impressive debut in *Chocolate*, Jeeja Yanin has solidified her position as the leading Thai female martial artist. She played central roles in *Raging Phoenix*, *The Kick* (Prachya Pinkaew, 2011), and *This Girl is Badass* (*Jukkalan*, Petchtai Wongkamlao, 2011), and appeared in support parts in *The Protector 2*, *Hard Target 2* (Roel Reiné, 2016), *Never Back Down: No Surrender* (Michael Jai White, 2016), *Europe Raiders* (Jingle Ma, 2018), *Oversize Cops* (*Owoe Sai Chut... Thalai Phung*, Phuwanit Pholdee, 2017), the HBO Asia original series *Halfworlds* (Ekachai Uekrongtham, 2016), and several Thai television soaps. Her most recent film, *Triple Threat* (Jesse V. Johnson, 2019), where she teams up with Tony Jaa and the Indonesian *silat* star, Iko Uwais, best known for *The Raid: Redemption* (*Serbuan Maut*, Gareth Evans, 2011), will likely promote her further. Steimer sees Jeeja's position within Thai martial arts cinema as both similar to and in contrast with Tony Jaa. She argues that 'Much like Jaa attempts to provide body spectacles that are "new" and distinct from those of Hong Kong performers, Yanin must consistently differentiate the visual pleasures that she supplies from those of Jaa' (2013: 151). This means that unlike Tony Jaa, who sticks to his acrobatic version of *muay boran*, Jeeja's fighting style is meant to be more versatile – currently including *taekwondo*, *muay thai*, *capoeira*, *kung-fu*, as well as the imaginary drunken style of *meyraiyuth*, *bike-fu* (fighting on bicycles, Figure 11.2), and a whole lot of dancing.

Figure 11.2 Jeeja in bike-fu action from a fight sequence featuring bike acrobatics in *This Girl is Badass*.

As a Thai martial artist Jeeja finds it impossible to escape *muay thai*. Having spent her formative years training in ballet, Jeeja switched to *taekwondo* at the age of eleven. At fourteen her skills were good enough to qualify her as an instructor and today she holds the 4th Dan Black Belt. Jeeja's *taekwondo* skills landed her a part in Pinkaew's Korean co-production *The Kick*, where she helps a Korean *taekwondo* family fight criminals. Thai action films, however, prioritise *muay thai*, both for ideological reasons and because *muay thai* can be quite cinematic. Additionally, Panna Rittikrai's fight choreography used to rely heavily on *muay thai* simply because it was familiar to him and his stunt team. In Jeeja's dynamic performance, however, *muay thai* – now simply one of many combat sports – is stripped of its ideological significance and appreciated solely for its body spectacle, graceful movements, killer moves and impossible acrobatics. Despite the fact that Jeeja could outmatch many male fighters, her gender excludes her from the grand patriotic narrative many Thai *muay thai* films convey. The conceptualisation of *muay thai* as the expression of 'Thainess' – a politicised quality related to the vague notions of 'tradition' and 'Thai values' – reinforces fixed gender roles that see women as subordinate to men. Thai culture restricts certain parts of symbolic life to men only. While women can worship at a temple, they are denied monkhood and need to follow strict protocol in contact with monks. Similarly, women may be encouraged to practise *muay thai* as a sport but they continue to be excluded from *muay thai*'s spiritual dimension and ideology.

The characters Jeeja portrays do not match the 'ideal Thai' persona of the male boxer. Zen from *Chocolate* is an autistic teenager with a talent to learn martial arts by mimicking the movements of others. She is also the daughter of a Thai assassin and a Japanese *yakuza* which makes her essentially un-Thai. In *The Protector 2*, Jeeja appears to be (part) Chinese, as indicated by her name – Ping-Ping – and stereotyped appearance (Figure 11.3). The locations of *Raging Phoenix* filled with foreign-looking architecture and Catholic iconography and the film's fighting style based on Brazilian *capoeira* also make it impossible to see her as the champion of the Thai nation. *This Girl is Badass* turns her into a teenage rebel mixing martial arts with bike stunts, generic action and jokes, its singularly un-heroic plot unfolding as a series of comedy gags in non-specified locations. In minor roles, Jeeja is cast as a fighter – a sportswoman, assassin, bodyguard or trainer – none of which require a national allegiance. Steimer attributes these differences to marketing strategies rather than gender, seeing that

Figure 11.3 Jeeja (right) and Theerada Kittisiriprasert (left) as a cute 'Chinese' fighting duo in *The Protector 2*.

the performers are sold as products to distinctive audiences; where Tony Jaa is marketed as 'a masterful martial artist and showman to cineastes and sports fans' (2013: 152) while Jeeja 'is presented to teens and other mall-goers as a shockingly physically adept, charming, and polite young woman with a perpetual grin and a keen fashion sense' (152). Obviously, with Jeeja being the only notable Thai female martial arts star any debate on gender difference in Thai action cinema is bound to be inconclusive, but since all Thai male martial artists are marketed similarly to Tony Jaa, while Jeeja continues to be promoted for her childlike fragility and cuteness, gender may well be a factor to consider.

Jeeja the star

Despite their occasional appearances in foreign films and the increasing international presence of Thai cinema, Thai actors rarely rise to transnational stardom. The global recognition of Thai martial artists as stars changes the dynamics of the local star system that prioritises dramatic actors and television celebrities over action actors. While Tony Jaa and Jeeja remain arguably the best known Thai actors outside of Thailand, this popularity is not necessarily reflected on a local scale. If stars are created by the film industry, the Thai film industry does not seem to put a lot of effort into the manufacturing of their stars. While it is debatable whether Thailand has ever had a stable studio system, or whether the operation of its film industry is compatible with the Hollywood model, the emergence of the *muay thai* film in the early 2000s is tied to a very specific film economy marked by the gradual dissolution or loss of influence of the existing Thai studios, reclassification of film studios as production units (notably the introduction of Pinkaew's Baa-Ram-Ewe as the in-house production company for Sahamongkol), the emergence of cineplexes as film marketing and distribution agents (specifically the rise of the Major Group as a significant player in the Thai film industry), and the rise of television channels as the main vehicle for creating and controlling star images, leading to the Thai audience's preference for television stars over film stars (especially Channel 3 stars). The shift in influence from Thai cinema to Thai television has had a profound effect on the way the star system operates in today's Thailand. It has also made it more difficult for martial artists to be acknowledged as stars on home ground even if their star status is recognised abroad.

Unlike in the case of dramatic actors or comedians, the possibilities for martial artists to appear in soap operas and variety shows that dominate Thai television are rather limited. It also does not help that despite its popular appeal the action genre is generally looked down on as lowbrow entertainment associated with 'provincial' cinema. The economic disparity between Bangkok and the rest of the country means that mainstream media production tends to be aligned with the tastes of the young middle-class urbanites seen as the most profitable segment of the audience. Since martial arts stars rarely appear in dramatic roles outside of action movies, they are often seen as incompatible with the images of celebrity geared towards the more 'sophisticated' Bangkok audience that dominate advertising billboards and gossip magazines. This ultimately means that outside of the narrow time period when studios and cinema chains promote the films they play in, martial arts actors do not receive much media publicity, which is usually directed at channel-promoted television stars. They also have fewer opportunities to endorse products or services, or appear in commercials, and often have to rely on fan-generated materials or on their own ingenuity to ensure the circulation of their images.

While Jeeja makes it to most fan-generated popular online rankings of top Thai film stars, her stardom brings her very few actual benefits in Thailand. Apart from the routine three months of promotion before the release of the film Thai studios/cinemas do not normally organise any events with their actors. Unlike in Hollywood, Thai actors are not necessarily seen in terms of the studios' greatest capital. The films Jeeja typically appears in do very little to glamourise her image through cinematography or lighting, partially because of their general low production value (poor lighting set-up, minimal *mise-en-scène*) and focus on fast-paced editing and the use of jump-cuts to speed up action sequences. Most of her parts foreground visual references to Hong Kong martial arts cinema rather than the actress herself, like repetitive Bruce Lee-style thumb nose flicks and vocalisations in *Chocolate*, or the fight sequence in the same film referencing Bruce Lee's ice factory fight scene from *The Big Boss* (Wei Lo, 1971). The most impressive 'glamour shots' of Jeeja, if they can be described as such, are those that showcase the incredible flexibility of her body in training sequences, most obviously in *Raging Phoenix* (Figure 11.4). Shots like these, however, highlight the agility or musculature of the body promoted as an aesthetic object and often do not feature the actress's face in close-up.

Despite her appeal, Jeeja's stardom does not lead to many offers to appear in commercials or endorse products. When I asked her why she has never recorded a commercial she replied that she was not the 'right type' of an actress to attract the target audience Thai marketers are interested in: 'Nobody would ever ask me to advertise cosmetics or beauty products, so what am I supposed to advertise? Maybe pain killers?' No company has ever made her an offer to promote sports clothing, accessories, or equipment, choosing to hire television actors

Figure 11.4 Jeeja and Kazu Patrick Tang showcasing their impressive martial arts skills in *Raging Phoenix*.

for this purpose instead. Tony Jaa has made it to billboards and a few commercials but they were specifically addressed to the provinces, seeing that the actor proudly identifies as 'the son of Northeast', and they were not promoted in Bangkok. According to the entertainment website *Thai Star News* the top earning Thai star in 2018, Nadech Kugimiya – a model and television celebrity, gets paid up to 400,000 Baht (over 12,000 USD) per event. The highest paid actress, Aum Patchrapa, also mostly known from television drama, gets 400,000 Baht per event in Bangkok and up to 700,000 in the provinces. Jeeja does not get asked to do events. Needless to say, her acting rates are also substantially lower than those of television celebrities despite her unique skills.

Jeeja's martial arts skills have won her a substantial fan base, but most of her fans are not Thai. The only contact she has with them is online, through her official fan page and Instagram account. Again, the Thai film industry seems to do very little to connect Jeeja with her fans. No public events are organised apart from the routine promotion of the movies and no offers have been made to organise promotional trips abroad to reach out to Jeeja's fans in countries other than Thailand. Her name appears in newspapers mostly in connection with the films she stars in and the juiciest piece of gossip about her seems to have been the announcement of her marriage in 2012 and the birth of her son. Jeeja does not seem to expect much promotion from the Thai media or Thai film industry. Asked whether she feels like a star she takes a humble approach: 'I am a human being. It is up to you if you want to call me a star. I am happy to be an action actress.' She stresses that when working on a film she is simply one of the crew and adds that Thai filmmaking is more a 'family' affair than business, as everybody knows what to do and how to take care of themselves. Explaining that a martial artist cannot act alone, she sees each film as a team effort and insists that nobody on set treats her in any way different because she is famous or because she is a woman.

Despite the fact that she is the only Thai female martial arts star, Jeeja does not see anything special about it. She argues that any actress can be trained to fight but most of them simply do not want to waste time on training. The number of female fighters in Thai cinema is on the rise, but most martial artists prefer to work as stunt persons since, unlike acting, stunt work guarantees continuous employment. For Jeeja, acting is both a passion and a profession. Her career choice is not a coincidence as she holds a degree in film with a minor in acting. She does not see her gender impeding this career – neither through training, which does not distinguish between men and women, nor through competition, as she can stand her ground against men. She points out that in film production actors do not actually fight but rather perform a set of movements that have to be repeated for various camera setups and the result of the fight is dictated by the script, which she sees as another equalising factor. Jeeja does not see her gender as the cause of any special treatment or discrimination. She has never been pushed to perform uncomfortable stunts or wear revealing costumes because she is a woman. She has never been told that women should stay clear of combat sports, nor called a tomboy, something she attributes to current Thai beauty standards that encourage a healthy lifestyle and privilege athletic bodies of women. Interestingly, however, she concludes that her fellow action actors treat her like 'a younger brother' – an incidental slip of the tongue perhaps, but possibly also a reflection on the female success in action cinema measured by her ability to be 'one of the boys.'

Conclusion

Steimer argues that Jeeja's star image, which focuses on her petite body frame and infantilised cuteness, is aimed at the teenage demographic (2013: 151), but this is also a generic way Thai female stars are marketed, regardless of the roles they play. Similarly, the fact that in films Jeeja is often paired with much larger opponents does make her appear childlike and vulnerable, but then with the height of 162 cm it is difficult to expect that many male martial artists will be smaller than her. Jeeja's star image appears to be split between that of a smiling youthful actress whose small, slender (and frequently whitened in photo-editing) body is perceived as feminine, fragile and childlike, and that of an athletic sportswoman with superhuman skills. None of these images involves a representation of 'Thainess', as it is often the case with male *muay thai* fighters, which makes her stardom more transnational. While Jeeja's star status is recognised both in Thailand and abroad, there is no doubt that her star shines less brightly at home. In the company of other Thai top female actresses, whose celebrity mostly comes from appearances in popular television dramas, Jeeja seems the odd one out. She also does not fit the mould of the patriotic hero/warrior, which in the Thai context is a mode of masculinity. The chances are that with more young women turning to martial arts inspired by Jeeja's example, Thai attitudes to locally made action films will change as well. And with the growing acceptance of *muay thai* as an all-inclusive sport rather than 'the burden of Thai men' we may see more Thai female martial arts stars in the future.

References

Ainslie, Mary J. (2018), 'New Thai Cinema', in Mary J. Ainslie and Katarzyna Ancuta (eds), *The Complete Guide to Thai Cinema*, London: I. B. Tauris, pp. 75–7.
Brown, Jeffrey A. (2011), *Dangerous Curves: Action Heroines, Gender, Fetishism, and Popular Culture*, Jackson: University Press of Mississippi.
Channon, Alex and Christopher R. Matthews (2015), 'Approaching the gendered phenomenon of "women warriors"', in Alex Channon and Christopher R. Matthews (eds), *Global Perspectives on Women in Combat Sports: Women Warriors around the World*, London: Palgrave Macmillan, pp. 1–21.
Dyer, Richard (1998), *Stars*, new edition with supplementary chapter by Paul McDonald, London: BFI Publishing.
Dyer, Richard (2004), *Heavenly Bodies: Film Stars and Society*, 2nd edn, London: Routledge.
Gomes, Catherine Jean (2004), 'Doing it (un)like a lady: rethinking gender in martial arts cinema', *Graduate Journal of Asia-Pacific Studies* 2:1, pp. 11–20.
Ingawanij, May Adadol (2007), 'Nang Nak: Thai bourgeois heritage cinema', *Inter-Asia Cultural Studies* 8:2, pp. 180–93.
King, Neal and Marta McCaughey (2001), 'What's a mean woman like you doing in a movie like this?', in Martha McCaughey and Neal King (eds), *Reel Knockouts: Violent Women in the Movies*, Austen: University of Texas Press, pp. 1–24.
Kitiarsa, Pattana (2005), '"Lives of hunting dogs": "Muai Thai" and the politics of Thai masculinities', *South East Asia Research* 13:1, pp. 57–90.
Kitiarsa, Pattana (2011), 'The fall of Thai Rocky', in Kathleen M. Adams and Kathleen A. Gillogly (eds), *Everyday Life in Southeast Asia*, Bloomington: Indiana University Press, pp. 195–217.
McDonald, Paul (2000), *The Star System: Hollywood's Production of Popular Identities*, London: Wallflower.
McWilliam, Kelly (2009), 'Star struck: fandom and the discourse of celebrity', in Jane Stadler and Kelly McWilliam, *Screen Media: Analysing Film and Television*, Crows Nest: Allen and Unwin, pp. 245–72.
Nayar, Pramod K. (2009), *Seeing Stars: Spectacle, Society and Celebrity Culture*, New Delhi: Sage.
Pinkaew, Prachya (2007), 'In conversation with Sronrasilp Ngoenwichit', *Asian Journal of Literature, Culture and Society* 1:1, pp. 86–97.
Rojek, Chris (2001), *Celebrity*, London: Reaktion Books.
Sangkhamanee, Jakkrit (2012), 'Thai boxing and embodiment: the construction of masculinity through sportsmanship', Asian Conference on Cultural Studies, Official Conference Proceedings, pp. 161–72, <www.iafor.org> (last accessed on 7 January 2018).

Steimer, Lauren (2013), 'Hong Kong action cinema as mode in Thai action stardom', in Russell Meeuf and Raphael Raphael (eds), *Transnational Stardom: International Celebrity in Film and Popular Culture*, London: Palgrave Macmillan, pp. 139–62.

Tasker, Yvonne (2002), *Spectacular Bodies: Gender, Genre and the Action Cinema*, London: Routledge.

Vail, Peter T. (1998), 'Modern "Muay Thai" mythology', *Crossroads: An Interdisciplinary Journal of Southeast Asian Studies* 12:2, pp. 75–95.

Notes

1. Alternative spelling JeeJa or Jija, also credited as Yanin Vismistananda, Yanin Vismitananda, Yanin Mitananda or Chanthathanisa Vismitananda.
2. The article uses information obtained through a personal interview with Jeeja Yanin conducted on 7 June 2018 in Bangkok with help of Solarsin Ngoenwichit.

Notes on contributors

Mary Jane Ainslie is Associate Professor in Film and Media Studies at the University of Nottingham Ningbo China (UNNC). She specialises in culture and media throughout Southeast Asia, with specific emphasis upon Thailand and Malaysia. She is the co-editor of *Thai Cinema: The Complete Guide* (I. B. Tauris, 2018) and *Southeast Asian Cinema on Screen: From Independence to Financial Crisis 1945–1997* (Amsterdam University Press, 2020) as well as the author of *Anti-Semitism in Contemporary Malaysia: Malay Nationalism, Philosemitism and Pro-Israel Expressions* (Palgrave Macmillan, 2019).

Katarzyna Ancuta is a lecturer at the Faculty of Arts, Chulalongkorn University in Bangkok, Thailand. Her research interests oscillate around the interdisciplinary contexts of contemporary Asian Gothic/Horror. Her recent publications include contributions to *B-Movie Gothic* (2018), *Twenty-first-century Gothic* (2019) and *Gothic and the Arts* (2019). She also co-edited three special journal issues on Thai (2014) and Southeast Asian (2015) horror film, and Tropical Gothic (2019), and collections *Thai Cinema: The Complete Guide* (2018) and *South Asian Gothic* (2021).

Thomas Barker is Head of School and an Associate Professor of Film and Television at the University of Nottingham Malaysia. He is the author of *Indonesian Cinema after the New Order: Going Mainstream* (Hong Kong University Press, 2019).

Jonathan Driskell is Senior Lecturer in Film, Television and Screen Studies at Monash University Malaysia. He is the author of *Marcel Carné*

(Manchester University Press, 2012) and *The French Screen Goddess: Film Stardom and the Modern Woman in 1930s France* (I. B. Tauris, 2015).

Jane M. Ferguson teaches anthropology and Southeast Asian history in the School of Culture, History and Language at the Australian National University College of Asia and the Pacific. She specialises in mainland Southeast Asia, Burma/Thai/Shan cultures, borderlands, insurgency, ethnic politics, popular culture, musical genres and passenger aviation.

Pujita Guha is a PhD student at the Film and Media Studies Department, University of California, Santa Barbara. Her work probes the entanglement of environmental media, forest histories, South and Southeast Asia media and cultures. Alongside her environmental interests, she works on popular cinemas and cultures of South and Southeast Asia, having published in *Industrial Cinemas and Networks of India, Popular Cinema in Bengal* and *Nang*, among others.

Annette Hamilton is a cultural anthropologist who has worked in Southeast Asia since the 1980s. She has published numerous articles on cinema, media and popular culture in Thailand and more recently has been working on Cambodian film including the work of Rithy Panh. She is Professor Emerita in Film Studies in the School of Arts and Media at the University of New South Wales in Sydney, Australia.

David Hanan pioneered the Film Studies programme at Monash University, Melbourne, Australia. He has researched film in Indonesia since 1983. He is the author of *Cultural Specificity in Indonesian Film: Diversity in Unity* (Palgrave Macmillan, 2017) and *Moments in Indonesian Film History: Film and Popular Culture in a Developing Society 1950–2020* (2021). He is currently an Honorary Fellow in the Asia Institute at the University of Melbourne.

Qui-Ha Hoang Nguyen received her PhD from the Department of Cinema and Media Studies at the University of Southern California in 2020 and is an incoming Postdoctoral Associate at the Yale University MacMillan Center for Southeast Asian Studies (2021–2). Her research interests include film historiography, postcolonial studies, feminist studies, film industry studies, sound studies, transnational cinema, Southeast Asian and Vietnamese film and media, and environmental humanities. She is currently writing a book manuscript titled *Figuring*

Women in Vietnamese Revolutionary Cinema (1945–1975): Representation, Affect, and Agency.

Chrishandra Sebastiampillai is Lecturer in Film, Television and Screen Studies at Monash University Malaysia. Her research focuses on stardom in popular Philippine cinema, particularly the film couple or 'love team', an aspect of stardom she has explored in both her Honours and Doctoral dissertations. Her research interests include stardom and celebrity, the romance genre and its film couples, and Southeast Asian cinema.

Katrina Ross A. Tan received her PhD from the School of Media, Film and Journalism at Monash University. She is an assistant professor at the Department of Humanities in the University of the Philippines Los Baños. Her research interest lies in the intersection of gender, class, ethnicity and nation in cinema. She is currently writing a book based on her thesis about contemporary regional cinema in the Philippines.

Index

100 Rifles, 128
30+ Single on Sale, 192

A. R. Tompel, 41
ABS-CBN, 14, 166, 167–71, 173–4, 175, 181n1
action cinema, 7, 132, 194–7, 203–18; *see also* martial arts
Adam Jawaqni, 136
Ahmad Mahmud, 40
Ahmad Nisfu, 40
Akibat Pergaulan Bebas (Consequences of Free Intercourse), 128, 130
Alda, Alan, 12, 84, 94
Alex Komang, 119
Ali Baba Bujang Lapok (Ne'er Do Well Bachelors Ali Baba), 42
Ali Shahab, 127, 128–32
Alonzo, Bea, 14, 166–81
Alpha Studio, 85
Althusser, Louis, 111
Aman, Zeenat, 103n8
Amir Muhammad, 1
Anakku Sazali (Sazali My Son), 41, 43
Anand, Dev, 96, 97, 103n8
Anderson, Benedict, 105
Antara Dua Darjat (Between Two Classes), 37, 42, 43, 44
Antonelli, Laura, 125
Apocalypse Now, 84
April Love, 55–6
Apsara, 23–4, 33n3
Aquino III, Benigno, 154
Aquino, Corazon, 151
Aranua Namwong, 27

archives, 20, 34n4, 92
Arifin C. Noer, 139
Asian Financial Crisis, 209
Association of Southeast Asian Cinemas, 5
Association of Southeast Asian Nations, 6
ATM: Er Rak Error, 192
Atsay (Maid), 154
Aubry, Danielle, 95
Aung Lwin, 53, 58, 61
Aunor, Nora, 7, 13, 149–50, 151–7, 159, 163
authoritarianism, 7, 8, 12, 52, 64, 70, 194
authorship, 6–7
Avellana, Lamberto V., 12, 38, 42, 86
Aye Aye Thin, 57
Ayu Azhari, 135
Ayu Yohana, 135, 137

babaeng martir (the long suffering female), 13, 149, 154, 155, 156, 177
Badai Pasti Berlalu (When the Storm is Over), 118
Bakti (Devotion), 40
Banaue: Stairway to the Sky, 154
Bang Rajan (Bang Rajan: The Legend of the Village Warriors), 189–90
bangsawan (theatre), 10, 39, 40–1, 43, 45
Barang Terlarang (Forbidden Goods), 132
Bardot, Brigitte, 125
Bayer, Rolf, 86, 97, 103n8
Begadang (Stay Up All Night), 111–12
Benyamin Jatuh Cinta (Benyamin Falls in Love), 107
Benyamin Raja Lenong (Benyamin, King of Lenong), 107

Benyamin S, 8, 12, 104, 105–9, 110, 112, 114, 119, 121–2, 126
Benyamin Spion 025 (Benyamin Spy 025), 108
Bernafas Dalam Lumpur (Breathing in Mud), 127
Bernal, Ishmael, 1, 154
Bernardo, Kathryn, 176
Betawi
   culture, 12, 104, 105, 106, 107, 108, 109, 114, 121–2
   language, 105–6, 108, 112
Big Boss, The, 215
Bintang (film magazine), 38, 41
Bishop, Cindy, 186
Bituing Walang Ningning (Star without Sparkle), 159
Blue Lagoon, The, 132
Bo Ba Ko, 57
bom seks (sex bomb), 12–13, 124–48
bomba films, 125
Bona, 154, 157
Boone, Pat, 55
Bopha Devi, 22, 23
Bophana Audio-Visual Resource Centre, 20
Born to Fight, 190, 204, 210
Brocka, Lino, 1, 154, 159
Brown, Judith, 125
Brunei, 5
Buddhism, 10, 23, 52, 54, 63–4, 85, 209
Bujang Lapok (Ne'er Do Well Bachelors) film series, 37, 42, 44
Bukas Luluhod ang mga Tala (Tomorrow the Stars will Kneel), 159
Bumi Makin Panas (Earth Gets Hotter), 127
Burma (Myanmar), 1, 5, 8, 10, 12, 51–2, 53, 54, 56, 57, 60–1, 63–4, 65, 97
Burmese way to Socialism, 10, 51–2, 55, 56, 57

Cambodia, 1–2, 5, 8, 9, 11, 12, 19–31, 33n2, 34n8
Camus, Marcel, 22
Caregiver, 13, 149–50, 152, 157–62, 163
Catfish in Black Bean Sauce, 94–5
Cathay-Keris Studio, 38–9
Catholicism, 14, 170
celebrity, 4, 41, 115, 140, 144, 206, 214, 216, 217
censorship, 10, 52, 54–5, 56–7, 64, 91, 120, 136
Chaibancha, Mitr, 8, 185, 195, 203
Champagne X, 186

Chan, Jackie, 203
Chaplin, Charlie, 41
Chea Yuthorn, 27, 33n3
Chen, Anthony, 1, 6
Cheng Pei Pei, 208
Cheung, Maggie, 208
Chiếc Bóng Bên Đường (Roadside Shadow), 90–2
Children of An Lac, The, 94
China, 22, 64, 77, 207
Chinta (Love), 40
Chocolate, 14, 203, 204, 211, 212, 215
Chou, Davy, 9, 29, 30, 35n20
Christine Hakim, 12, 104, 115–19, 120–1, 122
Chupong, Dan, 197, 203–4, 210
Cinta di Balik Noda (Love Behind the Stain), 139
Cinta Pertama (First Love), 116–17, 118
Clapp, Krissada Sukosol, 182
Coffin, The, 192
Cold War, 6, 11, 67, 85, 88, 96, 98, 99, 183, 184
colonialism, 2, 6, 9, 57, 71, 74, 94, 104, 105, 109, 118, 183–4, 187, 188; *see also* decolonisation; postcolonialism
comedy, 7, 8, 12, 41, 56, 106, 107, 108, 118–19, 132, 192, 212
Concepcion, Gabby, 159
Concrete Clouds, 190
consumerism, 11, 45, 74, 80, 81, 161, 184, 187, 193
Coppola, Francis Ford, 84
cosmopolitanism, 9, 10, 28–9, 37, 52, 60, 64, 65, 86, 95, 162, 183, 186–9, 190, 191, 193, 196, 198
Coward, Noel, 41
Crepuscule (Twilight), 28
Cruz III, Tirso, 153
Cruz, John Lloyd, 14, 152, 166–81
Crying Ladies, 159–60
cultural heritage, 9, 20, 33n3, 85, 205, 209, 210
Cummings, Lana, 186
Cuneta, Sharon, 13, 149–50, 151–2, 157–63, 177
Curtis, Anne, 181n2

Da 5 Bloods, 99
Dalagang Bukid (Country Maiden), 2
dangdut, 12, 104, 109–13, 114, 122
Darah Muda (Young Blood), 110–11

Daun di Atas Bantal (Leaf on a Pillow), 120–1
de la Rama, Honorata, 2
de Leon, Mike, 154
Dean, James, 10, 51, 116
Dear Heart, 159
Debbie Cynthia Dewi, 128, 129, 137, 138, 139
decolonisation, 2, 6; *see also* colonialism; postcolonialism
Depan Bisa Belakang Bisa (In Front Can, Behind Can), 132, 134
Derrida, Jacques, 20, 86–7
Destination Vietnam, 12, 86, 103n8
Dewi Perssik, 144
Diah Permatasari, 132
diaspora, 11–12, 86, 88, 92, 93, 99, 151
Diaz, Lav, 1, 6
Dibalik Kelambu (Behind the Mosquito Net), 117–18
Doea Tanda Mata (Two Souvenirs), 119
Dollah Sarawak, 40
Doris Callebaut, 126, 128
Double Crime on the Maginot Line, 34n8
Đức Hoàn, 72, 82n3, 83n8
Duo Kribo (Afro Duo), 128
Duterte, Rodrigo, 181n1
Dy Saveth, 9–10, 24, 26–9, 30, 31, 33n3, 34n12, 35n18
Dyer, Richard, 2–3, 5, 26, 39, 46, 70, 91, 105, 116, 125, 135, 136, 150, 205
Dynamite Warrior, 204, 210
Dynasty, 12, 95

East Timor, 5
Enny Beatrice, 132, 138, 139–40
Estella, Ramon, 38
Etang sacré, L' (The Sacred Pond), 26
Eternity, 182, 192
Eurasian, 135, 183–4, 185, 187, 188–9, 191, 198–9; see also *luk khrueng*
Europe Raiders, 211
Eva Arnaz, 128–32, 134, 136–7, 141
Everingham, Ananda, 14, 182–3, 186, 189, 190–1, 192–3, 194–9
Evil Within, The, 12, 86, 95, 96–7, 103n8

Fai Sang Am, 27
fandom, 23, 56, 171
Fantasy Island, 95
Fatherland, 191
Febby Lawrence, 135
femininity, 72–3, 74–5, 76–7, 78, 81, 126, 191, 193, 202n4, 207–8, 217

femme fatale, 125
Fenech, Edwige, 125, 128
Fighting Continues, The, 83n5
Filipino Channel, The, 151, 166
film festivals
    Asia Film Festival, 41
    Cannes Film Festival, 1
    Indonesian Film Festival, 118, 119, 132, 139
    Vietnamese International Film Festival, 99
Floating Village, 83n5
Flor Contemplacion Story, The, 13, 149–50, 152–7, 163
Fonda, Jane, 67, 125
Forest Fire, 83n5
Freedom Films, 85
French Indochina, 11, 34n6, 49, 71, 85, 94

Gadis Bionik (Bionic Girl), 132
Ganda, Vice, 175
Gangster, The, 194
Garin Nugroho, 1, 6, 120
gender, 11, 13, 14, 15, 27, 69, 71, 77, 124, 125–6, 135, 138, 141, 144, 156, 168, 183, 185, 191–3, 202n4, 205, 207–8, 212–13, 216–17; *see also* femininity; masculinity
ghosts, 19, 20, 25, 26, 31, 54
Giao Chỉ Film, 85
Gitty Srinita, 132
glamour, 11, 13, 25, 34n12, 46, 67, 70, 81, 92, 150, 162, 163, 168, 179, 209, 215
globalisation, 81, 209
golden ages/eras, 1–2
    Burma, 1
    Cambodia, 19, 26, 29, 30, 33n3
    Indonesia, 124, 127
    Philippines, 154
    Singapore, 10, 36, 38–9
    Thailand, 184–5, 196
    Vietnam, 67, 80
Golden Slumbers, 9, 29–30, 35n21
Golding, Henry, 8
Grier, Pam, 125
Guida, Gloria, 125
Gyllenhaal, Jake, 198

Hải Ninh, 68, 73, 78, 79–80
Halfworlds, 211
Hang Tuah, 37, 42, 44
Happy Birthday, 191, 192
Hard Target 2, 211
Harimau Tjampa (Tiger from Tjampa), 127

Heart Attack, 192
Hedren, Tippi, 93
Hi-So, 190
Hindi cinema, 4, 21, 25, 38, 103n8
Hitchcock, Alfred, 118
Hmone Shwe Yee (Glimmering Gold), 51, 52, 61–3
Hnit Yauk Te Nay Kyin Tay (Let's Stay Together), 51, 53, 56
Hồ Chí Minh, 67, 69, 71
Hồi Chuông Thiên Mụ (The Bells of Thiên Mụ Temple), 85
Hollywood, 1, 4, 21, 60, 71, 75, 84, 86, 88, 93, 94, 95, 96, 97, 108, 118, 162, 183, 184, 198, 204, 207, 208, 213; see also stardom: Hollywood stardom
Holy Day, 83n5
Hong Kong cinema, 1, 85, 203, 207–8, 209, 211, 215
horror cinema, 5, 7, 8, 14, 41, 127, 192–3

I Fine . . . Thank You . . . Love You, 192
Ibu (Mother), 41, 43
Ibu Mertuaku (My Mother-in-law), 37, 41, 42, 43, 47, 48
Ibunda (Mother), 121
Iko Uwais, 211
Ilo Ilo, 1
Indonesia, 1, 2, 5, 7, 8, 11, 12–13, 49, 104–23, 124–48
  New Order, the, 7, 12–13, 104, 109, 114, 121, 124, 144
Inneke Koesherawaty, 135, 139, 141–3, 148n30
Insi Daeng (The Red Eagle), 194–6
Instagram, 167, 171–6
Intan Perawan Kubu (Intan the Kubu Virgin), 128
Islam, 12, 109–10, 111, 112–14, 140, 141–2, 144

Jaa, Tony, 8, 15, 203–4, 209, 210, 211, 213, 216
James Bond, 7, 95, 121
Jenny Rachman, 128, 141
Jins Shamsuddin, 40
Johny Indo, 126
Joie de Vivre, La (The Joy of Living), 29
Jolie, Angelina, 19
Jones, Shirley, 56
Journey from the Fall, 12, 93–4
Joy Luck Club, The, 12, 93–4
Julia Perez, 144

Kaenjai Meenakanit, 125
Kapoor, Raj, 41
Kawin Kontrak (Contract Marriage), 140
Kemilau Cinta Langit Jingga (A Radiant Love in an Orange Sky), 113
Khin Lay Sway, 58
Khin Than Nu, 56, 61
Khmer Rouge, 1–2, 9, 19, 20, 23, 26, 27, 29, 30
Khomsiri, Kongkiat, 194, 196, 197
Khoo, Eric, 1
Khun Pan, 194, 196–8
Khun Pan 2, 196
Khun Phaen Begins, 197
Kick, The, 211, 212
Kickboxer, 203
Kiều Chinh, 11–12, 72, 82n1, 84–103
Kiki Fatmala, 132, 135, 136, 137
Killer Tattoo, 190
Kim Cương, 82n1, 90, 100, 103n6
Kinatay (Butchered), 1
Kittisiriprasert, Theerada, 213
Koboi Ngungsi (Refugee Cowboy), 108
Kong Sam Oeun, 26, 33n3, 34n12
Korean Wave, 192
Krishnan, L., 40
Kugimiya, Nadech, 182, 216
Kulikar Sotho, 9, 30
Kuswadinata, 43

Labu Labi film series, 42
Lâm Tới, 83n9
Langitku Rumahku (My Sky My Home), 120
Laos, 5, 11
Lara Croft: Tomb Raider, 19, 30
Last Reel, The, 9–10, 30
Latifah Omar, 40
Leap Years, The, 192
Lee, Bruce, 203, 207, 215
Lee Kuan Yew, 12
Lee, Moon, 208
Lela Anggraeni, 136
Letter, The, 95
Letters from Thailand, 184
Li, Jet, 203
Lina Budiarty, 137
Liquigan, Roxy, 176
Liv Sreng, 29
Love H20, 191, 192
Love Is Forever, 183
love teams, 7–8, 14, 166–81
Lucifer Complex, The, 95

luk khrueng (Thai Eurasian), 14, 182–99, 202n5; *see also* Eurasian
Lundgren, Dolph, 204
LVN Pictures, 169, 170
Ly Bun Yim, 26, 29, 33n3
Ly You, 26

M. Amin, 40, 41
Madu Tiga (Three Wives), 42
Mahathir Mohamad, 12, 37
Mai Châu, 72, 82n3
Majallah Filem (film magazine), 38, 43, 46
Major Group, 214
Mak Dara, 40, 43
Malarin Boonnak, 125
Malay Film Productions (MFP), 36, 38–9, 40, 41, 42
Malayan Emergency, the, 11, 39, 49
Malaysia, 5, 8, 10, 12, 36–7, 39
Malvin Shayna, 135
Mana Bisa Tahan (Cannot Hold On), 132
Manahan, Johnny, 181n1
Mandalay Film Company, 55
Mạnh Linh, 82n2
Mao Ying, Angela, 208
Marcos, Ferdinand, 12
Maria Menado, 40
Mariani, 40
marketing, 38–9, 162, 166–7, 171, 172–3, 175–6, 212–13, 214
martial arts, 8, 15, 196, 203–18
Martin, Coco, 175
masculinity, 57, 64, 95, 177–9, 192, 194–6, 199, 205, 207, 210, 217–18
M*A*S*H, 12, 84, 94
masquerade, 88, 94–9
Mat Sentol, 41
Maung Toe Cherry Myay (Our Favourite Land of Cherry), 55–6
Maurer, Mario, 182, 197
McIntosh, Willy, 182, 186, 187
Me . . . Myself, 193
Meas Sam E, 22
Megi Megawati, 135
melodrama, 8, 25, 40, 57, 64, 98, 113, 116, 117, 119
Mendoza, Brillante, 1
Merdeka Film Productions, 37, 39
Meriam Bellina, 132, 133, 135, 139, 141
mestizo/a stars, 13, 14, 152–3, 159, 168
Metanee, Sombat, 203

migrant workers, 149, 150, 151, 157, 160–1, 162
migration, 120, 151, 185
military rule, 10, 12, 51–2, 54, 65, 154
Minsa'y Isang Gamu-Gamo (Once a Moth), 157
Missing Picture, The, 1
Mistress, The, 172
modernisation, 13, 111, 124, 125–6
modernity, 9, 10, 11, 20, 21, 23–4, 25–6, 28–9, 37, 42, 45–9, 54, 57, 58, 69, 76–7, 80–1, 100, 118–19, 126, 162, 185, 187–8, 190
Molina, Cathy Garcia, 14, 166, 170, 171
Moment to Moment, 58
Monroe, Marilyn, 125
Montir-Montir Cantik (Beautiful Mechanics), 132
morality, 26, 43, 47, 52, 57, 63, 73, 111, 124, 125–6, 128, 135–6, 137, 141, 144, 167, 196, 205
Moreno, Alma, 125
Muay Thai Chaiya, 194
muay thai, 7, 14–15, 190, 194, 196, 197, 203–5, 208–13, 214, 217–18
Mui, Anita, 208
Mulvey, Laura, 118, 193
Munoz, Tita, 103n8
musical film, 12, 38, 44, 56, 109–15, 168
My Husband is Missing, 94
Myint Myint Khin, 58

Nada dan Dakwah (A Song and a Sermon), 113–15
Nadjib Abu Yasser, 109
Nai Khanom Tom, 204–5
Nano Riantiarno, 116, 121
Napas Perempuan (Breath of a Woman), 128, 131
Nary Hem, 22
Ne Win, 10, 12, 51–2, 54, 55, 57, 64–5
Never Back Down: No Surrender, 15, 211
New Thai Cinema, 7, 13, 208–9
Người Tình Không Chân Dung (Warrior, Who are You?), 88–90, 92, 99
Nguyễn Phương Hoa, 82n3
Nguyễn Văn Thiệu, 103n9
Nhiek Tioulong, 24
Nia Dinata, 1
Nimibutr, Nonzee, 7, 194
Niño Valiente (Brave Boy), 154
Nop Nem, 22
Nordin Ahmad, 40

Norodom Sihamoni, 24
Norodom Sihanouk, 9, 22–5, 26, 28, 29, 33n3, 34n8, 34n9, 35n19
Norodom Sihanouk: Roi Cinéaste (Norodom Sihanouk: King and Filmmaker), 22, 23
North Vietnam, 11, 67, 69, 71, 73–7, 84, 85, 92–3, 98, 102n2, 103n9; *see also* South Vietnam; Vietnam
nostalgia, 7, 10, 24, 64, 81, 82n3, 92, 93, 126, 144, 166, 167, 171–6, 209
November 1828, 118
Nurhadie Irawan, 113, 114
Nurnaningsih, 127
NV Productions, 154
Nyunt Myanmar Film Studio, 58

Oh! What a Lovely War!, 97
Oiseau de paradis, L' (Dragon Sky), 22, 28
On the Same River, 73, 82n2
One More Chance, 14, 171–7, 178
Ong-Bak, 15, 190, 203, 209, 210
Opera Kecoa (The Cockroach Opera) (play), 121
Operation C.I.A., 12, 86, 95–6
Osman Gumanti, 40
Overseas Filipino Workers (OFWs), 13, 149–52, 154, 157, 160, 163
Oversize Cops, 211

P. Ramlee, 10, 36–8, 39–49
P. Ramlee: The Musical (play), 36, 40, 46
P.S. I Love You, 159
Padamu Aku Bersimpuh (To You I Kneel), 141
Padilla, Daniel, 176
Pancharoen, Eve, 182
Pangky Suwito, 140
Panh, Rithy, 1, 6, 20
Pasan ko ang Daigdig (World on my Shoulders), 159
Pasir Berbisik (Whispering Sands), 120
Patchrapa, Aum, 216
Pembalasan Ratu Pantai Selatan (Revenge of the South Sea Queen), 139
Penarek Becha (Trishaw Puller), 37, 40, 43
Pengabdian (Devotion), 113
Pengantin Pantai Biru (Blue Beach Wedding), 132
Pengemis dan Tukang Becak (The Beggar and the Rickshaw Driver), 119
Perez, Jose (Doc), 169
Perjuangan dan Doa (Struggle and Prayer), 112–13

Perry, Rod, 103n8
Petit Prince, Le (The Little Prince), 24
Phetchakhat Si Chomphu, 186
Phi Nga, 73, 79, 82n2
Philippines, the, 1, 2, 4, 5, 7, 8, 12, 13–14, 84, 96, 103n8, 125, 149–63, 166–81
Phoe Par Kyi, 58
Pich Chanbomey, 27
Pinangan (A Proposal), 107
Pinkaew, Prachya, 14, 15, 190, 203, 209, 210, 211, 212, 214
Pleasure Factory, 191, 193
Ploy, 182, 193
Pol Pot, 12
popular cinema, 5, 7, 15, 19, 116, 122
popular culture, 26, 64, 105, 107, 108, 110, 115, 121–2, 172, 206
postcolonialism, 6, 8, 9, 11, 12, 25, 35n20, 187
Prabhu, P. V., 97
Presley, Elvis, 10, 51, 53, 56, 57
Prince of Persia: The Sands of Time, 198
propaganda, 64, 67, 70, 76, 205
Protector, The, 190, 203, 210
Protector 2, The, 210, 211, 212, 213
Puos Keng Kang (The Snake Man), 27, 28
Puos Keng Kang Peak Phii (The Snake Man Part 2), 27

Queens of Langkasuka, 194–5
Quiet American, The, 85

race, 8, 14, 36, 183, 186–7, 188–9, 190, 191, 193–4, 195, 196, 197–8, 199, 210
Raging Phoenix, 14, 204, 211, 212, 215
Raid: Redemption, The, 211
Raja Copet (King of Thieves), 107–8
Raja Dangdut (King of Dangdut), 112
Rajhans, B. S., 40
Rano Karno, 109
Ratanaruang, Pen-Ek, 1, 7, 182
Raymundo, Carmi, 170, 173–4, 175
Rd Mochtar, 2
religion, 8, 13, 126, 144, 180, 194, 209
Rembulan dan Matahari (Moon and Sun), 120
Reynolds, Burt, 95
Rhoma Irama, 8, 12, 104, 109–15, 120, 121–2, 126
Rika Herliana, 135
Rittikrai, Panna, 190, 203, 204, 212
Road to the Front, 83n6
Robby Sugara, 128
Roekiah, 2

romantic comedy, 7, 192
romantic film, 8, 14, 45, 56, 159, 166, 168, 170–1, 172, 176–8, 179, 192
Roro Mendut, 132, 133
Ros Serey Sothea, 27
Rose of Bokor, 34n9
Rothrock, Cynthia, 204, 208
Roy Marten, 128
royalty, 8, 9, 23, 24, 25, 29

S. Kadarisman, 40, 43
S. Roomai Noor, 40, 41
Saadiah, 40
Sabaidee Luang Prabang, 191, 192
Saksi Sbong, 22, 24, 34n12
Sally Marcellina, 132, 136, 139
Saloma, 42, 43, 46
Sampaguita Pictures, 169
Sanda Film Co, 57
Santos, Erik, 172
Santos-Concio, Charo, 170
sarsuwela (musical theatre) 2, 168
Sasanatieng, Wisit, 1, 194, 195
Satria Bergitar (The Knight with the Guitar), 113, 114
Saung Eik Met (Death is a Dream), 57–8
Second Chance, A, 14, 166–7, 169, 171, 172–80
Sergeant Hassan, 42, 44
Seventeenth Parallel: Day and Night, The, 68, 72–3, 77, 78, 79, 83n9
sexuality, 13, 124, 125–6, 132, 137, 138, 144, 193, 207
Shadow of Darkness, 35n17
Shadow Over Angkor, 28, 35n19
Shambala, 182
Shaw Brothers, 38, 48, 208
Shutter, 14, 182, 192–3
Si Doel Anak Betawi (Doel, Child of Betawi), 109
Si Doel Anak Modern (Si Doel, Child of Modernity), 118–19
Si Doel Anak Sekolahan (Educated Doel), 109
Si Genit Poppy (Poppy the Flirt), 128, 129
Siam Renaissance, The, 190
Singapore, 2, 5, 8, 10, 12, 36–7, 38, 40, 42, 46, 47, 48, 154, 156
Sinn Sisamouth, 27
Siput Sarawak, 40
Sister Tư Hậu, 72–3
Siti Tanjung Perak, 40
Sjuman Djaya, 107, 109, 118
Skylight Films, 166

Slamet Rahardjo, 12, 104, 115–18, 119, 120, 122
Slice, 194
snake film, 9, 27–8
soap opera, 134, 139, 186, 214
Sobasith, 26
social media, 14, 144, 167, 171, 172, 175–6; *see also* Instagram
socialist realism, 10, 52, 54, 63, 75–6, 83n7
Sorga Dunia di Pintu Neraka (Heaven on Earth at the Gates of Hell), 132
Sound of Music, The, 84
South Vietnam, 11–12, 72, 82n1, 84, 85–6, 88, 90, 92, 93–4, 96, 97, 98–100, 103n6, 103n9; *see also* North Vietnam; Vietnam
Southeast Asia, 1–2, 5–9, 11, 12, 15, 19, 21, 27, 34n4, 42, 86, 87–8, 95, 98, 103n8, 105, 125, 184, 192
Southeast Asian independent cinema, 5, 6
Sri Gudhi Sintara, 132, 135, 140
Stanislavski system, 72, 82–3n4
Star Cinema, 166, 167, 170, 173–4, 175, 176
Star Magic, 167, 175, 181n1
star studies, 2–5, 8, 15, 48, 70, 124, 126
stardom
  and extraordinariness, 39, 42, 135
  and ideology, 2–3, 13, 49, 125, 149–50, 152, 157, 163, 168
  and the individual/individualism, 10, 11, 12, 13, 39, 45–8, 76, 77–9, 104, 115, 121–2, 149–50, 153, 157, 162, 163
  and ordinariness, 39, 42–5, 70, 75, 135
  and proximity, 42, 43, 135
  Hollywood stardom, 3, 4, 5, 10, 11, 19, 25, 26, 38–9, 42, 70, 86, 105, 132, 205–6, 214
  socialist stardom, 11, 69–71, 75, 78
star systems, 3, 4, 12, 14, 26, 205–6, 213–14
star vehicles, 13, 14, 37–8, 151–2
stars as social types, 116, 125
transnational stardom, 86–7, 213
studio system, 23, 105, 213
Sudwikatmono, 120
Suharto, 12, 13, 104, 107, 114, 120, 121, 127, 128
Sukarno, 106, 120
Suksawat, Jarunee, 184, 186
Suriyothai (The Legend of Suriyothai), 189–90
Suzzanna, 127
Sway, 190, 191, 192

Tamruat Lek, 185–6
Tarsan Pensiunan (A Retired Tarzan), 108

Tarzan among the Kuoy, 34n8
Tatlong Taong Walang Diyos (Three Years without God), 154
Tawag ng Tanghalan (Call of the Stage), 152
Tea Lim Koun, 27, 34n14
Teater Koma, 116
Teater Populer collective, 12, 104, 115–21, 122
Teguh Karya, 12, 104, 116, 117, 118, 119, 121, 122
Tein Hlwa Moe Moe Lwin (Cloudy Sky), 52, 58–61, 63–4
Terang Boelan (Full Moon), 2
Teresa Teng, 64
Thailand, 1, 5, 6, 8, 14–15, 22, 27, 125, 182–3, 184–99, 201n2, 201–2n3, 202n4, 203–5, 208–18
Thẩm Thúy Hằng, 11, 85
Thành Được, 90
Thanh Nga, 82n1
Thirteen Beloved, 190
This Girl is Badass, 211, 212
Thongleng, Nonthawan, 194
Thorne, Dyanne, 125
Ti Na (Tina Leung), 125
Tiada Jalan Lain (No Other Way), 128
Tin Tin Aye, 57
Tjoet Nja' Dhien, 118
Tongraya, Mick, 182
Trà Giang, 11, 67–9, 71, 72–81, 83n4, 83n5, 83n6, 83n8
tradition, 9, 10, 13, 14, 22, 23, 25, 28–9, 37, 42–5, 46, 47, 48, 49, 56, 61, 62, 72, 73, 74–5, 77, 80–1, 102n4, 107, 126, 171, 177, 178, 185, 190, 192, 195, 198, 208, 212
Trần Anh Hùng, 1
Triple Threat, 15, 211
Từ Sài Gòn Đến Điện Biên Phủ (From Saigon to Dien Bien Phu), 11, 85, 97
Tuệ Minh, 72
Tun Tun, 57
Tuti Indra Malaon, 12, 104, 115–16, 121

U Tin Yu, 51, 53
Udo Omar, 40, 43
Uncle Boonmee Who Can Recall His Past Lives, 1
United States Information Service (USIS), 21, 26, 85

Valdez, Vanessa, 170
Van Chann, 29
Van Damme, Jean-Claude, 203–4
Vichara Dany, 34n12
Vietnam, 5, 8, 11, 21, 67–8, 69, 71, 74, 80–1, 85, 87, 93, 94, 95, 96, 99–100; *see also* North Vietnam; South Vietnam
Vietnam War, 11–12, 67–9, 72–3, 74, 76, 79–80, 84, 85, 86, 88–92, 93–4, 95, 97–8, 99, 184, 201–2n3
Virak Dara, 26, 33n3

Wajah Seorang Laki Laki (Face of a Man), 116
Warkop DKI, 132, 134
Watthanaphanit, Macha, 185–6
We Will Meet Again, 83n6
Weerasethakul, Apichatpong, 1, 6, 7
Wei Yin Hung, 208
Welch, Raquel, 125, 128
Weng Weng, 7
Westernisation, 74, 109–11
What's Cooking?, 95
White Flower River, 80
Wieke Widowati, 132
Win Oo, 10, 11, 51–4, 55–65
Winai Krabutr, 27
Windy Chindyana, 135
Wise, Robert, 84
wuxia, 203, 207

Yanin, Jeeja, 14–15, 203–5, 208, 211–19
Yank in Vietnam, A, 12, 86, 96
Yasmin Ahmad, 1
Yatti Octavia, 128, 137
Yenny Farida, 135, 136, 138
Yeoh, Michelle, 204, 208
Young, Tata, 186
youth-oriented films, 149, 153, 159
Yukari Oshima, 204, 208
Yurike Prastica, 135, 139
Yvon Hem, 22, 29, 35n17

Zaenal Abidin, 139
Zorro Kemayoran (A Zorro of Kemayoran), 107, 108
Zulueta, Dawn, 175

EU representative:
Easy Access System Europe
Mustamäe tee 50, 10621 Tallinn, Estonia
Gpsr.requests@easproject.com

www.ingramcontent.com/pod-product-compliance
Lightning Source LLC
Chambersburg PA
CBHW082116230426
43671CB00015B/2714